Holy Cats!

Dream-Catching at Woodstock

Praise for The Author

"I just LOVE the way you write. Your wit and turns of phrase and insights are so unique and beyond compare. You must write many books!"

Carolyn Cassady
(wife of Neal and love of Jack's life)

"My God, you're the very spirit of Jack! He would've *loved* you!"

Edie Kerouac Parker
(Jack's first wife)

"This is an exceptionally fine piece of work on your part. Marvelous dissertations and mightily written rapportage!"

Henri Cru
(Remi Boncoeur in *On The Road*)

"I like your distinctive narrative voice. You are a great stylist."

Sterling Lord
(Kerouac & Kesey's literary agent)

"Hombre, let me say right off — you are a hell of a writer! This piece you wrote is just wonderful. I love it! It felt like I was there ..... what a treat."

Walter Salles
(director of *On The Road*)

"You're not an *On The Road* scholar — you're an *On The Road* character!"

Teri McLuhan
(Marshall McLuhan's author/filmmaker daughter)

"You can write your ass off!!"

David Amram
(Kerouac's principal musical collaborator)

"You erased the period after 'Jack Kerouac.'"

The Wizard of Wonder
(21st Century Merry Prankster)

More Praise for The Author

"Brian Hassett is definitely NOT a typical scholarly researcher! Instead, like all good gonzo reporters, he set out on a personal journey to immerse himself in the movement that started with the Beats, went through the hippies, and has reached into so many corners of America. His memoirs are fascinating, must-read reporting for anyone -- from students writing term papers to young seekers searching for the meaning of life."

Lee Quarnstrom
(author, journalist & original Merry Prankster)

"I am so impressed by Brian's understanding of what he wrote. Other people have knowledge, but he really 'got it.' His impressions of those I know and love were lessons for me, too. He is an astute, keep-it-simple-&-real author ... and I'm proud to also say a Friend."

Anonymous
(aka Linda Breen, original Merry Prankster, who got On The Bus in Calgary in 1964)

"The stories of your adventures are always intriguing and fun. Despite what's going on in the moment — you have an outlook on the world that is just joyful. And I love your play with words."

Jerry Cimino
(founder & curator of The Beat Museum)

"You make lightning strike."

Brad Kepperley
(Aretha Franklin's horn player)

"If it's happiness you want, Brian Hassett seems to have found it."

Bill Sass
(Edmonton Journal)

"People like you are extremely helpful and inspiring."

Susan Ray
(widow of film director Nicholas Ray)

Holy Cats!

Dream-Catching at Woodstock

Brian Hassett

Gets Things Done Publishing

For more information and to stay up to date . . .

BrianHassett.com

Facebook.com/Brian.Hassett.Canada

or email — **karmacoupon@gmail.com**

To the half-million
who smiled at once

Table of Contents

Preface

This book was written in my ground floor apartment / studio / lab at 224 East 70th Street in Manhattan immediately upon returning from Woodstock '94 — so it's contemporaneous and percolating with the positive energy that that event created. According to my 1994 datebook, I finished the basic draft on Thursday, November 17th.

As I'd done at a prior epic Adventure to the Jack Kerouac *On The Road* Conference (captured in my 2015 book *The Hitchhiker's Guide to Jack Kerouac*), I brought a little pocket cassette recorder with me and basically dictated the whole damn trip onto tape as it was happening.

This Woodstock book was the first long-form Adventure Tale I ever completed, and although it was good, by the time it was fully finished the world had moved on, and I never really tried to sell it. I was making great dough as a freelance legal assistant in Manhattan in the mid-'90s, so I didn't need the cash

— but one thing I did do was perform the entire book live. (!)

My girlfriend at the time, who was also the first reader of every word of it, and an editor throughout the whole process, was working in the Manhattan head office of Starbucks just as they were beginning their massive takeover of America, and one of their locations had a whole second floor performance space, which we were able to commandeer in the summer of '95 and perform the entire book over three nights (like Woodstock). I remember the big room was full, and by the third night it was standing-room-only. And I had a couple versatile musicians next to me (Al Robinson & Rich Huarte) playing the songs that were being played from the Woodstock stage as I was describing them.

I dunno how we got crowds back then — I barely had dial-up AOL email in 1995. Was I phoning people? Was it the flyers? Was "Woodstock" a big enough draw? I have no idea how the room was full, but it was. I remember walking up the stairs and turning the corner . . . and being stopped-in-my-tracks by all the people in the chairs! *Who are these people?! Where did they come from?!* I'd only performed sporadically in my 15 years to that point in Manhattan. These three Woodstock shows were really the beginning of my performance career that's now spanned continents and millennia har har.

After the shows, I kept tweaking the book, and the surviving printouts of the different chapters are dated February 26th and March 10th, 1996 — so this book has been buried in the metaphoric trunk for 23 years!

I went on living my life, started a nice six-year run in the executive ranks of MTV in Times Square, and continued having nonstop Adventures. People would sometimes ask about the Woodstock book and I'd tell them (as I really believed) that it was a nice ace in the hole for somewhere down the road once I started writing books. And voilà! ☺

I was always writing back then, but more short story length Adventure Tales. Life was moving so fast with so much happening every day & night of the gawdamn week in Madhattan in the music business in my 30s & 40s, who the hell had time to write a book?! Who had time to *read* a book?!

My parents eventually needed caregiving, and being an only child who left home at 18, I finally got off the merry-go-round and came back to Canada to hold their hand through the final fade to black. And THEN it was writing season.

I wrote the start-to-finish draft of *The Hitchhiker's Guide to Jack Kerouac* in 11 days in February 2013. I put together *How The Beats Begat The Pranksters* from concept to published book in 13 days in 2017. Yeah — you read that right. That's a whole other story I'll tell ya sometime. Then I wanted to do a tribute to two close friends, one who passed away in late 2013 but did indeed get to read part of *Hitchhiker's*, Carolyn Cassady, and her only son, John, who is still Gratefully with us. I wrote that tribute book, *On The Road with Cassadys*, over the summer of 2018, and it came out on the same day as *On The Road*, September 5th.

Then we rolled into 2019 and it was going to be the 50th anniversary of Woodstock. In fact, in that Cassady book, I wrote in the opening story about the streak of 50th anniversaries that began with Jack Kerouac writing his famous scroll version of *On The Road* in April 1951 — making April 2001 the kick-off of the 50th anniversaries of everything of any cultural importance that, as far as I'm concerned, ends with Woodstock. It was basically an 18 year streak from Jack sitting down and scrolling Bill Cannastra's tracing paper into his little portable typewriter at 454 West 20th Street to Michael Lang & Company creating the magic they did in upstate New York, which Michael Wadleigh & Company captured in an Academy Award-winning documentary worthy of the original event. Then right after that everything went to hell. Jack died in October; Altamont was in December; The Beatles announce their breakup in April '70; Kent State was in May; and Jimi & Janis died in September and October.

I'm partially kidding about everything going to hell after Woodstock — but what's for sure is that the flow from Jack writing the new American Constitution to Jimi Hendrix playing the new *Star-Spangled Banner* was the coolest birth-to-voting-age 18-year streak in human history.

Then, somehow, despite my best efforts, I ended up still alive in 2019 (!) and it's like, "Oh geez, I better get that Woodstock book out."

And this is where it gets a bit tricky.

Y'see . . . computers . . . can't live with 'em, can't keep up with 'em. Of course the files were long gone. Who the hell still has computer files from 1996?!

You know who? You know anybody who knows me? They'll tell ya. "Hassett keeps everything."

And somewhere in one of 56 filing cabinet drawers around here were the 3-inch floppy disks. But a'course that and a dollar will get you on the subway. What the hell are you gonna do with floppy disks from 1996? Well, if you're an insane archivist like me, I still haven't thrown out the big old fashioned desktop from that era! So I cranked up the Model T, and sure as damn hell, the files on the floppies opened!! So I plugged a jack into the back to connect the dinosaur to a modem, and was actually able to email myself the old Word files! and then had some program on my 21st century Steve Jobs Macintosh Spaceship that was able to open them!

What you're about to read is pretty much exactly what survived from nearly 25 years ago when all this went down.

1994 was really the end of an era in that it was just before the internet and cell phones really changed the way we lived. From the Woodstock site, we used hardwired landline telephones to contact to the outside world. We used paper maps to find our way around. We read printed newspapers to get the news.

I hope that good reunions happen all over the world for the 50th anniversary this year. We sure need it. As Peter Gabriel said at the climax of the Woodstock you're about to time travel to —

"25 years ago,
People believed
You could change the world,
If you fought for justice,
If you fought for what you believed in,
If you fought for your dreams.

This is your Woodstock.
These are your dreams.

What happens now
is up to you."

Brian Hassett
May 3rd, 2019

Grab a cup of mud and hear the New York premiere of

ADVENTUREMAN PLAYS WOODSTOCK

NEW!

EXCITING!

The Woodstock Anniversary Readings
Starbucks Coffee, 1559 2nd Ave. (at 81st St.)

WEDNESDAY, JULY 19, 1995, 7pm--11pm
Sneaking in, Parking Behind the Stage, Discovering the Abandoned Cabin,
Crashing the Media Tent and Seeing Sheryl Crow

WEDNESDAY, AUGUST 2, 1995, 7pm--11pm
Roads Close, The Band Plays Music Near Big Pink, CSN Sings Woodstock at Woodstock,
it Rains a Little, there's Fireworks and an Epiphany at the Ancient Ruins

SUNDAY, AUGUST 13, 1995, 7pm--11pm
The First Anniversary of the Anniversary Concert ☺
The Allmans, Traffic, The Neville Brothers, Liquid Sunshine, Dylan, Cliff, Gabriel
and Seeing a God or Three

HOLY CATS!

Learn: How to sneak into concerts
Hear: Bob Dylan lead a sing-along
See: Behind the scenes
Smell: The coffee
Put: Your feet up and chill

Eat! Drink!
Get Buzzed On Coffee!

Adventure Card collecting in encouraged!

Please cycle

Adventureman 212-737-8296

The PreRamble

Grannies were reading newspapers on porches in the shade, rocking in their eighties and sipping lemonade. Mudpeople were riding bicycles in groups and in the nude, while others preferred walking, thinking cycling a little crude. Incoming newbodies were nervously looking around as they moved in tight clusters, rushing to get where things would be normal, but heading straight for the mosh pit of madness. But at least their shirts were nice and clean, and they were all well prepared with their Cheese-its and Wheez-its and Jeez-it's unreal.

All along the roadside outside were partying packs of wolves who'd commandeered embankments and were drinking beer and hooting and howling a running commentary on the passing foot soldiers. Men had been sent from their base camps deep within the site in search of more provisions. Some exhausted soldiers had dropped to the ground and were littering the curb like empties. Tents still covered every flat patch of ground in sight, and standing outside most was the hawk of the roost shaking his rain-soaked feathers in the temporary rain break ritual.

It was noon on Sunday and high time I found *The Times*. That phat New York rag has been my sacred tome for years. I've written odes to *The Times*, I've written poems to *The Times*, I've even written in *The Times* (once). And Sunday was their big sax solo climax of the week. I couldn't wait to see what they'd say about the magic we'd created.

Of all the Pavarottis and assorted Paul Simons who'd ever gathered a million in the Empire State, this was the crowd that faced the weather and pulled together. Never before have so many people assembled under such torrential downpours and actually held it together. (alright, once)

I was salivating to taste their first metaphor, their first multisyllabic impression (when a single syllabic would do) because I *knew* this would be the journalistic legerdemain that scholars would scrutinize for centuries to come on the digital chips implanted in their brains, because THIS was *The Goddamn New York Times*.

Imagine my jaw-dropped demise when I finally found a rare copy, only to read sentence after sentence, then paragraph after paragraph, about how people would rather have been in the Vietnam War than here. Huh? I was stunned. They were saying everyone was disappointed, disillusioned, and going home; How everyone had to walk 30 miles to their car, and it was a disaster in every sense of their hyperbolic wordplay.

Me heart sunk mum. This was what the world would think. I looked up and personally counted over a thousand people within eyesight smiling, singing, and dancing in the middle of the street, many of them still with their clothes on. I looked back down at the article in disbelief, and it wasn't *nearly* as fun.

In fact, it was dead. Wrong, that is.

And something had to be done.

Clearly this was a job for Adventureman.

Thursday

"I've got to get back to the laaaand, and set my soul free," I was singing out the van windows to all the birds and rabbits along the New York State Thruway. I was on my way to Woodstock and if anything ought to fire up the old feeling tree it was C.S.N.Y. In case you missed the first Woodstock, `C.S.N.Y.' stood for Can't Stand New York, a popular singing group at the time who later changed their name to Can't Stand Neil Young, after a prolonged stint as Crabby, Sore & Nasty.

But right now they were the Channeling Spirits Nab You as I was on a Road's Scholarship that would change my life for more than a weekend — although at this point I didn't know where I'd spend the night.

Unless, of course, I looked at my meticulously mapped out Adventure Itinerary which provided multiple options for every moment of my life. That's the key: Plan everything to a 'T' then do whatever you want. If you start with an amazing blueprint, you'll always be doing something even better before you have to fall back to "amazing." Once again I was

5

traveling into the unknown with a list of things to do when I got there.

It was the old Rent a Van and Load it for Self-Sufficiency routine outlined in Emerson's famous essay, "*Creating A KarmaCoupe*." Or, as our great *Adventurous Emeritus* U.S. Grant once said after a few afternoon encouragements, "So goes an army or a man; Be self-sufficient wherever you can."

So I threw in some warm clothes, cool clothes, rain clothes, mud clothes, blue clothes, red clothes, plain clothes, No Doze, and a fire hose. I had a cooler, coffee, kind bud, milk, maps, snacks, tunes, Tums, a harmonica, camcorder and bike. I got my ears, I got my eyes, I got my nose, I got my mouth, I got my brain. I got freedom, brother; I got good times, man; I got million dollar charm, cousin; I've got life, life, life, life LIFE!

Anniversary observances for The World's Most Famous Party reunion were happening all over America this weekend. The festival that changed the world's perception of the most successful counterculture since old Sam Adams and the boys went boozin' back in Boston was in full bloom. Before Woodstock, flower power was a seasonal fad. After Woodstock, it was a continental divide. A half-million kids regressed to a cow pasture and evolution was actually advanced. Skinny musicians were suddenly more powerful than Evil Empires, and little-known businessmen like Bill Graham and Joseph Papp suddenly had their calls returned.

Underwear became optional.

Sheer numbers — and a really cool movie — changed the world. A president inhaled, some babies went boom, and suddenly this great nation, under God, had a new birth of freedom, proving that music of the people, by the people, with lots of people, was obviously way more fun! And it was so.

Over on the original site at Yasgur's farm, starting in about April and running through whenever they wandered away, was the Free Hippie Gathering. These were Woodstock's strict Constitutionalists, preferring original performers only, such as Richie Havens, Arlo Guthrie, and Melanie. They had long since set up encampments, and word was Richie Havens would bring a flatbed and mega sound system this year.

Original promoter & Woodstock visionary Michael Lang was initially planning his anniversary there until the local tweezers nitpicked his proposals until he just went, "Hey, this sounds familiar," and moved to Saugerties. Then no less a concert authority than the Multiple Sclerosis Foundation stepped in to promote their version of a Woodstock anniversary, but sadly history would never know that once-in-a-lifetime moment of sunset over Yasgur's farm with the smell of cows and history blowing across us on closing night and finally Dione Warwick and – NO! – Neil Sedaka!! come walking out together singing *God Bless America*! But even *this* was too wild for the town council of Bethel, so they voted these guys out of town too!

Then when old Sid Bernstein showed up with his "vision" thing they starting picking at his threadbare pocket until by the time some insurance heirs finally bailed him out, they had exactly two minutes left to promote the show. The final result was thousands of people were heading for Bethel, only nobody was ever allowed to set up fences and gates to collect tickets. And if that isn't what town councils are for, I don't know what is.

In between the two sites were about sixty miles of creek-filled Catskill Mountains and a chasm of debate. For six months the coffee klatches and newspapers were spilling all over each other regarding who had rights to the mantle peace. Were the rainbow people gathered at Yasgur's the true descendants of the first festival or just a bunch of homeless on acid? Were the original promoters actually disguised yuppies selling-out their legacy of peace for a corporate buck? How could a half-million mosh-pit skinheads get together for three days and not kill several people? How many kids were there in this MTV generation who could find their way off a couch and negotiate life without a remote control? Or to paraphrase the sixties: What if they had a Woodstock and no one showed up?

I'd been secretly communicating with the people handling the Gumbofest's International Press, which by some stretch of my imagination I could be considered. I thought I'd go there first to try to seal the deal and secure the access to the only event of the weekend that wasn't free. Things were not looking hopeful since they told me they were cutting way back on press, which probably meant me, but what would I be if I didn't try? I had to try. But worse, no vehicles of any kind were being allowed onto the concert site itself, so not *only* would you need an all-access pass to get inside to have an Adventure, but you'd also need some sort of car pass or you'd have to park in about Boston and shuttle back and forth. Plus, you might remember all the press accounts were reporting 12-foot electric fences, helicopters, metal detectors, stun guns, dog-sniffing cops, drugs on horseback, and a hastily constructed prison for 600. I realized sneaking in would take longer than usual. I figured, best idea is to get a master key to Moneystock, then bolt to Yasgur's for a quick olde timey vibe-check.

The first "Woodstock Parking" signs started appearing about twenty miles from the site, and the main Saugerties exit was already shut down with a wall of flashing squad cars two days before the official opening. Then I saw it. Stretching like Disneyland for more than a mile along the side of the freeway were the spires and flags of the newly-minted site. I turned open-mouthed to the imaginary buddies in my van and the whole Coupe started buzzing. "Hey, keep it down back there," I yelled, feeling us listing to the left as everyone crowded to the window for a look.

I imagined Johnny Dodger, my childhood friend, smiling in the passenger's seat. He was your standard manic Woodstock buff who would have loved this. In fact, he and I used to stage Woodstock reunion concerts — if you can imagine such a thing — back in Winnipeg, Manitoba, the small prairie town we never grew up in. Since there was nothing left to do by the middle of August (or after breakfast, really), every cool young person of a certain musical persuasion in our school would gather in a field those three nights, wear love beads, smoke rope and listen to Woodstock cassettes on a prototype boombox powered by a car battery.

I brought the music and Johnny brought the people. He loved everyone, and vice versa. He was my partner in pranking, and when I walked into the designated medieval-style Friar Tuck Inn in Catskill, N.Y., to scam my credentials — there he was holding court at The Round Table bar!

"No Way!" we both screamed with our eyes as we fell into a spinning, hugging, drink-splashing whirl. We'd changed each other's lives two or three times way back when, but it had been years since we'd actually Adventured together. Suddenly the person who was there for the starting gun on this long strange trip was shaking my shoulders outside of . . . Woodstock!

Johnny had grown a little rounder over the years like most of us, but it was much more in keeping with his happy personality. He wasn't quite roly-poly but he was definitely off-his-rocker. He had an open cherubic face you'd trust in a heartbeat, because all he ever sold was good vibes. For the most part he was absolutely normal except for the bit where he'd tell elaborate and untrue stories to strangers just for the fun of it. But most importantly — he was one of the few sailors I ever shipped with who would still travel a thousand miles to hear a good band. After all the wars on drugs, marriage, kids and other causes of rock n roll death, Johnny was one of the few left like me — with absolutely no life, nowhere to go, and nothing to do.

So instead of getting married and having kids, we met at the Friar Tuck on Thursday.

But now – the most Critical Mission of the whole entire weekend lay ahead. One of us, namely me, had to descend into the dungeon of this huge papier-maché castle and penetrate the central command of the International Press to fight and plead and smile to get what was rightfully not mine.

Apparently there were 11,000 other people who wanted to try the same thing. And most of them were already on line when I got there. Rows of tables were ringing the room, and rows of phones were ringing off hooks. Walls were covered with taped-up announcements of rule changes, fax numbers, schedules, and travel tips. The road-weary warrior reporters were hungry for service and the highly strung tension wires were buzzing: The French were complaining, the Italians were laughing, and the Canadians were politely plotting their takeover.

Even though I'd parlayed pre-approved status, as we stood in line I heard them denying passes and restricting access to almost everyone. It was like watching your brethren walk up and get slaughtered right in front of you and there was nothing you could do. At least I had time to work on my routine.

By the time I reached The Judgment Tree, the pivotal exchange went something like this:

"What are you doing here?"

"I need to file four stories, one a day, and the first one's due in ..." (artist looks at his watch) "Four hours. I need three things: access to press conferences for quotes, access to some sort of table with electricity and modem jacks on-site to write and file, and access to the stages and audience for the story."

A mere two hours later I was bounding back up the dungeon steps with an all-access site pass, *plus* the V.I.P. parking pass, good for nearest lot to the site! He shoots! He SCORES!

"It's a free concert from now on," I heard the voice of the original '69 stage announcement echo through the alcoves of the castle. There were two Woodstock reunions happening simultaneously that no one ever thought would happen — and suddenly both were free and open. The leaves had changed from green to golden in Sherwood Forest, and there was Friar Johnny entertaining his Merry Men with mythical tales of the road.

We had 45 minutes to squeeze in one Adventure before the 7 PM Press Briefing at the Tuck so we made our excuses and bolted for the site on our first Reconnaissance Flight. "Lets find this V.I.P. lot on Churchland Road before it gets dark," I suggested as we sprinted for the KarmaCruiser. Johnny was busy outlining his elaborate plan to sneak in on the press bus, because at this point he didn't technically have a ticket per se.

All I kept thinking was, "I can't believe I'm going to Woodstock with an all-access pass and Johnny Dodger!"

There's something divine about playing with someone you've known for years. You quadruple your strength by the two of you joining, which is to say, once you've been through the war of adolescence, peacetime's a blast. Neither one of us shut up for the first hour but we heard everything the other one said, playing with the between-the-lines digressions without explanations in a seamless free-flowing jam. We were together, we were on the road, and we were going to Disneyland!

The traffic had turned rush-hourish, but our new fluorescent-yellow parking pass dangling from the mirror got us waved through every State Trooper checkpoint like we was contendas. Cops were directing buses and semis with their arms in a constant swirl of inching wheels over rerouted roads. Around the site, thousands of backpacked teenagers were already eyeing the fence by the Thursday night of a concert that wouldn't officially start until noon on Saturday.

As we crept along the southern perimeter looking for a Churchland Road sign, I noticed one little middle-aged woman cop in the middle of the intersection conducting traffic like it was the philharmonic. She seemed so petite to be holding down the center of the biggest traffic jam in the history of the county. She asked me with her white-gloved hands if we were going in the delivery entrance, and I shook my head through the windshield but a big smile grew on my face. She was glowing with that rural sweetness that only comes from a lifetime of big family dinners and knowing your neighbors. For the first time I saw the face of the company we were going to be keeping this weekend and it was just as country as it was rock 'n' roll.

The site would officially open at 9 PM, but the press was promised an advance go-see, which also sounded like Plan A to sneak Johnny in. "You want to go back for the 7:00 press thing?" I asked.

"Yeah, better," Johnny said. "So *then* ... the guy comes back, turns on the light, but we're behind the couch, eh?" he was laughing. Before he could even finish half of his embellishments from the trip here, we were back at the Friar Tuck for our only shot at an official scouting of the sea before the storm. But by the time we found the hidden Maid Marian

Suite in the labyrinthian dungeon of the Friar Tuck Castle, reporters were backed out the room and down the hallway steaming mad like sports fans after a bad call. *This sounds fun.* Without saying a word, we both turned around and went back to the parking lot to shoot some beers.

A funny thing happened as we were toasting the fact we'd actually both made it: suddenly neither Yasgur's nor Saugerties's line-up seemed worth going to. "I *knooooow. Where's Neil Young?*" Johnny asked, just like he does every morning as soon as he wakes up.

"And Joni Mitchell," I said. "She only wrote the song that kept this thing alive."

"And Johnny Cash was supposed to play but he cancelled cause they put him on the wrong stage or something? What a mistake! He would have *killed.* He should fire his manager," Johnny advised.

"And his agent and roadies and hire us!," I said. "Imagine him strolling out at night in his black gunslinger get-up and slaying the audience the way he did at that Dylan tribute at the Garden," as we both took off designing our own fantasy Woodstocks just like we did as kids, only now we were parked outside two real ones.

At some point I decided I had to go to the Hudson River for sunset, and Johnny had to go to town for food, so we decided to meet back at the Friar Tuck right after sunset. *Seemed* simple.

It was time to be alone and find The Perfect

Spot of The Day — the abandoned turret, the battle site, the ancient ruin, whatever was available. Once a day, and twice on vacation, I uncover some sacred spot to be quiet and alone. Been doing it since I first found it more enlightening than school. Plus I collect another Adventure Card each time I sneak past a security guard or catch a full 4-color sunset from the top of a place you shouldn't be.

I negotiated the KarmaCoupe through Saugerties, an old mill & quarry town of 18,000 people an hour up the Hudson River from Manhattan. Fortunately no industrial revolution ever ruined the place so none of the buildings were higher than the trees, although several of the people were. Downtown was lined with beautiful Victorian bay window storefronts displaying arts & crafts, real antiques, and of course glowing-orange Woodstock '94 T-shirts.

I followed Lighthouse Drive in my determined search for The River. I always look for the center-heart of where towns started. It's how I see the world. By beginning at the core, you can fully experience how any place grew up. And like the rest of us, it's always water-based.

I followed my maps and instincts out towards Lighthouse Point which formed one side of a very funky bay. Or so it all seemed from the map, which failed to mention that the entire area was private property with signs every seven feet, each one reflecting a different generation's attempt at privacy:

old rusted tin signs said, "Please Keep Out;" cracked wooden ones that read, "No Trespassing;" withered cardboard ones cited the statute; and the nice new plastic ones said, "I Don't Call 911."

Normally a no trespassing sign or two has no effect on Adventureman, but even I knew it was getting harder and harder to pretend you didn't see them with each successive bend. Maps don't tell you these details, and I think they should. Someone needs to make a "Cool Roads and Fun Places of America Map," and maybe it's me. (Please turn to the map section of your Adventure Manual.)

Never to be deterred in my search for bliss, and knowing all roads lead to it, and also that all towns have to have something along their waterfront — preferably a motherfuckin' _park_ —I persevered in my sniffing out of the source, of the forest lining the river, of the — YES! There was a worn footpath through an open gate near an overgrown hedge that looked like it was heading off to the Nowhere I was searching for.

Zing zang zoomer, I docked the Couper; got loaded for beer, and slipped through the gate quiet as a deer.

Finally alone in the private Buddha Garden, I closed my eyes and listened to the sunset's symphony — the creaking of the cottonwoods, the whispering of the willows, the panting of the dogwood, and, finally, faintly, the steady backbeat of the waves lapping at all of us. I kept walking with my ears towards the cush

cush cushing until suddenly the gliss gliss glistening watershine came bursting through the trees and I was on the edge of the flowing-wide Mississippi of New York that could take me anywhere in the world.

Reaching out above the mighty waterway like a sturdy arm was a long-fallen cottonwood, its branch-fingers reaching into the rushing river and holding the muscular forearm like a bridge. I realized I was going out on a limb, but that was sort of the point. I tight-roped out to the end, sat in its palm, and watched the golden flames do their nightly dance on the river's playful ripples. I leaned back against a branch and heard myself singing *Brokedown Palace*: "Going home, going home – By the waterside I will rest my bones. Listen to the river sing sweet songs to rock my soul."

I raised a Heineken to the sky. I'd just been handed an all-access press pass to the most expensive concert in television history, hooked up with my oldest friend in the world who'd first dreamed with me of doing something like this, and was bang on schedule with my Itinerary! Couldn't be happier! Then, right at that moment, just when I had it totally together, I reached for a beer in my bag, broke a branch, lost my balance, and fell into the damned river!

Ha ha. Only kidding. Not even close. I was so balanced I could do cart-wheels on a sunbeam. I was tingling, maybe channeling, certainly vibrating. Everything was new to the touch. The breeze against my lips was so sensual I had to cover my mouth. Goosebumps shivered my arms. I could no longer feel the tree below me as my body floated up, light-headed, dreaming, spinning, shimmering like the waves, blazing like the sunset, and flowing like the river. I drifted away.

I didn't know it then but I know now. This was more than a sunset on a day, it was the sunset on a life I'd been living in search of something I would find in the freedom of this weekend. This was the last night of the first half of my life.

* * *

When I came back to reality, it was dark and I was on my way to the Tuck. By the time I got there, Johnny was nowhere to be seen. Nor was his one-of-a-kind dust-covered, hubcapless red 1972 Whateveritwas. So while he was off exploring the universe, the Adventure Manual clearly stated I needed to fly one more Reconnaissance Mission past the site.

On the way, I swung into a submarine joint in one of those tiny country strip-malls. All the storefronts had been gussied up like royalty was coming with "Welcome Woodstockians" in every window. The locals had gathered in every store to watch the hippie invasion, or whatever it was they were dreaming of. But the onslaught must have been caught in traffic, because I was the only non-local in the joint. I'm sure by Sunday they weren't disappointed, but word of a solo flier spread through the mall like a Clearance Sale rumor. People were coming from as far away as Hank's Bait & Bagel Shop just to watch me buy a hoagie. I did not feel so all alone, but I got out of there before I got stoned.

Down by the site, the scene had become like a late night horror-movie set. Colored smoke drifted in clouds under high freeway floodlights. Squad car cherries were silently spinning and troopers were waving their flashlights. On one side towered a Berlin wall with spotlights and sentries drawing a clear dividing line between the party & music inside and the scary police-state highway I was currently trapped in on the outside.

The traffic may not have been moving, but I was twirling like a dervish. All the Heinies and hoagie were hot on my tail and I knew I better keep moving or they'd nab me. In fact, for the first time I felt myself a cog in something turning really slow. Whoa! Sirens were spinning like an airplane crash, cars ahead – Brakes!

Road round site. Party full swing. Swirling boomboxes blending with police radios in dizzying surroundsound. Too many people. Too many lights. Gotta get out of here. There's that little traffic cop woman again — yeah — it's her, white gloves pointing, pointing me again, flashing, flashlight, pointing, her finger, looking me in the eye, seeing the V.I.P. pass, pointing with her eyes, with her finger, pointing me, in, steering me, pushing me, in, pushing me, God help me, in, through some checkpoint, no troopers — green t-shirts, guard house – gulp for breathe, totally bleary, no squad car, waving me, saying go, green shirts saying go, go, go through, waving me on, waving me through the looking glass.

Trees reached their hands down over the road and grabbed my roof. Shadows were dancing in the corners like devils around my headlights' flame. People were streaming toward an ominous bright light ahead. Figures appeared out of nowhere. Sudden cavities in the old dirt road made the van lurch from side to side, and AdventureGear was tumbling to the floor all around me. People were everywhere, like a parade, and I was the float. Light towers, production pony-tails, t-shirts, muscle-heads, bikers, roadies, flashlights, arrows, trees, lights, cameras, action everywhere! And then suddenly — there it was: the stage! *"Holy cats!"* I thought.

But there wasn't a moment to relish it as I was constantly making second-by-second driving decisions because there was nowhere to park and too many people and nothing but moving traffic and no where to even *stop.* And I don't mean all the spots were taken, I mean there was *no where* to park – there was nothing but one road and fences and guards and things. I was blindly following flashlights wherever they twirled me.

The thick fog engulfing the site cast everything in an otherworldly haze, and caught the different colored spotlights, painting the air with brilliant washes: blue halos glowed like a werewolf's moon — white spotlights embellished like a stadium at night — yellow emergencies were going off like flashbulbs — and jeep headlights were bouncing like skiers over moguls.

I knew I couldn't slow down long enough to smell the rose-colored clouds because someone might ask what in the hell I was doing behind the stage exactly, so I just kept moving, blissfully bouncing along like some rich Rodney Dangerfield knocking over his own urns with the Rolls, and scattering guards like pigeons. I drove like this all the way to the other side of the site and almost out the other gate! Whoa! I hung a fast U-ie at the last possible bulge before death by exitcution and started back the other way beside the trail of semi's that led to the stage.

I had to hide. I had to stash the van. How do you hide a van for God sakes? I thought back to the stage crew area but all the roads were fenced off and I'd look pretty obvious in the morning. All around the stage there was so much activity you couldn't even stop let alone park. Just as I realized there was no possibilities I saw a tiny two-tire track leading between some semi-trailers. I pulled the wheel hard and went shooting up the embankment to God knows! — Past a little van, past another van, trees, ahhhhh! I cranked a hard left just before wiping out a port-o-san and skidded to a stop on the dewy grass with my nose brushing the bright red vinyl of some poor puppy's tent.

I hit the lights, scratched my head to see if I was dead, and said, "Kay. I think I'm parked."

Everyone around me was so busy working that the TV crew I pulled in beside didn't even notice. Each vibrating second was bringing the light of the enlightenment closer. "I just parked the van," I thought to myself as words would form. "Backstage. ... At Woodstock." I sat in pulsating Buddha-beer silence with my ears throbbing with microphone checks, hollering roadies, and slamming doors. "And I think that might be the stage I'm looking at!"

I didn't move a muscle because I knew that made me invisible. Hours of seconds later the sun actually rose again in my brain garden, and I realized: "Hey, they can throw me out if I'm sitting here."

And I was out the door and down the hill in under a minute. Even though I'd had a few beers, I felt okay to walk. I entered the actual concert field for the first time, and for the very last time I was able to go straight across it. Well not straight, exactly.

It was 10 PM, the gates had just opened, and beaming faces were exuberantly discovering the field by the thousand. Fresh hay had been laid all over the natural amphitheater and it glowed like cashmere in the moonlight. A back-log of ticket holders had built up because there was some delay in getting identification bracelets or something, but now they were all running around like kids in a playground, exploding with hours of pent-up energy. Tents were being pitched, property staked, lawns pampered, hair brushed, and bottles popped. People were even setting up tents directly in front of the stage. "And I thought I had a good spot!" I said out loud to the ghosts of everyone I ever knew who was right there with me on this dewy field of Woodstock.

Futuristic gizmos and interactive cosmos were buzzing everywhere. Up the hill behind the sound mix tower a huge spaceship had landed. On closer inspection it appeared to be a giant mist machine for cooling people off. As you walked underneath huge white space tubes, a gentle steam hissed out as though you were cooling off beside a waterfall. Near that was a big wooden corral for horses, which on classroom detention — I mean closer inspection — turned out to be a frame to hold the piping that carried water to a hundred faucets pouring off it. Surrounding this dead center water shed were layers of lava shale like a manicured garden. The whole place looked like Versailles just waiting on ice for Josephine.

Across the entire quilt of a field there wasn't a wrinkle anywhere. But there were more rides than Disneyland! Over by the stage I noticed some bleachers and immediately penciled them in my Itinerary. Surrounding the massive field was a ring of huge striped tents that housed God knows what at this point. Here and there, new things were everywhere!

Then some Wink Dinkerson deejay wanker came out and made a few straight-street opening remarks, welcoming us to history but sounding much more like Big Bird's tour of a farmyard than the marching orders for a generation.

All of a sudden right above my head a giant light exploded! I was standing directly underneath when they suddenly began projecting *Easy Rider* on movie screens approximately the size of the sun. It seemed a little late to be starting a movie turned up so loud you could hear the pot crackling in the joints Fonda and Hopper were sharing. The sound was Clean, Big & Precise, it certainly bore well for the music ahead, but probably not for those who hoped to sleep tonight. I was suddenly overcome with a profound sense of joy and happiness that my tent was made out of a van, and wasn't pitched in the middle of this decibel testing zone.

I crossed the giant drive-in — I mean sit-in — with all the kooky colored tents parked pell-mell as the campers watched the flickering road story or made love behind zipped flaps or just whispered collectively, "This is amazing!" Wide eyes beamed white like headlights. But this was only the jaw-dropped calm before the storm, while everything was still perfectly laid out the way the host prepared it before all the rowdy guests showed up and trashed the joint.

And speaking of a joint, it felt like it was taking a *really* long time to cross that field. But by tomorrow the same route wouldn't be passable in any amount of time. The hay-laid bowl directly in front of the stage was currently free and open but would soon become a bodycrushing mosh pit for the rest of the weekend. I crisscrossed its fresh carpeting several times, watching as wandering fans walked closer and closer to the stage like Lilliputians tentatively approaching Gulliver. The structure was so huge it was intimidating. It was loud. It was alien. But it was ours. And very slowly we were getting used to that idea.

We were drifting in the islands, sailing in the tropics, singing on the road. Easy rider. Joy rider. Raft slider. Rum runner. Song hummer. "Mama, mama, many worlds I've come since I first left home," as someone kept playing *Brokedown Palace* on the jukebox of my brain. The peace. The place. The field. The space. The resonating bliss of the chimes of freedom ringing, people singing, memories zinging, bodies swinging, karma calling, mattress falling, pillow mauling, dream installing.

> "In a bed, in a bed,
>   By the waterside
>   I will lay my head;
>   Listen to the river sing sweet songs
>   to rock my soul."

Brian's Map of Woodstock

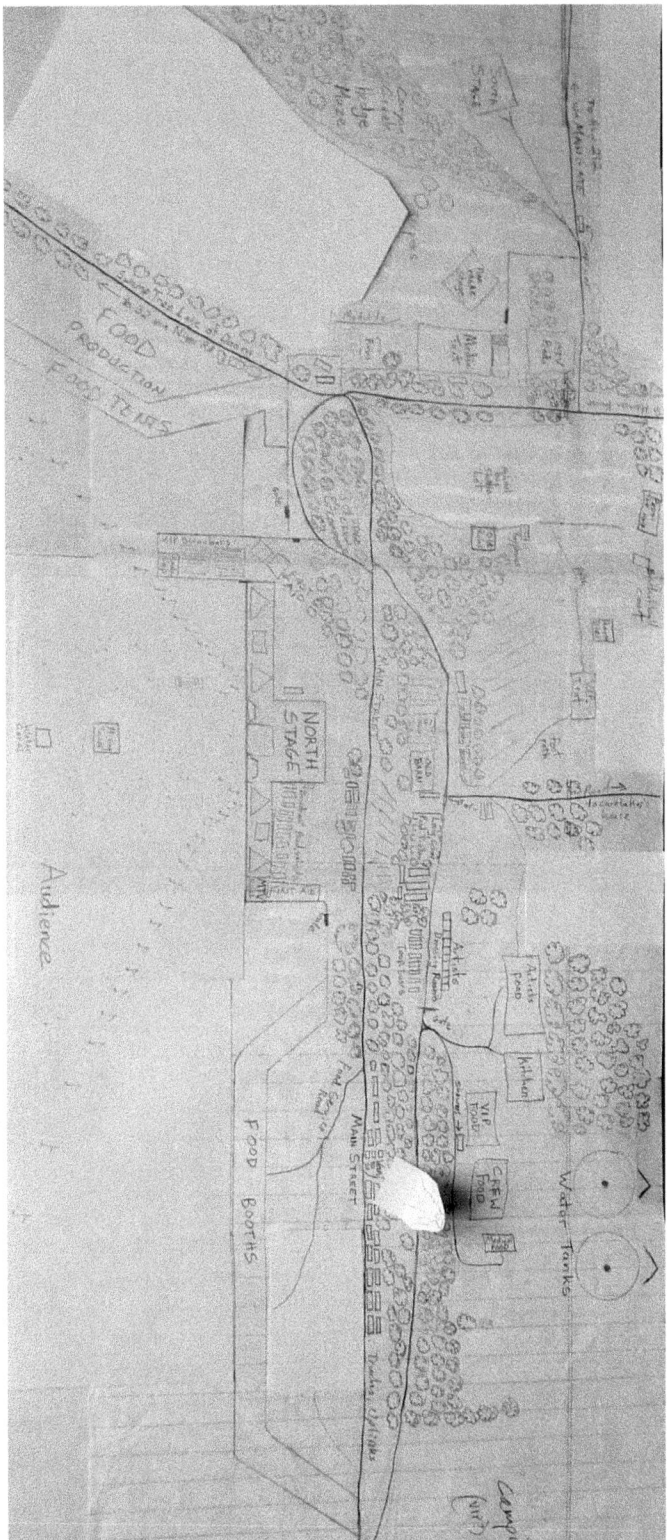

Friday

"Cockle-doodle-*doo-oo-oo*."

"I could have sworn I just heard a rooster," I thought, struggling against the world to go on dreaming.

"Cockle-doodle-*doo-oo-oo*."

"I *did*! I did hear a rooster!" My eyes popped open. "This is even better than dreaming!" I leapt to the window but couldn't see a thing. "It's still dark! No way!" I smiled wide and high. "That was a rooster *at Woodstock*! I can't believe this!" I thought, as it began to dawn on me and the day. "And I have a feeling I'm in a pretty good spot."

Fresh Hudson Valley morning air gushed in like water as soon as I opened the door. "I'm surrounded by million dollar satellite dishes ... and *roosters*?!" I thought as the morning milk trucks began to make their deliveries of brain cells. "Okay, I got back to the land. Now what?"

"Cockle-doodle-*doo-oo-oo*."

29

"I can't believe this," I fumbled, as I mumbled to my feet.

By tomorrow morning no one would be hearing any roosters.

Rising up behind the stage was a fairly steep ridge, which I was parked halfway up. In my ever-expanding quest to be at the highest point in any given place, I threw the bathroom sink in my Guatemalan daypack in case I discovered running water, dangled the #7 press laminate around my neck to see how far that would get me, and marched into the glory of the daybreak.

It was still dark but just past the impenetrable blackness of night — more like what night looks like in the movies when you can still see everything. I climbed up the first part of the rise behind my KarmaCoupe home and came out on the car road that angled up the ridge. I could have followed this up the hill the long way, but instead cut straight up the rocky slope until it abruptly broke at the crest of the ridge revealing another road lined with production trailers, and behind them, massive tents hidden like the officer's mess they were. I immediately snuck in and snagged some cold lemonades for breakfast and went snooping to see what else I could find before this rock 'n' roll fantasyland came to life.

As I walked along the top of the ridge the first trailer I came to had lights on, and whadda ya know, its door ajar, I swear, so naturally all I did was just peak inside, and YES! — a pristine clean shower machine! Literally! The closest production trailer to my van, contained six new showers with hot water, sinks, and *flushing porcelain toilets*! Knowing you have to ride your gift horses to win the race, I immediately took all my clothes off. This blessing only grew when I found out later it was the only shower trailer on the entire compound!

"I'm good till Sunday," it dawned as I sudsed. "I could live on a farm," I was thinking. "You go for a hike, scoop some lemonades, and have a shower before breakfast. This is easy."

When I stepped back out of the soul-cleansing soap center it was like coming out of a matinee and into the light. Good morning sunshine had opened the day the first music would play at Woodstock.

I walked along the road to the break in the trees that I'd climbed up and suddenly the entire City of Woodstock opened up. Over to my right loomed a gigantic mile-long stage, all glistening new and shiny. Scrimmed wings stretched for miles off a 2001-like black performance cube in the middle that looked like it had to be built for something much bigger than a temporary rock show.

Down the ridge where the KarmaCoupe was parked ran a mile-long row of white semi-trailers parked end-to-end, each with its own mammoth satellite dish balanced on top, and — this is the key — little production vans littered all about. My mini-cargo blended in like a relative.

During the night thousands of different colored nylon patches appeared out in the field, covering the 90 acre mattress like a giant quilt stretching all the way to the horizon. Surrounding the rainbow dotted center were the large red & white food tents, and beyond them, a fluffy line of dark green treetops. Across everything a thick fog was gently obscuring the scenery as the lost clouds dropped in for a visit.

"I can't believe there's this many tents *in the world*," I was whispering as some young volunteer medic walked up shaking his head and looking worried. "What's the matter, Doogie?"

"How are they ever going to get those kids to move all those tents?" the poor innocent wondered.

With a half-million teenage moshing American beer beasts on their way, I wasn't too concerned. I explained to the med school grad that nowadays fans pack so tight in front of the stage they can actually climb on top of each other's heads, and that some go so far as to jump right on top of the audience so their bodies get pushed around above the crowd in the recently sanctioned Olympic sport of *moshing*.

"You'll wish the tents had stayed when you meet the moshers," I smiled, thinking of the group that would give him the most work of the weekend.

Then he started worrying about them and I bid his neurosis adieu. I no longer listen to people who whine or worry. Life's hard enough without hearing complaints about it. I mute them like a TV commercial and return to my regular programming

of bliss and happiness. He saw tents and trouble.
I saw an odyssey and ecstasy. "Holy cats," I was
thinking as I plodded down the hill. "Are there ever
going to be a lot of Adventures around here!"

So I promptly unhitched old Ranger, my trusty
traveling bicycle, for a morning survey of the new
Adventurefield. Ranger had been with me from the
beginning. We'd done Clinton's first inauguration
together – oh boy could I tell you some Ranger
stories, including Arlington Cemetery as the sun set
on the final night of the Reagan-Bush nightmare just
before saxy Bill's assumption — but that's another
book (coming January 2020). Here we were, together
again, cruising the American epics. There's just that
one basic rule I try to live by, I think it comes from
the old Tao-Chi Lou: Take the train to the end of the
line, but have your bike in cargo.

I pulled out the hokey little cartoon map they
gave us and proceeded to entangle the entire area.
As I rode along desolate Main Street, the whole
compound felt like a Mad Max ghost town. There
were modern behemoth satellite trucks and banks of
electronics and movie screens with tentacles of cables
and wires – but not a single person. I had the bike
of the place! I was in the middle of a half-million
people but I couldn't see a one of them.

Naturally I rode directly to the stage to see
if it was really as big in person as it looked from a
distance. I weaved and whoa'd between pot holes
and semi's and finally glided up to the giant island-

sized stage. And there on the deck was Captain Stage Manager and a few of his cronies sharing a roasted brew right on cue.

"Nice bike," the Captain called out.

Ranger hadn't heard such talk in years. She and I met in the East Village nearly ten years ago through a mutual friend who'd fallen off the wagon and banged his head. Back then Ranger was a real looker – a skinny black racer with a carefree youthful style. Now, she'd been living in New York for ten years and was brittle and bruised and barely worked anymore. But she didn't take any shit from anyone.

"It gets me there," I yelled back, as I rode big circles in front of them.

"I'll bet you're the envy of all your peers," he said. "'Hey man, who's the guy who remembered his bike?'" and they all laughed and toasted their coffees in my direction.

Here was the stage manager of the biggest concert in history blessing my Ranger at the start of the weekend, and articulating the key to any successful Adventuring: Bring your bike.

I rode around the loading dock in circles like a young cowpoke on his horse with the Big Boss Man knighting his young apprentice, knowing his training was complete and he was ready to ride out on the range alone in search of his fortune. I rode past him one more time, raising both hands in the air in triumph as he nodded and toasted me again with his steaming sword in a slow deliberate canonization, as

I let out a loud "Eeeeeee-yaa-hoo!" wheelied, and pealed out with a fresh bolt of energy to explore every nuance of this wild coral.

"I'm the envy of all my peers, yeah, that's it," I said, as I galloped straight down the center of Main Street toward the Media Tent.

I was the very first person there as the phone man was wrapping up after laying in about a hundred phones in perfect lines on the new rows of tables. A food production trailer was nearby so naturally I snooped through every cupboard but couldn't find so much as an soggy Saltine. I decided to ride to town and reconnoiter the civilian stockades.

As I was negotiating the same Mud Mogul Road I came in last night, suddenly I heard, "Cockle-doodle-doooo!"

"Not again!" At this point I was a mile from the Coupe but still in the middle of the site. Through a fence, I spotted a huge weathered henhouse with a surrounding pen full of bobbing white heads and cocky red roosters. Just beyond the pen were a half-dozen *sheep* grazing in a pasture. "Yeah-sure," I thought. "I need some more sleep."

Not yet knowing my luck with the van in the old In-Out Department and whether I'd ever be able to get out of here and find Johnny again, I pulled Ranger over beside the guard house and watched the security guards letting vehicles in. Or not letting vehicles in, as the case happened to be. An ABC News station wagon pulled up full of reporters, camera crews and whatnot, and he wasn't letting *them* in! Then two band's tour buses came up with one lead van in front, and he told *them* to pull over! So the lead vehicle continued to pull through the gate and but the tour buses assumed they had the go-ahead and just kept driving toward the stage. This caused the Don Knotts Guard to go running off down the street after these big buses yelling, "Hey! Come back here ...."

Very quickly these bozos had a jam of cars clogging the gate and the first traffic confusion of the weekend was setting in. Nobody seemed to have the right passes, but obviously ABC was supposed to be here. Point was — they weren't letting *any* vehicles into the site. "There's too many cars in here already," I heard the Rent-A-Local tell a driver.

Then a mini-van pulled up dangling both a V.I.P. parking pass like I had and a special red "S" pass, which apparently stood for "Special Site Access." The guard said, "Tear that thing off," pointing to the type of yellow pass I had. "They're useless. Don't let me see it again. Just show the `S'. Okay, go ahead," he ordered, and waved the guy on.

"Oh-oh, they're on to me!" I realized. "I'm stuck," I thought, as I pushed off the fence on Ranger's two wheels. My parking spot was suddenly shooting up in the stock market. Access had become incredibly restricted. "If I pull out I'll be over in hell zone parking for the rest of the weekend. If I move I'll never get through those gates again," I warned myself as I rode along the empty morning streets.

Another Woodstock Lesson: If you're planning to beat the authorities, get there before they arrive.

"The only way I could get to Johnny is by bike," I thought shaking my head and picturing that long road we drove to the Friar Tuck, the crowds, and then him not even being at the Tuck when I got there. "There's no way," I realized, trying to convince myself not to try.

"We're all in this alone," I remembered Lily Tomlin saying. I was facing riding solo for the rest of weekend, just as I was at that very moment, on the virgin morning blacktop surrounding the bigtop.

All along the perimeter, they'd erected a solid ten foot tall wooden fence so people outside could only imagine all the fun they were missing inside. Each panel of the wall was a mural by a different artist expressing one of the themes of Woodstock: Rainbows, golden roads, doves, naked people. You could actually follow it like a visual conversation about the best parts of life actually. Or at least I did that morning.

The highway lines were dotted with fluorescent-orange rubber road markers (three times fast) to try to keep the cars in their lanes. But the only thing on the road other than me at this hour was the first of the big yellow school buses, each with a destination sign reading: "Employee Shuttle," "Green Lot," "V.I.P.," and so on. Uniformed State Police were at every intersection directing the minimal flow while wearing these huge grey flat-brimmed Stetsons that made them look like dorkie Ranger Smiths with flying saucers on their heads.

From the look of the front yards, the fateful families that found themselves unwittingly located along the road to paradise were taking the opportunity to throw the wing-ding of a lifetime. That simple twist of fate that places your peaceful country dreamhome in the middle of history reminded me of old Wilmer McLean whose front yard became the Manassas battlefield to start the Civil War, and then he moved as far away as he possibly could but his front parlor became the surrender site in southern Virginia. But this being the 20th century, these Wilmer's strung up colored patio lanterns and sold off parking spots.

One of the local bands was waiting outside the Woodstock Ventures office on Churchland Road because security wouldn't let them in the gate, and worse, they had to play in a few hours. For this warm up day's entertainment the promoters had lined up a bunch of semi-known acts to test the sound system and entertain the shoppers: Sheryl Crow, Blues Traveler and the Violent Femmes shared the bill with names like Candlebox, The Goats, and Peacebomb.

None of the Woodstock staff had arrived yet, and people had written graffiti all over their dew-covered window: "HELP", "Peace", and "High Time" — which I thought pretty much summed up the weekend.

Friday

Since musicians at 7 AM are not your preferred first class traveling companions, I continued riding through the beautiful farmland fog that bathed your face like an airy river. Evaporating dew from the tall, wild grass gave everything that healthy sense of daily renewal that country folk live with and city folk yearn for.

Here we were at Winston Farms, the rolling 800 acre rectangle of creeks and hills at the corner of a couple of old highways (212 and 32), a mile from the Hudson River and a million miles from anything else. It was built during the Rowdy Twenties by James O. Winston O. Boogie, a reservoir-building Virginian who was trying to recreate an opulent southern estate, with orchards, horses, a race track, and your standard 34-room mansion.

In fact, these are the very same magic fields that Michael Lang discovered in '69 when he first dreamed of staging an Aquarian Music and Art Festival near a cool little artist's colony called Woodstock. And it's a much more functional location than Yasgur's: It's right off a Thruway exit, has highways running down two sides, farmer's roads had already been running through the property for years, seven buildings were already there with electricity and plumbing, and it's got a natural concert bowl right in the center.

Ironically, just as Lang got kicked out of Saugerties in '69 before ending up at Yasgur's farm, he got kicked out of Yasgur's this time before ending up in Saugerties! In 1969 he was in negotiations with the Saugerties farm owner, a German frankfurter magnate named Schaller. When Schaller discovered they were a bunch of hippies he abruptly broke off discussions. Of course his kids never forgave him because Yasgur went down in history while they went down the tubes, so now that the kids inherited the place, they set out to redeem the family name. Or at least have free sex.

Covering the boulevards, driveways and front lawns around this rural museum were old silver Airstream trailers converted into hot dog stands not yet open for business, and wooden booths for T-shirts, fruit, sandwiches, programs, souvenirs, "you make it — we sell it," under every tree. Tables had signs for "Authentic Woodstock Posters," coffee cups, t-shirts, hammocks, fertilizer; carpetbagger's tents were set up to sell watermelon, homemade cookies, or cold beer if you asked with a wink; or visit the pick-up truck speak-easies for fresh fruit daiquiris. It was a perfectly arranged still-life county fair that was about to become an abstract riot.

Over at the highway intersection near the Thruway, there was a little rinky-dink bar-restaurant, a two-horse gas station, and a rundown Norman Bates Motel. And there in the parking lot was the first official awake body of the festival – an extremely strange looking local farmer with Woodstock patches all over his clothes and three or four free plastic cameras dangling around his neck.

We had to talk.

"Ah'v lived roun here aull'a ma lahf and ain't nothin' lawk this ever happen roun here befo', an Ah'v bin livin' roun here aull'a ma lahf," he told me, staring off into middle distance at something that may or may not have been there. "Ah don't reckon Ah'll ever see nuthin lawk *this* a'gin," he said, as he abruptly spun around and snapped a picture of an absolutely vacant parking lot. "An' Ah'm takin' pictures of the whole thang."

You certainly are. "Hope you have a lot of film," I smiled.

"Why?" he squinted at me, appearing to think. "You wan me to take yer picture er somethin? I ain't got <u>that</u> much film."

"No-no-no. I was just, I was looking for a beer actually. You think this bar'll be selling it later?" I asked, pointing to the Rinky-Dink.

"Sho they be sellin beer. Real fine place to get a beer," he said, leaning over but looking both ways to see if anyone was watching. "Fer ten bucks a glass they'll sell ya beer." Then he squinted at me ever closer, crunchin his nose. "You ain't from aroun' hair, er ya?"

"No sir, I reckon I ain't." When in Rome.

From then on he seemed to trust me. I think we were actually developing a bond of some sort. Which mildly frightened me. He looked up and down the road one more time, and when he figured the coast was clear, he leaned over sideways, real natural-like, and whispered out of the corner of his mouth, nodding behind him, "See the hump behin' me?"

I looked for a hump in the ground, a bump in the road, a lump on his back, but finally decided he was a Gump in the flesh.

"Thah — thah — the hump, the hump in the road righ' thah," he said, pointing at the overpass.

I felt so stupid.

"You go righ' over tha hump thah, and thah be all the stores you evah wanna see in ya whole lahf!" he said.

I thanked him, rode over the "Hump," and sure enough there was your Stewart's Good Food store! Your McDonald's! Your Dairy Queen! And a strip mall with your all-purpose Jamesworld K-Mart type joint, a Pizza & Beer place, a Subs & Beer place, a Liquor & Beer place, a Beer & Beer place, and a 24-hour Grand Union grocery store! Holy Score, Ranger! And like the real Gump, the guy's chance remark had changed my weekend.

I walked into the bright clean Grand Union with all its picture perfect racks of fruit and mile-wide aisles of unadvertised smiles on sale this week only. I had a long talk with the stage manager of the store, or I guess that makes him a s*tore* manager, and pumped him for details on the Union's preparations for the impending invasion. He said he thought it might be a little more hectic than usual, so they were closing at 11 PM because they didn't want anything to happen. The daytime was likely to be safe, he figured. I figured he was probably from Uranus.

"Just kind of like the day before a long weekend, huh?" I said.

"*Exactly*. Like a Saturday, but with more kids, I suppose," he said.

"Or like Times Square on New Years except with more people," I mumbled.

"How's that?" he asked.

"I say, expecting more people, are you?"

"Yeah," he said, balancing the last apple on top of his tall pretty pyramid then stepping back and admiring. "We got a couple extra girls coming in both days. We're ready, boy."

"Like a lemonade stand in a cattle drive," I thought, wheeling my cart away before his pyramid collapsed. I bought an excellent large salad and chocolate milk for breakfast, six cold Heinekens for lunch, and as a non-perishable dinner snack, two boxes of disgusting fake granola bars that were so gross they're still in my cupboard if you want one.

I went out on the front lawn and found a unused picnic table and had a quiet breakfast reading every newspaper in the state. Over at the next table a group of homeless Saugerties street hippies were recounting stories of the aluminum can stashes they'd found overnight, and how they got drunk to celebrate their good fortune, only to wake up to find out somebody else had walked off with their returnable fortune.

After I finished the last of the articles and croutons, I cruised around preforming a careful reconnaissance, taking precise mental notes on every service or product available within reach of the site, including the beautiful rough-cut Visitor's Center nestled in a natural collage of arches and benches — a very welcoming place for a visitor to smoke some kind bud.

With the heavy yet still cold six-pack barking on my back, it was time to head back to the BaseCamp KarmaCoupe to drop off supplies and see who else the roosters woke up.

As soon as I rode back over Gump's Hump — sure enough — the Woodstockian mother had birthed a nation! The first shuttle buses had dropped off the Eager Morning Beavers, and there were bright-eyed people roaming the roadside with their tightly rolled sleeping bags at their necks with vodka hidden in the center. Ticket holders were stashing supplies because they had to pass through the metal detectors and skin searches before they could even get on the shuttle buses, and security guards were confiscating everything of any actual value. The promoters played an Ambassador Card, saying it was for our own safety, when what they meant was it was for their own profit. Why let us carry it in when they could sell us a perfectly good new one instead?

To combat the marketplace with the $135 entrance fee, the front boulevards of the Howard Johnson's and Super 8 across from the site had become a free-for-all of homemade wooden stands selling homemade Woodstock castanets, kool-aid, fruit cakes, or whatever they had in the basement they wanted to get rid of.

"Official Woodstock comic books!"

"But this is a *Superman* comic."

"I know, but I lived in Woodstock when I read it."

"Oh."

I didn't buy it — been kicking myself ever since.

As I proudly rode up to the guard at the gate with my dangling press pass and no vehicle, the inside-the-gate Rent-A-Local-Lowlife suddenly held up his hand in the universal Stop signal. This Overly Officious Bowling Team Alternate wannabe looked me in the eye and said, "No bikes."

"What are you talking about?" I bounced back, but I was really thinking, "Oh-oh."

"I've been biking around here for days. All the staff has bikes. How long have *you* been here?" I fabricated and pushed it all at once, living by Robert E. Lee's dictum of a bold confident front being the best way to overcome a stronger opponent.

Unfortunately this prompted him to immediately get on his walkie-talkie to the No-Man who says "No" to everyone and who naturally confirmed the fact that NO, I can't bring my bike in. But they would allow me to lock it by the gate for the weekend.

Yeah, that would be *really* safe. But then it got

worse. After he said "No," I countered with, "Well I've at least got to get it back to my car and store — "

To which he calmly asked, "YOU'VE GOT YOUR CAR IN HERE???"

"No-no-no, not my car, of course not my car, I mean . . . *our production truck.* Yeah. The bike goes with the truck wherever we go. I can't come back without it."

"Yes you can," he smiled like Arnold on *Green Acres.* "You can pick it up on your way out, oink-oink. No bikes."

"Oh *yeah,*" I thought. But I said, "Well I guess I'll go ride around once more before I lock it up, okay?" and took off, never to return here again. Unfortunately, it was the main gate.

I immediately started scouting Route 212 for that risky long-shot that no one but me would take. But this being Friday morning all security systems were intact. In fact, there were farm-fresh State Troopers with eggnog and Woodstock Ventures Peace Patrols at every possible twig in the fence. There were A.T.V.'s on the hilltops, and easy-chairs with shotguns under the elms. Christ, there were barbed wire ribbons running along the two rows of fences and for the first time it became obvious I was going to have trouble getting in.

As I coasted down the gentle hills outside the site, the road next to the mile-long mural was now a parade of people in all stages of back-packing, from barefoot Apaches portaging canoes (not really) to shirtless locals pushing shopping carts stacked like totem poles of Budweiser (really).

The bus loops for the school bus shuttles to pull into and drop people off from the parking lots were against the site along the edge of Route 32. I strategically fell in behind one of the yellow buses, drafting as we coasted along the skinny country highway, until as soon as it pulled into the loop, I cut Ranger in on the blind side from the guards and was suddenly past the first row of security at the rim of the bus loop. Then, before I could be detected by any human radar survey, I ran a quick evaluation of every gate guard where the shuttled people entered, scanning for the most innocent face blocking my road to paradise.

Once radar detected the friendliest smile, I made sure my laminate was visible, then rode confidently through like I lived here. Both guards just stepped aside, smiling at the sight of the dangling press pass, and we each nodded in knowing recognition of us scamming the same show.

Boom boom boom I was back in the site, smiling as I negotiated the Swiss cheese earth which was not exactly biker-friendly. Once out in the main field, I was riding among all the new arrivals who had just had their Swiss Army Knives confiscated, and who were going, "Hey, how did that guy get a _bike_ in here for chrissakes?!"

It was Friday morning in the universe and you could already feel this was going to be huge and insane. The whole field was nothing but tents and people as far as you could see. Encampments were already stringing up fences and tweaking their bonfire pits, with a steady stream of new migrants pouring past, longingly looking for that elusive flat patch of pasture to call home.

And there on the range was one of the official wild west banks where people exchanged real dollars for Woodstock scrip so they could shop at The Company Store and buy their $12 pizza or $4 hot dog or official $3 condom. It sort of stood out because it was the only enclosed building on the field and it had these little tellers' windows like old west banks to exchange money through. The armored trucks that were constantly rolling in and out with the cash became one of the symbols of greed that the more radical and displeased of the patrons began to take their frustrations out on. By tomorrow, Rainbow Family lifers would spot these behemoths groping along the roads and attack them with mud. But this morning they were just another weird sight among millions that none of us had ever seen before.

"Here come old flat-top, he come groovin' up slowly, he got joo-joo eyeball, he one holy roller, he got hair down to his knee, got to be a joker, he just do what he please," I kept singing for some reason. "One thing I can tell you is you got to be free."

"Hey look at that naked guy!" I rode past somebody whispering. Sure enough, there walking along the earth like the first homo erectus of the weekend, was a long-haired, ape-man strolling through the people like a prehistoric sleepwalker.

I continued to bump and roll like a small boat on a choppy cow field seas, past The Wiz, yes The Wheeze! The Great American McCheese of fast-food music who successfully put all the mom 'n' pop stores started by people from the first Woodstock out of business. But now here they were with their six semi-trailer warehouses, golden dividends and theft-protecting radar guns so you could safely spend your official Woodstock scrip on your official Woodstock disposable camera for taking pictures of the Eco-Village and put it all in an official Woodstock plastic bag so that you could walk around the official concert Knowing you were Officially having a Grand Time!

The field was full of fresh optimistic people scouting the site for cleanliness and hay and girls and food vending people stapling paper doilies to their booths, whisking off the sawdust, patting down the tablecloths and smoothing out the wrinkles with worn hands. It was 9AM on a sunny Friday morning of a long, long weekend that was going to end in a muddy flood with all rules and doilies thrown out the window, but for now it was, "Woodstock Scrip Only Please," and just a minute while I pleat my skirt.

Like life, this weekend began with hope, hard work and careful preparation, all of which was going to be jumbled upside-down in unknowable ways before it was over. Something unexpected grew from the hard work, and it changed people. It allowed people to play, be free, and express themselves in ways they always wanted, to stretch in ways they needed, and bend in ways they were scared to. It was just another weekend, except that it changed people forever. And it was just a cow field afterwards, except for the life it celebrated while it was here, except for the people it opened like flowers while it lived.

* * *

Camped right next to me on Guerrilla Ridge was New York-1 News, the brand new 24-hour New York City news station. Slogan: "Because this is New York. And you live here."

I love these guys. They're like the first year of CNN: Real-people reporters and cardboard sets, instead of the other way around. No face-lifts, just raw data round the clock. I watched them constantly.

They had a fancy trailer home with its awning pulled out, and underneath they'd created a bona fide control room, with monitors, tape players, coffee tables and couches. Running cover for me were their own mutually white mini-vans. The coolest, most radical news crew in town, the cats who I already invited into my living room when I'm sitting home in my underwear, were my table-mates at the big feast.

I talked to their crew chief, a tall, tanned outdoor camp counselor type named Andy. I saw him at every press briefing, and he was the only media guy I ever noticed out the actual concert field. Sometimes he was a cameraman, sometimes a sound man, or the reporter, and the whole time he was directing a crew of ten. He was also the clearest of mind to talk to. I felt I could trust him. He was a general. He knew warfare and troop placement. When you find yourself on the frontlines, a general doesn't question how the neighboring regiment got there. You know they're one of you, or you wouldn't be fighting side-by-side. Generals know battles. And all privates wanna do is have some fun. It's those ladder-climbing snake oil middle-management captains you have to watch out for.

"We go live two or four times an hour until the music stops each night, then we're live again at 9," he told me, as we stood side-by-side overlooking the battlefield. "There's six of us sleeping on-site, and a few others shuttling from the Days Inn. They're the relief squad. We bust their butt and make them do most of the work cause they get to shower every day. They don't know about the ones here," he smiled. "What's your story? Why are you here?"

"I've been circling this thing for years," I said. "My friend Phil grew up near Yasgur's and called me when the first town meetings were held about two years ago, and we've been following it ever since. Woodstock always had this sort of mythical stature in our lives, maybe cause we both just missed it, I don't know. But it seemed like such an pinnacle of everything we ever believed in, you know? So when there was even a hint of acceptance by Sullivan County for the 25th, he was right on top of it. That whole area around Yasgur's is so conservative, they still haven't gotten over the first one. So when they actually held town meetings and the locals weren't burning the buildings down we knew something had changed," I said, smiling.

"Their local daily, *The Times Herald Record*, did a great job of covering the meetings, and his mom was mailing us the clippings. We both got in touch with Woodstock Ventures, and I read every book about how they did the first festival and their hiring practices, so we knew roughly what the advance hiring schedule would be like. Then all of a sudden Lang pulls out of Bethel and comes over here. So Phil and I drove over to this site back in April, as soon as they announced it. I think we had the sight-lines scouted before they did," I winked.

"Why were you talking to Woodstock Ventures?" Andy asked.

"Phil and I used to produce concerts together. He's doing it out West now. We were going to be production assistants or anything we could. I must have spoken to them fifty times. They actually ended up hiring me at one point. I was like `YEAH!' and then the next day they called; `Ooops sorry, we're going to use a free intern instead.' Ahhhh shit!" and Andy smiled like he knew the feeling.

"Meanwhile, I was simultaneously playing

each of the revolving promoters at the Yasgur's farm
site. First Lang, then M.S., then Bernstein, then the
Rhulens, and finally Delsener. I talked to every one of
them if you can believe that, but of course there was
never a show – just a roller coaster ride," I smiled.

Turning from the battlefield, General
Andy looked me straight in the eye and paused.
"Something worked, brother."

"Yes sir," I stood there thinking of all the times
I'd driven myself crazy going for something I thought
I needed and almost getting suicidal for godsakes
when it wasn't happening, but in fact it wasn't
supposed to happen you idiot because something so
much greater was just around the corner, and how
come I never remember that?

"Hey," Andy said, looking at his watch. "We're
live in 15," he saluted me out of my trance, and we
both fell back to our camps.

* * *

In order to keep the spirit lingering, I lit some . . . uh,
incense, yeah, and stuck it in the door frame. How I
remembered to bring all these little perks I'll never
know, but it just goes to show the importance of
traveling in a van capable of holding most of your
worldly possessions. When in doubt, throw it in. My
Principle Packing Tip: bring everything you touch
the week before you leave. Don't go looking for the
harmonica that's pushed in the back of some dusty

drawer (which I still do anyway), but do bring the dish towel, the pen, the pillow, the *cutlery*, the toilet paper, the coffee maker, the sink, and *both* soaps. I should have a TV show. Or at least be a guest on *Tips For the Poor and Crazy*. I think I could be a lot of help to a lot of people.

Or is that, I need a lot of help from a lot of people?

But here I was camping on Main Street — or was this a dream? The KarmaCoupe Cabin was set back a serene 20 feet from the only road that cut through the site, camouflaged by a cluster of support vans, with a huge yard, nice neighbors, hot showers, and a private port-o-san for me and the crews.

"But the point is, I'm *trapped*," I muttered as I puttered around on Camp Duty. "If I move: I'll be out in Hell for the weekend. I'd have to sleep in the shuttle lots which would be about as much fun as a Jersey commute. But if I hang around the van too much, security might come questioning me. Things have gotten *much* tighter," I said, thinking about the security at the main gate and the kids getting searched for everything they owned.

Out front, the close curb of Main Street was a mile-long wall of semi-trailers connected together end-to-end like a train all the way from the stage to the broadcast flatbed caboose at the far end of the line, which was covered all weekend by reporters standing with their backs to the crowd to give the viewer the sense they were really "with it" when in fact they never strayed closer than a fence or two from any actual members of the audience. All weekend it was buzzing with hair-puffing women in red dresses and skinny bald guys with blush brushes and cameramen adjusting lenses on this weather-beaten, cattle-hauling truck that served as the launch pad for every satellite broadcast around the world.

Beyond this caboose was the continuation of Main Street along a few different propped-up cow paths leading out to the highways surrounding the site.

To make sure that the masses couldn't mingle with the reporters and vice versa, they built large overhead pedestrian footbridges like funnels for human gerbils. These temporary wooden bridges of Ulster County lifted the paying customers up from their Camp Dewy Meadow, over top of the backstage roads that plainly led to kitchens, showers, and fantasy fulfillment, and dropped the $135ers back in the next pen with The Company Store and Automatic Teller Machines.

Staying in this privileged pen was no place for me. "Clearly it's time to see some stages," I pondered as I wandered off down Main Street, skirting the edge of the ridge and flickering through the morning shade of the trees rimming the train of trailers. In what was just the beginning of the contrasts between earth and technology that were to permeate every image of the weekend, up against a black video truck was a vibrant bush of white flowers in full bloom. Tiny bell-shaped flowerheads were reaching up, open-mouthed to the sun, exactly like the white satellite dishes above.

I walked past the stage again only they'd cordoned off the entire loading dock area I'd been riding cowboy circles in earlier. I could see my stage manager general off in the distance yelling at somebody.

The whole scene had taken on the look of a front-line M*A*S*H unit — and this would stick for the weekend. We were like a huge temporary army set up in a field location where we never were supposed to be, but were. There were doctors and nurses rushing along the roadsides with Red Crosses around their biceps. There was this feeling of people meaningfully running around on missions, which by their faces were of grave importance. We were in a functioning, self-contained encampment with a chain of command, half-a-million soldiers, and a mission from God. The golf carts were the jeeps, the laminates were dog tags, and the press corps were scrambling to get the "real" story.

While I was stopped behind the stage carefully taking notes on the human traffic flows, I heard the promoter John Scher start talking from the stage. "Holy smoke! It must be 10:00!" I realized. "Sounds like he's opening the show!"

In the press kit they gave us at the Friar Tuck I noticed a sheet on Native Americans they'd scheduled for the Opening Ceremonies, and knowing they'd be the most direct spiritual masters of the weekend, I was in the crowd before Scher could finish his sentence.

The front of the field was surprisingly open, so I sashayed right up to the stage. These amazing gurus in their full peacock feathered regalia were chanting and dancing and blessing up a storm. And there was Michael Lang on the side of the stage in his fringed leather jacket, grinning his cherubic, beatific grin. I kept wondering: If the guy's such a capitalist prick as so many bitchers complain, what's with the full hour of Indian tribes *opening* his Woodstock II? Even if he "sold out" to Pepsi, he didn't have to invite all these spiritualists and give them their own tepee field for the weekend . . . and then stand on the stage and watch them in crossed-hand reverence. If they would have appeared for five minutes it would have been a perfunctory gesture. But he had them on stage for an hour with their various blessings, speeches and prayers in different languages, eliciting that singular tranquility only felt in the presence of true spiritual masters no matter the faith. It hushed the crowd. For an hour this supposedly heathen generation of moshers paid attention to a tribal overture about listening to your heart and how we're all a part of our future. It may have been the last time they were quiet until about next Tuesday, but they were quiet now.

And a wide variety of blessers it was too, including that pop art pillar Peter Max who said, "We've come here in the name of peace and music.

The whole world is watching, as it did 25 years ago. Let us conduct ourselves with peace and love, and let it shine all over the world."

Even after the recent widespread yuppie epidemic, with its *Beavis and Butthead* aftereffects, we proved that a half-million nineties kids could still find their way to a designated location and stand on their hind legs in unison. And maybe it was even more than that. But it was these ancient Americans who were putting a voice to it before it even happened.

Chief Jake Swamp was the Grand Poh-Bah of the whole shebang. He introduced a gorgeous singer named Joanne Shenandoah who looked like a goddess in a white flowing gown, while all around her were sage burners, flag wavers and drum players celebrating her arrival. They created with voice and music a transcendental sense of oneness, of all of us being part of a single body. We were hypnotized into a silent unity by a harmony and a beat. And it's pretty much stayed that way through Gabriel on Sunday.

* * *

Gliding like a dream over ice, I slid down the hill and found myself floating in the Media Tent with a million other fish. "Holy Doodle! School's out dude!" It was like falling into the most popular class in school just before the teacher arrived and everyone was standing around holding notebooks and chattering away like birds on steroids.

I felt a little lost, a little late for the party. Everyone was in full schmooze like they'd been drinking for hours and talking for years and vice versa.

I weaved my way to the back corner which seemed like the perfect place to watch and, of course, it later turned out to be where the International Media set up their Base Camp, as well as the north pole magnet for all the Canadian journalists. I was home again.

Apparently everyone was waiting for the first "briefing" of the festival. For those of you who haven't been to a "briefing" before, which I hadn't either, it's a kind of military-style operation where men in uniforms come out and tell you what they want you to believe happened, and then you get to stand up and ask them how to spell different vegetables.

First up was John Iaccio, the Department of Transportation guy who never removed his hardhat all weekend. He told us what percentage capacity the parking lots were at (70), the flow reports of every major intersection as of 30 minutes ago (moderate), and how many emergency vehicles they had standing by (tons). You knew he was losing sleep in more ways than one this week and you had to admire the people holding the safety nets for the party. And traffic was moving faster here than it does in Manhattan. I imagined being in Central Command at the D.O.T. watching the aerial photographs coming in, and scanning the radios, and responding to disasters. They were monitoring as many people here as were in Saudi for Desert Storm, only this was an army of blasted beer-heads on their summer blow-out, set in a sleepy seaside resort, with rock stars singing, *Eat The Rich*. What I'm saying is, these guys did an amazing job.

Next came the police spokesman, Colonel James O'Donnell. He told us the number of arrests and complaints during the weekend, and as of Friday, this was the total damage: Four `suspicious person' complaints, one medical emergency, one D.W.I. arrest, and eight illegally parked vehicles (although nine would have been more accurate ☺). With 500 State Troopers in the area, there were less arrests-per-cop than any night in New York State history.

They kept telling us how there were 75,000 people here now and how they were expecting it to double by this afternoon. When you looked out at the people and tents reaching all the way to the horizon and beyond, it was hard to imagine it <u>twice</u> as big. Yet it would be five times the size before it was over.

Then John Scher came out, a guy I used to work with, and it was good to see him promoting this. There's a lot of really sleazy people in the music business and for the most part he's not one of them. He's no angel, but if Bill Graham's not here in '94, there isn't a better heavy to be in charge.

He was being all nice and helpful, explaining how it was originally planned to only be Saturday and Sunday, but this day was added because of the demand from people who wanted to arrive today for the weekend. He explained who the new bands were, and was just trying to be as nice as he could be.

After not laying a glove on the cops, the tough-guy reporters were sitting back just waiting to hit the poor portly promoter with everything they had. And John was up there trying to smile and put the best face on their questions, but they started to get more and more offensive. "Yeah - but how many people got in for free?" a reporter yelled, and I raised my hand until I realized I wasn't supposed to.

A lot of us came to this expecting it to be about as authentic a Woodstock as Jerry Rubin turned out a radical, what with the Pepsi banners, $135 tickets, and ear-bleeding bands. A blind man could see by Friday morning that something special was happening. There were thousands of people from all over the world filling the field. An entire extra day of music & magic had just been added to channel the energy of the assembled thousands. We were on a huge farm that we could roam around on and was so big you could walk for hours in any direction without hitting a road. Okay, this might have been a problem later when you wanted to leave, but the point is, I was parked in the bull's-eye center of the whole thing! No, the point is, the place was *huge*! And if you weren't having a good time where you were, all you had to do was move a few feet.

That's another Woodstock Lesson: There are 360 degrees worth of ways you can always change your life.

So John Scher was up there taking the questions from the cynical whiners until finally he stopped being polite. After one too many, which I think was along the lines of, "Isn't this whole thing stupid, and our generation had the Vietnam War, and what do these kids know?" he just sort of snapped and said, "Alright, alright. You're really opening yourself up to something here," and it reminded me of Laurie Metcalf's centerpiece monologue in Lanford Wilson's *Balm in Gilead*, where her friend asked one question too many and she lit into the most riveting single monologue I've ever heard on a stage. It began with, "Okay, alright, you asked for it," before she told the whole sad story of her life and had everyone in the theater in tears all six times I saw it. When Scher started with that, "Alright, alright, you asked for it," you could just hear the tension on the spring about to twang:

> "I think mostly it's media people who have trouble growing into middle age and letting go of their icons, letting go of the thing that was so near and dear to them, and not wanting to share it with their children or younger brothers and sisters, which, candidly, I think is disgraceful.

Calling it `Woodstock' was a very conscious decision by two groups of partners. **This isn't *like* Woodstock, this *is* Woodstock**, in every sense of the word. If you guys walk through and talk to that crowd I think you'll find that to be true. Having some 48 year old journalist sit here and say, `We had the Vietnam War, and Nixon was in the White House. What do these kids know about that?' Well you know something, one of us is *in* the White House right now. And to be serious for just a moment, these kids are faced with things that we were never faced with. I don't know how many of you in this room went to the Vietnam War, but many, many more people have died of AIDS than ever died in the Vietnam War. And unfortunately, many more people *will* die of AIDS. And these kids don't have the opportunity to go to Canada or to stay in college or go to graduate school."

"At the first Woodstock, the word `homeless' was something you had to look up in the dictionary. These kids have to trip over people on the way to school. This is the first generation that's never had the expectation of doing as well as the generation before them. They have issues that are as important or more important than the issues the first Woodstock generation had to deal with. Environmental issues, health issues, sociological issues, political issues, and I think everybody ought to open their eyes and talk to the kids that are here, and talk about those issues and stop worrying about the comparison to what happened in '69.

"It was a magical time in '69. These kids are going to create their own magic."

Right on Brother John.

* * *

Many of the assembled media were members of the Church of Jesus Christ I've Got To Make A Phone Call sect, and they were beginning to freak out. There weren't a lot of working lines in the middle of this cow pasture. All the new phones that had been laid out so nicely this morning had become a cord-tangled non-working octopus's nightmare. One in a dozen had a dial tone, and once you found it, the line would go dead as soon as you punched a number. But I'll try anything once. Of course the first phone I picked up was the one that was working and I actually broke through to the outside world. It felt like Radar O'Reilly reaching Seoul.

I got through to the Friar Tuck and had Johnny paged, so at least my conscience was relieved. He was probably off on another adventure at Yasgur's farm by my watch. I left a message with the bartender, which was the most obvious flare I could fire, and left it to fate from there.

Before leaving the Media Tent, I coaxed the time schedules from Miss Versa Manos, the Clara Barton angel of the International Media who made sure we stayed alive but didn't want to release the schedules to the press because she thought we'd all report that the show wasn't running on schedule. I don't know whatever gave her that idea.

The afternoon's line-up was filled with such appealing performers as Lunchmeat, Jackyl, and Roguish Armament, all of which sounded like Tylenol pushers to me.

The first act I wanted to catch was Orleans, with John Hall, who wrote *Still The One* and *Dance With Me* and basically put together that *No Nukes* concert and movie. He actually lives in Saugerties, so he was doing the "Local Boy Sings The Hits" routine, and I wanted to be there for the homecoming, which according to Maestro Versa would be 4 PM. This would be followed by Blues Traveler doing their "Real Music By People Under 30" routine, so I was well-primed for the acquisition of some musical options at that juncture. Indeed — starting with Orleans around

4:00 today there would be non-stop amazing music for the rest of the weekend. That made the next few hours the last chance to bike The Big Picture.

I checked the Adventure Itinerary and the only thing left to do was find Cheri Roberts, the Woodstock Ventures person who wanted to hire me. We almost got married over the phone two or three times, but never met.

Mission One: Find the girl — win the prize. Mission Two: Stay the heck away from the van. If anybody comes checking vehicles and asking, "Excuse me sir, but who the fuck are you?" I didn't have a real funny comeback, so I figured I ought to split.

I rode past the radio active flatbed caboose and out the "Not a Truck Route" road, and boy did they mean it! It dropped like a rock off the ridge and landed in a marshy wetlands with a creek and a narrow one-lane bridge. Just as I was reaching peak gravitational speed at the bottom of the hill, the Abandoned Building Radar Screen began blinking, indicating a small wooden structure hidden behind bushes along the creek. "Holy cats!" I skidded. "A totally abandoned cabin right here on-site!"

I honked a brake-slamming foot-dragging motocross speed-turn and shot down an old weed-covered path that may have once been a road. Finding abandoned buildings was *usually* Mission One on any given Adventure, but this weekend would be fairly crammed with music and other stuff so I'd shelved my regular dust-raising explorations until less life-altering patterns prevailed. But NOOOO. Here, right in the middle of my busy schedule, was an overgrown cabin *on a* creek flashing an ultraviolet neon sign:

"Cool Cabin ! !" "Space Available" "Cool Cabin ! !"

The entire Catskillian region is flourishing with very affordable abandoned hotels, barns, castles, houses and such. This is because of an old Ulster County ordinance still on the books which reads: "No structure standing five (5) feet or higher may ever be torn down for any reason whatsoever no matter what its condition, and that's final."

This peculiarity of law has resulted in the richest mother lode of cobwebbed crawlspaces in the Western Hemisphere, or at least in Upstate New York.

"Hi kids. I'm your host, Scott Phree, here for another episode of *This Old Abandoned House*. Last week we taught you how to climb into condemned train stations. This week, we'll show you how to pull secret cabins out of thin air, and how to how to build a hang-glider out of standard prison-issue clothing."

I can't help it. Wherever I go I climb into anything that doesn't move, irregardless of climate, custom, or continent. It's a way of exploring a city's past, of walking with its ancient local ghosts, seeing the way people used to live, and what they left behind. It's crawling under the skin of the community and seeing it from the inside where you're not supposed to be. The forbidden portholes to history. The all-access pass to the secret, sacred places of earth.

In fact somewhere on this thousand-acre spread there's a 3-story mansion built in about 1700 which clearly fit the profile of A) potentially abandoned, B) Gold Adventure Card, and C) conveniently located. If you have any leads let me know, because it's on the Itinerary.

The whole cabin had turned a uniformed shade of Confederate-grey like old buildings and people sometimes do. The windows were now your open-air variety, with fragile cobweb ribbons where the pains were once framed. A knotted trap of weeds covered the door and floor in a gnarly web. Vines grew up the outside walls and in the windows then out again through holes in the roof.

I stepped up onto what was used to be a porch, balancing on the foundation beams like railroad rails. The marshy creek had eaten away most of the floorboards and the ones that were left crunched to dust under my boots as I balanced from beam to beam. I tightroped to the wooden door that was propped ajar, and pushed through the weedy net to the solid floor inside. Camouflaged windows provided excellent spy radar look-out views in every direction.

While standing at the windowsill and filling up a Commemorative Bowl to celebrate this rich discovery, I noticed across the creek through the trees ... was the stage! Through the filter of only a couple of leaves I could now watch the entire show from my own private abandoned cabin! I quickly pulled the Itinerary and made a special report: "Private on-site KarmaCabin 2 minutes from the Coupe. Meditation ground beside trickling creek. See Stage. Bring beer."

"How much better is this going to get?!" I grinned. I'd already collected one Adventure Card and hadn't gotten out of sight of the stage yet. Tea-hee. "Find Magic Secret Spot within inches of my house." Check. Next!

I slid the Card in my pocket and said, "Thanks a lot, eh?" to the friendly ghosts of families, strange trappers and fishermen who still lived there. "See you in a bit," and I pushed off to resume The Mission.

I continued down the dusty little Mower's Mill Road until I reached the State Troopers barricading the end of it. They were stopping all but the few farmers who lived here, but they didn't even blink at my bike so I knew I'd found free passage, which was the good news. The bad news was I'd also found that the rim of my wheel was riding on the pavement. Sure enough – Ranger had a flat!

The poor old girl just about had it. Originally a ten-speed, she was now more like a no-speed. The back wheel mostly rubbed against the frame, while the front brake mostly rubbed against the rim. Mostly it was like riding a stationary bike with the tension on High. It may be time for the old girl to be riding the great highways of the sky, but I'd never admit it. And besides, even as I steamrolled along on a steel rim over pavement, my dear old Edsel Ranger with one flat tied behind her back was faster than the plodding pedestrians. "I better get this fixed or I'm going to be that slow for the rest of weekend!" I scared myself into action as I rolled into Cheri's Woodstock Ventures compound.

I bounded up the stairs to her office with my ha-ha funny story and a full-grown happy face to finally meet the voice I'd grown to love by phone. "Oh Cheri just moved on-site this morning," the receptionist said. "You just missed her."

With the large "Loser" sign flashing in the middle of my forehead, I asked if there was a bike shop in Saugerties. Of course no one in the room was from closer than Brooklyn and they knew less about the area than I did. When I checked the phone book, there wasn't a single bike shop in the entire town of Saugerties. Yeah, I know what you're thinking. "You just didn't find it. *Every* town has a bike shop. How do people get their bikes fixed?"

"They drive to Woodstock," the guy told me over the phone. "That's the only bike shop for thirty miles."

This was no time to miss Manhattan. The clock read 4:15. The Woodstock store closed at 6:00 and

I was ten miles away on foot, times the number of people stranded along the highway, divided by the hypothesis, equalled, "Holy cats! I've only got 14 protractors to get there!"

If there's one thing I've learned, it's that the most time-consuming part of any shitty job is the time spent putting it off.

Out on the road around Paradise the masses had gathered for mass. Tourists were having their pictures taken by the murals. Kids were scanning the fences for ways in. Every second vehicle was a big yellow school bus making it look like a gigantic Bill Murray summer camp, with fresh campers leaning out the windows taking pictures, singing songs, and planning how many rules could break by Sunday.

"All I need is a damn inner tube," I thought. "Quick — run a scan on the paperwork and maps. Play back the morning's surveillance tapes. Good, okay, there's Stewart's Good Food store, the McDonalds, the gas stations, that K-Mart place, — right! *That's it!*"

I bolted to the first locals I could find, in this case, lounging under a homemade wooden shelter with "Watermelon for Sale" signs out front. These were just a decoy, however, as they were using the stacks of fat fruit to hide their buckets of Budweiser. These industrious hosers had gone to the trouble of constructing an entire fake fruit stand in the middle of the action just so they'd have somewhere in the shade to get drunk. And it was apparently working!

Between the lot of them they were able to remember that the K-Mart I was looking for was called "Jamesworld."

As I crossed Gump's Hump, I was trying to picture the lines at a K-Mart next to a Woodstock at 4:30 PM on the Friday. As I swung the door open expecting a department store 2-for-1 New Year's Eve frenzy, standing before me all alone was the sweetest grey-haired matron in a checkered apron you'd ever want to see. Her hands were crossed in front of her like a bed & breakfast hostess and you were the first guest coming through the door.

My precious savior led me all the way to the bike section in the back corner of this warehouse-sized store that you knew sold one of every single thing made in the world and I was all set. Except they had every inner tube size but the one that would fit my bike. Now it was 5:00 and I could feel the "L" brand burning back into my forehead.

I looked around for Pride and it was no where to be seen, so I went off in search of Help. Up in the front of this Twilight Zone-empty store, the only person who wasn't a teenage mutant check-out girl was this blond Californian Bandanadude. I asked if he knew anything about bikes. Of course he was a pro cyclist looking for a tube himself! *What?!*

"Come on man, we'll fix you up," and he walks me back to the rack and rigs me a new tire and tube and explains how to make it fit my rim. Ranger's Bike Angel Cometh! Her ninth life was granted!

There was hope for the old girl yet!

> Synchronicity for 100, Alex: Was this
> simply the time of day bikes broke down,
> or was it something more? How could
> I be in a store that sold everything, but
> had no people in there except one bike
> expert?

Promising to never do anything wrong again as long as I live, I went to the check-out counter where all the girls were wearing tie-die for what you had to figure was the first time in their lives. I quickly found out these were your hardcore soap opera buffs, and I don't just mean TV. I'd stumbled into one of the key gossip centers of Saugerties. Entire families were gathered round the registers swapping stories like it was high-stakes poker.

"They're just *lettin'* people in. They're not checkin' or nuthin'."

"I heard they're selling 6-packs over the fence for $20."

"I heard somebody got a ticket for $80!"

"I heard old man Kendle bought one for 30 off some guy on the road!"

"Tootsie Bennett got hers for 20 from her old man."

"Wally said there's a big hole in the fence just past the front gate that you can just walk right in!"

Then suddenly a young girl came running

in the exit door all out of breath like a female Paul Revere. "You can drive in the delivery way," she panted, holding up her hand. "We just did it," she said all out of breath and looking back as her dad came strutting in like a bronco rider after winning the rodeo. Good old-fashioned American competition was in action, with each local family striving to out-scam the other. By the fervor of the announcement I could tell this was the first vehicle to get in and out, and dad planned to milk it for life. Until someone could produce a card ranking higher than, "Oh yeah, well I've just been driving in and out all day," he was the reigning Jamesworld Champeen.

I'd love to have heard the winning entry on Monday morning, especially if getting your car in and out was in the lead by Friday afternoon.

Somehow in the Woodstockian KarmaSoup mix I had extracted an inner tube from the town of Saugerties. Now I'd need about the same luck extracting a crescent wrench and bike expert from Cheri's office. But pins and needles to say, within 10 minutes I had a team of three giving Ranger a complete overhaul! And the handlebar mustache chief fix-it guy also happened to be the Director of Transportation for the whole freakin' site! I didn't mention where I was parked.

Oh, and on top of that, the very helpful Bicycle Brothers were keeping company with a half-dozen blond Dutch models who were here on some promotion that involved expensive bottled water and very short shorts.

Put that in your corncob and smoke it. And we did, in the trailer, with cold beers and gorgeous Pam Anderson lips wrapped around a twisted fatty if you will. The air conditioner was blasting but I was melting like butter on a skillet. Golden delicious flesh flashed under sleeves, under halters, under shorts, understand? Trust the God of Heineken to find it's way home to roost! It heard the lyrical call of the Dutch-accented songbirds singing their mating melodies and it brought me to the hash bar of its bounty.

An intoxicating blend of perfume, oils and herbs transformed the room into a sensuous garden of youth, where each bouquet was more beautiful than the last. "As long as we're off by 10:00," Ryah said, wearing nothing but a silk bra and panty-shorts and passing me the joint. "If I don't see Sheryl Crow I'm going to die."

"She's great," I said, sucking in the air behind the smoke. "Can't believe you've heard of her."

"I knoooow," Ryah said, flashing open her green eyes in amazement. Then really slowly she said, "She's *so* great."

"'There's such a muddy line between the things you want and the things you have to do,'" Janna sang from the front of the mirror, pulling at the top of her jumpsuit, then at the bottom, then the top.

"That's one of our warm-up songs," Ryah said, bending over till her elbows almost touched her feet. "And Melissa [Etheridge]," she said, letting out a long steady breath. "But she's not till tomorrow. Can we just give away all this swag today and take the rest of the weekend off?"

"I wish," Janna said, nodding toward the window and fruitlessly trying to pull herself into something she was spilling out the top of. "Oh well," she shrugged. "It'll be fun anyway."

"Have you seen the mist machines in the field?" I asked.

"We haven't been *any*where," the oldest one said, getting up from the couch and brushing past Janna to the front room.

Ryah just rolled dismissive eyes and smiled like we were the bad twins in the corner. "I'm having fun," she mouthed to me, then nodded a fussbudget nose toward the Matron Complainer.

Janna shook the joint backhand to Ryah as though trying to get rid of it before someone saw. Ryah feigned fear in a lingerie disguise, then reached out for it like a mime spy, but mom's the word, don't catch her eye, just you and I. Bobbing curls of prankster girls in smoky swirls, we were bouncing our smiles and rolling our eyes like riffs off of drum rolls, and dodging the meanies by rubbing our genies. But only till Mother Hen comes back again.

She passed a change of clothes to Janna like a football hand-off, saying, "Here." She just held them to her tummy and looked at Mama Hen, then down at the denim top. "That'll fit," the eldest one said as she cushed back onto the couch. The two of them smiled at each other real quick, then Janna disappeared behind a curtain.

An hour and two lives later I felt myself floating down some stairs off the runways of Amsterdam and back into the dusty highways of, "Oh my God — .... " The infant scene I'd left a generation ago had grown into a full-blown adult-on-the-make. Dusk had ripped the innocence from daylight, and the decadence of night was just ahead. There was noise coming from everywhere. People were screaming and laughing and different kinds of music were spilling from every direction. And you could sense that the security & rules routine may have slacked off just a little.

Out on the highway there was a shirtless guy holding up a sign and yelling to the traffic, "Prices Inside Are A Rip-Off, Bring In Food." This fired-up rebel soldier, A) could obviously get in and out of the site, and B) felt so passionate about prices that he'd rather be out here telling people about the injustice than inside enjoying the show. Not a happy camper, but a dedicated democratizer.

As amazing as this meandering tie-dyed river of humanity was, I had overstayed my welcome in the outside world and was overdue back at the KarmaCoupe. I teetered off down the highway on my re-shoed Ranger to the "Local Access Only" road, which was being efficiently manned by your tax dollars and mine shootin' the breeze with the babicious hippettes such that a fighter jet could have flown past and they wouldn't have noticed.

As I started back along the road to the secret abandoned cabin, I suddenly stopped. Stretching out before me all the way to the horizon was that scene out of the *Woodstock* movie of thousands of young people straggling down a narrow dirt road carrying everything they needed in a flowing rock 'n' roll pilgrimage.

They were in pairs, families, or street-wide gangs, but thousands were heading in the same direction. And each of them had to walk several miles from wherever they parked to even get to this road. But this troubled pilgrimage meant that every person who danced in that field had to work to get there, and we all knew it and respected each other for it. We had to put a lot into it just to be in position to get anything out of it. And it worked.

As I glided down the Main Street hill towards the Coupe I nearly flattened a doddering Larry "Bud" Melman who seemed to be staggering drunk in the middle of the road. I'm just glad nobody gave him a golf cart. It turned out we were neighbors on Guerrilla Ridge and he was going to become one of those reoccurring images of this TV festival. Except he was always alone, his "suit" costume looked even more geeky on a farm, and he always seemed to be in about as festive a mood as Andy Rooney. Or are they the same person?

Back at the KarmaCoupe there was good news: First, there was <u>no</u> note on my windshield saying, "Please remove this vehicle from the site." Second, there was in fact another white mini-van parked directly behind mine, blocking my exit. "This is great," I thought. "I'm *literally trapped* at Woodstock – couldn't leave if I had to!" This was exactly the kind of break a guy like me needed to run with. I promptly popped a frosty.

It was 7:00 Friday night and the group Live was on stage sounding surprisingly like *The Pusher* by Steppenwolf in last night's *Easy Rider.* "My God, I haven't even been here 24 hours!" I realized. "But what a ride!" I thought, as I lay down on the foamy, put my feet up, and smiled at my KarmaCamp. "A flat tire and *fixed*, all before dinner."

Here I was with food, herb, clothes, tunes, beer – beer is important. And no one around to bother me. "I can be kicking back with cold ones and listening to the show until something interesting happens on stage, then be over there before the song's over," I realized, toasting the Holy Goof who makes these things happen.

I laid back and let the reverberations ripple as I listened to the fluttering helicopters overhead. Both the police and the promoters were constantly flying surveillance over the site keeping close tabs on all troop movements, and using ultra-violate night-vision cameras to see if anybody was leaving with any money still in their pockets.

"Dream-come-true or what!" I laughed, shaking my head in disbelief. "How am I ever going to explain this? There's finally another Woodstock, and where am I? In a freakin' mobile fort parked a hundred feet from the stage with total access and no job!"

Another Woodstock Lesson: The right things will happen in ways we can't predict. Nothing will be as great as your dreams, but lots of things will be even better. Every General loses battles on the way to winning wars. Just fix the flats when you get them, and keep on riding.

Just then a New York-1 news anchor came up and started fixing her make-up in my windshield. It had gotten so dark she couldn't see me inside staring at her as she fingered her face and poked at her hair.

"Well, this is good," I thought. "At least I'm providing a service. I'm the mirror!"

But my keen journalistic instincts were telling me I was not experiencing the true and complete essence of Woodstock by being here in my van, so I raised my weary bones and give them one more roll.

As I dove back into the darkness of the unknown I realized the difference between the site by day and the site by night was like day and . . . . No, it was like . . . *real* by day and *sur*real by night. It was like staying in the shadowy woods too late. Lighting became sporadic, like a full moon blinking behind fast moving clouds. Flickers of dancing white leapt like candlelight, splashing to life the faces and parties and clusters and tents. Seductive eyes and shadowy fingers reached out at every bend of the road and lured the body into dens of the unknown. Bouncing headlights bobbed like jeeps in an uncharted jungle, with mystery paths in every direction, some parts lit, most parts not. There were flashes of young people, grey-hairs, blond hairs and no hairs walking the roads in the dark and light, dark and light, like a strobe machine flashing to music playing on the biggest boombox in history, filling the farm with one bouncing rhythm after another.

Back in the Media Tent things were even weirder: Hundreds of reporters were ranting at full-bore. The evening press briefing had just ended and everyone was buzzing with facts and figures. They'd just suspended ticket sales at something over 200,000, but there was already more people than that here already. It was starting to be accepted that this was going to be bigger than expected and the pool was beginning to bubble.

You had to hand it to these guys. A bunch of them were over at their laptops typing away or doing stand-up evening news reports or talking to their editors on rare working landlines. There was an amazing flow of focused energy zapping through the tent as hundreds of reporters scrambled to get the story out under very rural conditions.

The phones and cords had become an impossible nightmare of twisted wire after each user would carry the phone around and wrap it around chair legs and human legs and then somebody else would step on the jack and disconnect it and the guy would be sitting 10 feet away yelling his story into a dead phone until you heard him say, "Hello? Hello? Can you hear me? I can't hear you. I'm going to try another phone." Then he'd curse, slam down the receiver and immediately trip over the cords as he tried to storm off, falling face-first into a cluster of folding chairs and no one else even notices.

I calmly walked into the corner, picked up the last phone that was working in the tent and called my girlfriend. By the time I got off there was a line behind me like a crack house on Avenue D.

"Um, does that phone work?" the first news junkie asked as I winked a Yes and passed the baton.

* * *

It was nearly 10:00 and Sheryl Crow was about to come on. There's something about a great female voice singing rock 'n' roll, as in, haven't we heard enough *guys* for a while? And these promoters tapped the mine fairly fine, inviting Sheryl, Melissa, The Cranberries, the Sisters of Glory, Salt-N-Pepa, Arrested Development, WOMAD, and Rita Marley.

When I first heard that her label A&M was doing the soundtrack I figured she was a natural, but she wasn't added until two weeks ago. The new artist I've been the most excited about in my whole life, and who is still currently a "new artist," was actually playing at Woodstock in a few minutes! Don't you think that's weird?

I believe in her as much as I've ever believed in any entertainer, and now she was actually playing the show that meant the most to me of any show in the world. Do you think that's strange, or are these all just unrelated coincidences?

By the time I walked back into the audience – oh my God! It was like Mrs. Jack finding a Beanstalk where her garden used to be. While we were off eating our curds and whey, this audience had grown into a Jolly Green Giant!

It was huge, it was huge, it was huge. *And* it was crowded, and inconceivable to even see the front of the stage let alone imagine standing there this morning. Wait: that was *this morning?!*

It became frighteningly clear that if you wanted to see any act up close, you'd have to spend the whole day with the insane mosher loogans in the front. For the first time I understood what people meant when they came away from the first Woodstock saying they never really saw a single band.

But I decided to step out into the madness. The once-beautiful hay-covered carpeting the promoters had prepared for us was torn asunder and mud was beginning to peek through. And you couldn't help thinking, "This thing doesn't even officially *start* until tomorrow!"

The enormous field that was supposed to hold

the weekend's audience was already spilling over the rim. I had to step over and around people for a half an hour before I could even get out to a place where you could see the stage.

Ah, *the stage*. It was big. If you took the Empire State Building and laid it on its side and multiplied it by about 12, it would probably be way bigger than the stage, but still . . . it was the biggest stage ever! It made the pyramids look like a sand castle. It made the Mona Lisa look like a sketch. It was so big, even if you left now, with no traffic, you wouldn't get to the other side until next week. This stage was so big it could NOT have been built in Rhode Island.

In the very center was the actual performance stage itself, a shimmering cube of scrims in organic blues and greens lined the stage walls and ceiling. Across the back was a giant, arcing full-color rainbow, and all over the thousand feet of flapping cloth were different colored birds and animals. In fact, the entire performers stage was a magic nature center where tiny fairies fluttered and make your dreams come true. Or at least they did mine.

On either side of this singing songbird soulcenter were enormous paintings, each as big as the performance stage itself. In the middle was the Woodstock dove & guitar logo, and it was surrounded by a blue & yellow kaleidoscopic stained glass color pattern that moved the more you looked at it. But these were actually the speaker covers that hid the 750,000 watt cones they had crankin' in the cow patch.

On either side, beyond the stained glass murals, were mammoth fluttering triangles which by day were just another rainbow-colored eye treat, but by night became a projected 3-D patterned web that was pulled up like a quilt at a cabin on a cold night.

Then beyond these matching fluttering pyramids were the giant drive-in movie screens that showed us *Easy Rider* last night and close-ups of Sheryl Crow in a few minutes. Beyond the screens were yet another pair of enormous 3-D pyramids, just to balance out the empire I guess. So you see what I was getting at about "big." It was like a giant blue aircraft carrier. And *we* were the sea she sailed in. And music was the birds she launched! And love was the fuel in her engine! I don't know, but that stage really inspired me.

So after I stepped over and around people for about two hours, I managed to get to a point where I could at least see one of the movie screens. It was like going to *Woodstock: The Movie*. At a drive-in. From the other side of the highway.

I had gotten used to people not knowing Sheryl Crow. I'd seen her three times at little clubs in New York where you could tell she had exactly 200 fans. But every person I mentioned her to all day, from young kids to old hip people, were suddenly saying they loved her. I was surprised. When you pick up on somebody no one else has heard of, well if you're me, it's usually the kiss of death. I loved the TV show *My*

So-Called Life. I loved *704 Hauser.* I loved the *When Things Were Rotten* Robin Hood series that lasted 13 episodes. I loved Steve Forbert, Manfred Mann, Paul Tsongas – people who turned out to be about as popular as homework. I never really had a knack – The Knack, ya'see? I couldn't stand them and they were huge!

The fact that Sheryl Crow was in some way "making it" was just amazing, and I still don't really believe it. The week after Woodstock, her new single *All I Wanna Do* was the Top Airplay Gainer of the week in Billboard, at #36, and was actually number one in Tulsa, Oklahoma! (And I bet you think I'm making some of this up.)

It's pointless to try to describe what an artist does for you. Most people feel that magic tingle at some point over someone, that shivering chill when you're transported by an artist of any medium to a different dimension. It's what keeps us going – that moment – that fall-in-love goosebump chill that fires the best voyages of life.

And like the bumper sticker says, "I'd rather be tingling." As often as physically possible, I snag that blood-thumping buzz, that joyous pious frenzy when we reach up and grab the humming golden rod of clear-flowing spirit – one-on-one – channeling the connection through the heart so the whole body vibrates and fills with positive energy.

Sheryl did that for me. And as she walked out onto the biggest stage of her life that night, she was about to do it for the world.

She opened with *Can't Cry Anymore* and her new hit *All I Wanna Do*. She seemed to be looking even more stunning than usual on the giant screen. In fact, she suddenly seemed without question the sexiest woman to have ever sung rock 'n' roll. She may have been a dot on a stage a thousand miles away, but on the screen she was my whole day.

She had a 40 minute set before the most important audience of her life, so what does she do? Break out a new song. (No, you wouldn't want this person on your team or anything.)

It seemed to be called *Love Is A Good Thing*, the choruses ending with an "Ouuuuuu-yeah" refrain in case you ever hear it. If this is any indication of what's to come, she's gonna be number one in the world I thought, as a hand-held train of girls went choo-chooing past, harmonizing the new "Ouuuuuu-ouu"'s and dancing in synch. She played acoustic guitar, sang her heart out, and it was becoming increasingly obvious that she was nailing the whole joint between the eyes.

Man and I'm not kidding but her screaming out to where her voice breaks during this song is about the sexiest sound I ever heard. Carefree, gutsy, out of control, pushing beyond the limits, like we strive for ourselves or look for in others, going over the edge that holds us back and beyond where its safe. And God knows she was doing it in front of a quarter-million strangers. Thank you Great Spirit for delivering this one to us.

Then she did *Run Baby Run*, which opens her debut album like a resume of the madness that got her here: "Mama got high, high, high; And daddy marched on Birmingham singing mighty protest songs." All they taught her was "the only thing she'd need to carry on was to run baby run baby run baby run."

Scary stuff. Why do the most beautiful people come from the most torn lives? Could it be that adversity makes us better? Don't we all know a bunch of silver spoon pukes? And the one who's had everything go wrong in their life is the nicest, most generous person you know? Appreciate the disasters. If you have enough of them you might end up singing at Woodstock. And playing in the pocket, hitting the notes, and stroking a half-million ears with silk and leather.

By the time she played *Leaving Las Vegas* she had the whole field dancing and half of it singing the words. Not that I care at all. I spent the best part of my losing streak in an army jeep, for what? I can't recall. So I checked the odds and placed my bet. I wonder what I'll find? I'm just standing in the middle of this farm waiting for my ship to come in.

There's such a muddy field between the things you want and the things you have to do. I'm leaving New York. I'm going to get myself back to the garden.

She switched to keyboards for *The Na-Na Song* which sounded a lot like *Give Peace A Chance* but instead broke into Lennon's part of *I've Got A Feeling*: "Everybody had a hard year; Everybody had a good time ...." and by this point the audience sounded louder than the stage.

She ended her show like her CD, with *I Shall Believe*. It's a gutsy choice because she's just brought her audience up to a dancing rock 'n' roll frenzy with something like The Beatles in The Nineties, then drops it down to this quiet, hopeful chant. And a quarter-million bodies were swaying under her spell . . .

"Not everything is going to be the way you think it ought to be.
   It seems like every time I try to make it right,
     It all comes down on me.
      Please say, honestly, you won't give up on me.
       And I shall believe. I shall believe. I shall believe.
      I shall believe.
       I shall believe.
        I shall believe.
         I shall be .... "

Saturday

"Hear about the riots last night?" Andy the New York-1 Newsman said as I was performing the old morning post-Heineken Tai-Chi moan-&-groan.

"Mmmm?" I mumbled, fumbling for the socket to plug in my morning eyes to the world.

"A bus overturned and none of the shuttles could get in or out," he said, furiously unpacking and repacking camera gear as I worked on pushing my eyelids to half-mast. "It was pretty bad. There were four or five hour delays and people couldn't get off-site all night. They started rioting and overturned a bus and I don't know what-all," he said as he clip-closed a clasp. "Then the drivers all quit."

There's nothing like the smell of fresh disaster in the morning. "But then they'd just hire more drivers, or go to a back-up list," I computed as he added — "Oh, and there's at least two people dead."

"New information, new information. Situation fluid," I chugged faster and faster. The reports were growing grim to grimmer as I grimaced out at quiet

Main Street. The field was still a still-life collage of fluttering nylon without so much as a yawn in motion.

"There's a briefing at 9:00," he said, clasping shut a lens case and leaving in a deadline flurry for the broadcast trailer.

"Thanks."

"Oh, and there's a storm-front moving in with lightning and heavy winds. You may want to cover up," he imparted as he departed, disappearing between white semi's.

. . . "Some rooster."

I looked out at the field in disbelief, scanning the horizon for signs of trouble but only hearing the wind blowing across the sea of sleeping tents. It looked like a few million more people had shown up. The entire field was now covered with tents from the stage all the way up to the food stands at the top of the hill. As I turned around, tents had moved in all around my van, and over by the port-o-san, and cock-eyed half-way up the rocky hill.

"This isn't the same Woodstock I went to sleep in!" I realized, as I grabbed my towel off the clothes tree steering wheel. "I wonder if the Bliss Motel showers are still part of the program?" I thought, as I walked me out in the morning dew.

Sure enough — door's open! Except it wasn't 6 AM on the Friday before the festival anymore. My golden goose had turned into the golden arches and the morning rush was on. There were muscular black roadies and fat white nurses and tattooed pasty bikers and skinny little pale-faced writers, and a hundred other circus freaks all jockeying for space. Everyone fell undirected into an assembly line at each of the different porcelain functions. Of course there were lots of friends with friends so there were always talking and people being funny, unlike myself at the moment. Imagine all the people in the city where you live being in the same room at once, except there's only six showers, two mirrors, two sinks and two crappers. But the funniest part was, there was no toilet paper!!! Ha-ha. Toilets but no toilet paper! Those Woodstock guys are such kidders. But as it clearly states in The Adventure Manual, Rule 12B: Never cry — Pack two-ply.

In fact, porcelain became the most precious element in the burgeoning Nation. People would have done anything for it. Most never laid eyes on it until they got home on Monday. In fact, most people had stopped eating and drinking because they couldn't face the port-o-sans. So you either had to cramp your style or cramp your gut — or find the Bliss Motel and get out of your rut!

The shower stalls were now littered with enough empty hotel shampoo sample bottles to fill a Vidal Sassoon commercial, spanning the spectrum from exotic perfumes with foreign labels to your generic Motel 6 SHAMPOO. There were sunglasses, razorblades, wine bottles and bras behind every curtain. Intermittent shrieks of howling laughter from the co-ed locker room broke the waterworld every few seconds so even with your eyes closed you could never forget the rules were no longer the same.

It's 8:30 Saturday morning when I get back to the KarmaCoupe completely refurbished. "Staying cleaner than I do at home," I smiled in the rearview mirror. After each bike ride or adventure, I'd run up to the water trailer to take a quick splashing refresher because I kept thinking at any moment they might catch on and close it off. But so far so clean.

I buttoned up my twelfth shirt of the weekend, loaded up the day-pack, and hopped on old Ranger to go see what these deaths were all about. I began humming *Ohio* by Neil Young as I pushed off on my bike, and was singing, "Two dead in old Woodstock," by the time I hit the road.

Everything seemed so normal riding down Main Street. There was more traffic than yesterday but the systems still seemed intact. The gates were manned, the fences up, and huddles of green-shirted Peace Patrols were conferring at every checkpoint.

Inside the Media Tent, General John Iaccio from the Department of Transportation was up on the platform working with the four-by-ten foot plexiglass map they were using to show transportation and parking. I watched as he systematically drew a big red "X" over every single access road in the region. And he didn't stop putting markers over the parking lots until every one read "CLOSED". It didn't look real promising if you weren't here yet.

As General John was standing there closing every road while 300 globe-trotting correspondents watched in stunned silence, the P.R. emcee was nervously making announcements that everything was under control and they'd definitely begin the briefing in just five more minutes. By 10:00 the 9 AM spokespeople finally got their stories straight and came out to lie to us in harmony. Or, not exactly *lie*, just professional alterations.

For this morning's example, we'll take a look at this excerpt from the promoter's opening statement:

> "There's something more than 200,000 people on site. To the best of my knowledge the security perimeter has not been broken. The shuttle system has not broken down. It had little blips late last night, but it seems to be running right now."
>
> Translation: "There's something more than 200,000 people on site [a half-million is *more than* 200,000.] To *the best of my knowledge* the security perimeter has not been broken. [That's an old Ronald Reagan line meaning I haven't got a clue and you can't make me.] The shuttle system *has not broken down*. [Which is to say it's not exactly up and running.] It had little blips late last night, [like the Hindenburg was a blip

in the blimp business] but it *seems to be* running right now [although I could be completely wrong.]"

Colonel James O'Donnell of the New York State Police, clearly the most serious chaperone at the dance, was sent out to deliver the hard facts and bad news. In his no-frills Jack Webb monotone, he broke it to us straight —

"With parking lots and the festival site filled to capacity, the decision was made to close off all access to the site as of last night. There is no more room for cars, buses or people in the area. To try and squeeze in any more would jeopardize the health and safety of those already here. We have established roadblocks to turn away all non-local traffic at a 15 mile radius from the site," and low whistles went off around the room from even the oldest "been-there" reporters.

"Man, what is this, *Woodstock?*" I thought. "Now all it has to do is rain."

Then O'Donnell confirmed the two people who died: A 19-year-old woman on Thursday when she fell off her bike and was hit by a truck as she rode to the concert; and a 44-year-old man last night of complications from diabetes.

My main-man Gen. John came back out with his hardhat still balancing a foot above his head and informed us that all 48,112 parking spots were now taken, and every lot was filled to capacity. Apparently many of the lots had no one show up to supervise them, or were manned with under-trained staff who ended up letting people park pell-mell which only utilized 70% of the actual parking space. And inefficiency in parking *really* peeves the D.O.T. I think that's why they shut the whole area down.

As usual, the-powers-that-be were saying that things were really dangerous out there, and once again we'd been really naughty and they were shutting us down. Personally I'm sick up and fed of hearing uniforms telling me how dangerous the world is. Seems to me we got this far.

Seems to me I was up for seeing just how bad the damage was, how about you? Actually, I kind of like dangerous over-crowded disaster areas, especially when the devil's music's on the schedule.

I pried Ranger away from the bar she'd saddled up to and rode out Main Street into the greatest unknown I've ever known.

* * *

The backstage Main Street was constantly flowing with the people who ran the show, from the promoters and site coordinators to the doctors and reporters to food vendors and little kids in their birthday suits. It was 10:30 AM show day, and everyone was moving. We all had an-hour-&-a-half before Joe Cocker would be officially opening this thing.

I dropped off Guerrilla Ridge to my secret abandoned cabin and the whole marshy field was now covered with tents and homemade shelters. The number of people making the pilgrimage along the road grew thicker and thicker until by the time I reached Route 32 the artery was clogged. Many of them had been walking all the way from their distant parking lots because the shuttle buses just weren't running.

Route 32 was jammed with wandering people and creeping cars. Down by the fence some guys were pretending to pee while they were actually cutting open the corner of the fence with wirecutters. This whole upstate Woodstock area originally began as a creative artists retreat, and the newcomers were picking up on their ingenuity.

Suddenly I saw the mustachioed Director of Site Transportation who doctored up Ranger yesterday spinning in the middle of the intersection like a dizzy traffic cop directing a riot of school buses whirling in every direction. Ambulances, support vans, tour buses and cop cars were all trying to make the right call at each impromptu turn-off while kids engulfed the roadways like a flooding river. If there were herds of humans yesterday at the mural walls – today it was a National Monument in August. Oh wait, ... *that's exactly what it is!*

The Howard Johnson's parking lot and lawn had become a full-fledged marketplace with rows of Marrakesh-like stalls set up like a mall. The police had so effectively shut down incoming traffic that there were hardly any vehicles going through the main intersection, just people, and people, and people, like a human dam burst and the flood was washing through. There were people pushing grocery carts stacked to the clouds with beer, while others pulled kids' wagons with groceries and camping gear. Some were building monuments, others jotting down notes. The money-makers were raking, the P.T.A. moms were baking, the crew cuts were faking, and I'll bet that you think I'm making, this up. You could buy stickers, sneakers, flowers, frisbees, buttons, bongs, brownies, burgers, comics, posters, or fresh fruit baskets. You could buy pot, doses, quaaludes, mushrooms, hash or beer. It was Amsterdam without the coffee.

As I rode through the main intersection of 32 and 212, the Rinky-Dink was completely surrounded by people like a donut 20 feet thick — before noon! It looked like they were going to squeeze the tiny building and pop it right off the ground. "Human Donut Squishes Rinky-Dink," I pictured the headline as I rode closer. Standing at the door was the owner selling "Trips for $10." But not LSD: To the bathroom! Toilet paper included. But the line-up went out to the street and all the way to Portland. The people standing two or three hours from the beginning didn't look so healthy. I just kept exploring.

As I rode back over Gump's Hump, suddenly, stretching out before me like a huge golden necklace was a beaded string of school buses all the way to the horizon — and it was complimented by a sequined gown of flickering faces, smiling, each finally walking along their own private road to Paradise.

The Stewart's Good Food had 500 people pushing around the door with no room to get inside, and the Dairy Queen had a line four people wide and a hundred feet long! "Good thing I don't want ice cream," I smiled. "Can't wait till I get to the Grand Union for some real food."

I coasted down the Hump, cut into what was once an empty lot but was now a crowded cocktail party, and I came upon yesterday's breakfast benches with every blade of grass now a camping area. Then I saw it: Growing out of the Grand Union and stretching all the way across the parking lot was a single, thick line of people, 8 or 10 wide, and stretching maybe half a mile. It was like L.A. after the riots, or the Moscow McDonald's, or any New York subway token line. It was a disaster scene without the disaster (my favorite kind!) An army of KarmaCampers buying a ton of supplies for no other reason than to have fun.

I figured the store hadn't opened yet because the line was so long and unmoving, but as I rode all the way to the front, inside the store you couldn't see a thing but more people. There were so many bodies the cash registers and even the shelves themselves had disappeared. And worse — there was no way to get beer! It would take an hour just to get to the door.

So I immediately rode to the back exit to sneak in, but they already had it manned by two football players who looked like they had shoulder pads on, except they didn't. Piled outside the exit door however in case you were bored was a 20 foot Matterhorn of empty beer cartons you could climb.

I asked one of the lucky contestants leaving the store how he planned to smuggle in eight cases. "Oooh-dude — there's nobody at the gates. You just walk right in, Aaaouuuuu!" he howled, punching the sky with his tattooed beer-hoisting arm and pulling out of town with the cart.

Talk about a beer run! These guys were leaving with enough to open distributorships. I thought of Barbara Kopple's 11 roaming film crews and hoped one of them caught this. A grocery store more crowded than the trains at rush hour and 5,000 people in a line for Corn Flakes was definitely the weirdest image of the weekend so far.

But as yippie-yi-yo as this picture was, it didn't put beer in my pack, so I rode out to the road and found a couple of local Farmer Joes gawking at the mayhem. I asked if there was another store around here and one told me that there was a store down in the Village. "Where am I now?"

"This is the Town."

He explained how the Village is down in the Town, and the Town is everything not in the Village. Got that?

I coasted down the gradual descent to the Hudson River, into the Village of Saugerties, population 18,000, not counting the Grand Union, because that's in Town. It's a drift-back-in-time place, when everyone had little pink houses with little front lawns and big pink flamingos. The townsfolk alternated between families who were out on their lawn chairs watching and waving, and fearful shut-ins peering out from behind curtain cracks like petrified chickenhawks. I glided past some nearly-naked loony running full-tilt down the middle of the avenue. Flowing next to us going up the hill in the opposite direction were pick-up trucks full of beer-drinking yokel locals using their Resident Vehicle Pass to cruise the streets and go nuts – because they could. By this time on Saturday morning, locals were getting the sense that something very big was at hand and yesterday's rules were no longer in place.

The first store down Ulster Avenue was a Quik-Mart with a little two-pump gas station out front. Think they were doing any business? To feed the howling circus that was raging around their little convenience, they had simply opened the back of a beer truck and were selling cases right out the door. There was some barker balancing on a barrel, boasting, "Bud to go, right off the truck." But of course only Bud. Something was starting to smell like the wrong end of a Clydesdale.

Just then the naked loogan I'd just passed on the road came flying down the hill and into the parking lot yelling, "I'm on a beer run! I'm on a beer run!" which must have been some terribly funny joke he'd been working up all the way from Kansas or wherever he started. But in his enthusiasm to deliver the line he evidently forgot to also stop running and all the spectators just delicately backed out of the way revealing the fairly stationary table that they were using behind the beer truck. An'a' course I don't have to tell you, he bowled over the barker on the barrel who took a bath, bonking his bean on the bumper of the Budmobile, poor bastard. At which point about 70 kids took off with free cases.

"Have a nice day!"

Inside, the little store had less room than a Yugo and the poor guy working there was running constantly as the shelves were being depleted faster than he could ever keep up. "Do you have any more Snickers bars?" "Hey do you have any more bread?" "Cookies?" "Granola?" "Heineken?" I'm sure the guy still wakes up in a cold sweat with faces everywhere asking him for things he doesn't have. "I need electricity." "A wedding dress." "Back issues of *Boobies*." "Fireworks." "That cap gun you stole from my brother when you were 8."

Amazingly the line-up was only about 10 people long, probably because most people weren't bothering with the actual "paying" formality. The ones who stood on line just kept piling more stuff on their arms as they stood there. Or at least I did. I grabbed one of every newspaper they carried, the requisite 12-pack, beef jerky, and popcorn, which was about all this little oil change carried. The scrupulous part of the story was that they didn't seem to hike their prices for the weekend, and the small town girls behind the counter couldn't have been nicer despite the fact they were handling more people per hour than they did all last year. I found the 50¢ local newspapers to be the best souvenirs of the festival, while others maintain it was the free beer they walked away with.

But I wasn't picky. I was at Woodstock. I had my Ranger. And I had a hell of a hill to hoe to get out of the Village and back to the Town if you have a clue which I certainly didn't.

I rode back past the Grand Union Army Surplus Feeding Trough, and the final two lines of Troopers that were turning back all the pick-up trucks full of yahoos. By this checkpoint you had to either have a really good story or be running an illegal, high-priced taxi service with your Resident Vehicle Pass, a popular local pastime. I stopped on the peak of Gump's Hump once again just to sit there so contentedly and watch the river flow.

You couldn't help thinking about the 200,000 crowd estimates they kept using, and about how thick the mobs were this far from the stage. I pictured Simon & Garfunkel and all the other big Central Park shows that were estimated at a million people. And I thought about the crowd I just rode through, and inside the stores, and all around the Rinky-Dink, and the Howard Johnson, and every piece of public grass, and down every road in every direction, and camping all through the woods and swarming over every vending area at the site, and all through the Surreal Field, the Eco-Village, the South Stage, until you got to the North Field and a half-million people in front it alone.

Suddenly a kid comes running up. "I want to know how come the fascist pigs have been seeding the clouds, man." No sorry, wrong movie. But I was miles from the stage and there was twice as many people here as Paul Simon, not half as many.

The other thought was — that all of us were pretty damn lucky. We'd each made it inside the 15-mile perimeter before they shut it down. The cops said they were now turning back people even with tickets because there was nowhere to park their cars. But every one of these backpack-wearing, sandal-shuffling kids on the road to paradise were the ones I'd be spending the next two days with. All of us were locked in a giant 15-mile-wide stadium together. Each of us had made it somehow, for some reason, and now the gates were closed. For the next 48 hours, or until we went crazy or to heaven, we were together.

Bus load after bus load rolled past with spankin' fresh campers arriving from the parking lots, some of them drooling on the windows like puppies, and others hugging their sleeping bags like a life preserver, staring petrified at the throngs in the throws of madness this early in the morning. On the other side of the road empty buses roared back past on the way to wherever all these people were coming from. Steady as she flows, o Captain my Captain – our fateful trip begun.

* * *

It was High Noon on the High Seas, Saturday in Woodstock, America.

It was high rows of the V.I.P. bleachers. Count down. Chills. Crowds. V.I.P.s, other artists, medical personnel, and scrawny little pale-faced writers all scamming the bleachers, maybe 12 rows, maybe 100 people across, maybe just *a few* thousand people want to cram in every inch for Joe Cocker opening the festival that he defined and that defined him.

Getting above ground level you could see how far back the crowd went, which was forever. A million skinny arms waving like a wheat field. A million voices blowing like a tempest. And every one of them was cheering — "I've make it! I'm here! I never thought this would happen, but I'm _here!_" All arms raised and voices roared like a human lion, a howling phoenix rising, growing off the ground and growling to life.

And into this roaring Sphinx-sized jaw struts Cocker, center stage, with that funkiest of all white bands, as he grooves into *Feeling Alright* so smooth it was like it was already playing. "Ya feelin' alright, New York?" and the whole world just kind of snapped.

For all the talk of new bands and MTV and playing to these kids who want whatever it is they want, there was nothing like the audience's bone-chilling shrieks during Cocker that rumbled the ground and trembled the weak. The bleachers were shaking so much you had to have faith in divine providence or really good construction workers preparing for this. The field, the bleachers, everything became a sweating bouncing mash of sexy bouncing body heat. And Joe seized it, cooking us to a sizzling hot broil but not overdone. Simply burning.

Then he broke out John Sebastian's *Summer In The City* — a nice nod to the guy who wasn't invited but who helped carry the first festival. The lyrics were written by John's little brother Mark when he was in grade 8 and his brother's group the Lovin' Spoonful was just starting to make it. The little kid's teacher told him the poem was stupid and the wee-poet was crestfallen. His big brother John disagreed and turned it into the number one song in the country that summer. Which is why to this day the songwriting credits read John and Mark Sebastian, and you should never listen to teachers who tell you you suck.

Of course Cocker sang *Unchain My Heart*, which sort of turned into *Unchain the Fence*, because right at the same time in front of the V.I.P. bleachers, a bunch of yahoos began unclipping the fence. I was standing beside the last security guard in the house and asked him if maybe he shouldn't do something. And he said no, he was going to make sure the bleachers stayed secure. So both of us just stood there and watched as the only fence that separated backstage from the belly of the beast came down.

Granted they didn't storm the bleachers,

possibly because people had already jammed them like an elevator at rush-hour, but everyone now had free passage backstage. And this was only the first official performance of the festival. Suddenly there were swarming, sweaty shirtless moshers banging into polo shirted doctors and their families who thought they were safely behind the lines. It was the beginning of the complete collapse of security that we'd later learn was happening at this very moment all over the site. And I had the unique pleasure of watching the backstage fences cut down while standing with one of the few remaining people who could have done anything about it. Kay. I had a feeling this was definitely going to get stranger before it got normal again.

Meanwhile Cocker was performing the entire History of Soul, including his early hit *The Letter*, as in *My Baby Wrote Me A*, until finally his set built to *With A Little Help From My Friends*, and once again I felt the earth move under my feet, and once again I was asking, "They only booked three acts from the original?!?!"

While this song was likely being played at this same moment on several radio stations around the world, here was the original guy, singing the original song at the event that made both a legend.

In front of the bleachers raged an ocean of surging hormonal expression, of punching arms and tossing dinghies of moshers in a foot-flying free-for-all of first-time weekend freedom for these teenage euphoria machines. Beside me on the bleachers were the politely astonished older crew who were trying to keep what little cool they had left, raising their hands nearly over their heads at the really good parts.

On stage Joe was spasmodically flipping out and singing in that wonderful, shameless, rough-edged passion that exemplifies free expression, and in a way, a whole generation.

"See ya in 2019," he said, and it was over in a wave.

* * *

It was time to execute the practice of Protecting Perfect Moments (as Spalding Gray calls them), of shutting down all the senses and completely immersing yourself in what just happened – of letting it resonate for as long as possible, reverberating through the memory banks, and implanting itself deeply and firmly in the soil of the psyche. It keeps the worst things from leaving a mark, and makes the best things last a lifetime.

And in this case it was the completely unexpected power of Cocker's Foreman-like punch. It was the graceful way he could lull you into a safety groove, then knock you senseless with a platinum hit. And how this was only the latest in what was emerging as a pattern of expectations being blown out of the water. Including that any of this was happening at all!

Before the second act Blind Melon could shatter

my blind trance, I moved at a lama's shuffle through the crowd, riding the molecules of music still floating through the air, slowly, gliding off like dust . . .

Until one of the oddest, briefest moments in the human experience occurred as a few thousand of us were leaving. We've all felt it at one time or another — that beautiful human bonding when strangers are thrown into mirror-close proximity squeezing out the exit door bottleneck after an event.

Whether its a church, concert or whatever you attend en masse with strangers, there's that brief opening into the soul that we share with each other because we've just finished opening ourselves up on a private level to whatever was happening on stage, and then Boom suddenly it's over, but each soul still has their chest wide open and their heart still exposed as they walk out in a group together, pulsating, naked, strangers facing strangers with tears on their cheeks, resolve on their tongue and fire in their eyes, oxygen gasps of disbelief and composure, of openness to everyone. But before the tingles of the magic collective moment have stopped or the goosebumps receded, we share what just happened face-to-face with one another. We share our hearts. We share our eyes. And just for a moment, we share each other.

Just like the movie, megaphones kept announcing, "Clear the road, please," at the exiting mass of humanity. The thousands who traipsed over the fence were now spilling into the backstage area. It was like the Really Big Tent at The Really Big Circus with things going on in every direction and it didn't matter where you went or what you did, it was all going to be wilder than you ever imagined. Or you could just sit still and watch the Grand Central flow of people rushing to catch their next adventure.

The human swirl of faces was a Global Village mix of generational Adventurers: young black rastas and old white hippies, dapper-suited doctors and birthday-suited patients, bikers hauling coolers and Buddhists holding flowers, even scrawny little pale-faced writers and cool people, each and every one of these heart-souls was floating on the Beatles buzz and glowing like a lantern. It was the widest spectrum of blissed-out faces ever assembled in the Melting Pot state and we knew it.

The Cranberries were opening the South Stage as Joe was opening the North, and all the young dudes were streaming from that to Blind Melon and Cypress Hill who were coming up on the North. And all the old cooters were heading from Joe Cocker to The Band on the South Stage. It was a funny generational ships-passing-in-the-daylight kind of thing and everyone noticed it and smiled along. With the two line-ups constantly playing on both stages all weekend, this traffic pattern would happily continue throughout the festival. The trip between stages took about an hour if you went through the audience, or about 15 minutes via this backstage road.

I stopped in at the Media Tent on the way past to collect my free hamburger lunch, and good ol' Colonel

O'Donnell was back at the podium. If you recall there was almost zero security at the gates, a few extra kids had shown up, and the cops were starting to freak.

But then they went too far.

"As of 12 noon today we have suspended all beer and liquor sales, indefinitely," he said.

"*WHAT!?*" I blurted louder than I should have. "Nooooooo."

There was no warning — what is this? It was already 2:00, for the love of beer! Even Optimisticman couldn't hope to con another six-pack this far past the wire! I pictured the red totem pole stacks of suddenly-appealing Bud cases rolling out of the Grand Union a couple hours ago. NO BEER!?

Then, just like a green genie bottle's wish granted, I suddenly pictured the twelve I bought at 11:00 swimming in ice water in the KarmaCoupe. "<u>That</u> was making last call," I smiled.

I cashed in a KarmaCoupon and took Cold Ones for 500. "The answer is, `So much more than just a breakfast drink.'"

"What is beer?"

With everything in flux in 360 degrees, I knew I had to get out of there. Once again it was time for . . . Adventureman!

The Band was due on the South Stage at 4:00, so I only had two hours left to explore the teen show on the North Field and the rest of the site. This was finally the moment of truth: I would force myself to get hit in the head by "Generation X" whether I wanted to or not. It's what some Canadian writer coined these poor kids — its no wonder they have an identity crisis. To tell you the truth, I've been avoiding them like the plague. But there was no getting out of it this weekend. The X-Factor was here.

Whereupon our intrepid Adventurer debonairly trips over the legs, tent-pegs and mud holes of the mosh mine field in search of the truth for you the reader to benefit from all dry, mud-free and well-fed in the safety of your own comfy-chair right now.

But first I had to get past those beautiful triple X girls. And this year's model apparently called for cheek-bouncing faded jean cut-offs, see-through shirts, tattoos, and multi-colored hair. They were young, they were topless, and they were dancing. This wasn't a family show.

I only mention it because it was true, and would be the first thing anyone would notice if they wandered into that Gen-X Babestock. I felt really old. Not only because of the entire sexual revolution that seemed to be raging in front of me, but because of the moshing and how these kids actually seemed to enjoy slamming into each other and flopping around in an uncontrollable scene which I could stand for maybe three seconds.

But to watch, they were a single undulating mass of bouncing flesh, slithering and sliding against each other so it was impossible to tell one from the other. And maybe that was the point.

I was beginning to like these kids. Couldn't

stand the music they listened to, but they definitely had The Spirit. They braved the elements, the prices, the rules, the bullshit, and made it.

Blind Melon was on stage and to tell you the truth I can't even remember what they sounded like except that they didn't drive me from the field, which is exactly what the next group, Cypress Hill, did. They seemed to make a big deal out of the fact that they smoked marijuana, but I know they don't. No one who gets high can possibly make music that sounded like that — that's a scientifically proven fact.

As I was leaving I thought about the rookie bands who only had one album out when they played the first Woodstock: The Band, Crosby, Stills, Nash & Young, Joe Cocker, Santana . . . and wondered how long this year's freshmen would last.

I walked up to the temporary exit gates that were built along temporary fence walls being maned by these poor "Peace Patrol" guys. I don't know how much they were getting paid, but there was always about a hundred people out front trying to get backstage, and a hundred people backstage trying to get out front and these poor guys were the traffic cops in a madhouse.

The poor paying patrons had no idea this was a restricted backstage area since it looked exactly like all the other exits from across the field, so they'd walk about a hundred hours through the crowd toward it only to be told they now had to walk two hundred hours in the opposite direction to leave. So anyway, along comes this seven foot giant mountainman carrying his girl, a cooler and six or seven other people. And he wanted to leave. The Peace Patrol Weight Lifterman said no, and mountainman said yes, and Peace Patrol said no, and they set to shoving and the seven foot mountainman was getting wilder and wilder and demanding to push himself & his ducklings backstage until finally the weight lifter gave him one good shove and sent the mountain avalanching backward through all the people, crushing entire cities as he went.

Meanwhile of course the two crowds on either side of the fence had pulled back and were already throwing in their cheers, jeers and advice. Basically, the Peace Patrol guy was just securing his perimeter, and holy cats I wouldn't argue with the guy. So the giant mountain's ego's been bruised and he throws his cooler about twenty feet, and bellows, "Alright, that's it," and came charging back from his big shove. I was standing right beside the Peace Patrol guard because this was too good to miss until suddenly I saw this seven-foot whale of a wall rushing straight at me and suddenly I thought, "I'm going to be crushed like an ant on a runway."

But at this very moment everyone was collectively realizing, "These guys are way too big to fight." And just before the rock hit the hard place, a cloud of people surged forward without orders, leaders or authority and engulfed both the rushing bulls, pulling them back. Peace Patrols were tugging at one end and a gutsy consortium from the audience had grabbed the giant around his tree trunks and actually held the disaster back. It became a tug-of-war without the rope, with two armies pulling back as hard as they could with nothing in between but the thread of violence.

Disaster narrowly averted by the people once again.

What a day, though. Holy Doodle! And now Youssou N'Dour, and then The Band with a bunch of "friends," which would be immediately followed on the North Stage by Crosby, Stills & Nash singing *Woodstock*. Since that was going to be quite a stretch of happeningness which would take us all the way into darkness, I stopped in at the KarmaCoupe for a final pit stop before the big Saturday night rock 'n' roll show at Woodstock, America.

Oh bliss, oh home to running water & clean clothes. There underneath the New York-1 tarp was a bunch of TV news crews drinking brews and shooting flies like cowpokes on the edge.

"You're from the city too, are ya?" the toughest one high-fived me. "Is `All Star' that post-production house in midtown?"

"Yeah-yeah," one of the speedy techies chimed in. "We worked with them on the Grammies."

"`All Star' — no that's the West Side photo studio, isn't it?" Debbie Feyerick the on-camera reporter said, then all three of them abruptly turned toward me waiting for the answer.

"All Star . . . All Star," I scrambled. I had no idea

what they were talking about.

The chief honcho seemed to suddenly freeze-up like Clint Eastwood just before he shot someone, and without moving his teeth asked, "You don't work for them then?"

I quickly ran a word-search on my hard disk to see if I'd ever used the name in some scam but nothing was accessing. I knew I had to either give up, or attack 'n' bluff — I've never surrendered yet.

"Which `All Star' you talking about?" I countered.

"Where you work, or that's what I thought," the big guy said, standing up to about six-and-a-half feet and whipping out his summons book and a badge. Or that's what it felt like. Without taking his eyes off me he stepped over to the KarmaCoupe and I'm thinking, "I don't like the looks of this, Ralphy-boy."

"Right here: `All Star, 325 West 34th Street, N.Y. N.Y.,'" he said. "Isn't this your van?"

I walked over and on the side of the door was the name of the van rental company: *All Star*. "No wonder I blended in for days!" I thought. Finally I had a lead I could run with.

"All Star. Oh sure, it's a video production house in the West 30s. We have offices all over. I didn't know which one you'd heard of."

Suddenly I'd been given a promotion! I worked for All Star "Whatever I Wanted It To Be", and it was written right on the side of the damn van! And the even weirder thing was that this little off-track rental place changes its name about every six weeks. If Woodstock had been held in April instead of August it could have read "Scam's Vans." But today it said "All Star" — and suddenly I felt like one.

I celebrated the good news by loading up my day-pack with a couple of the final remaining Heinekens on the Eastern Seaboard, plus the usual first aid stuff I boy-scouted with me to keep everyone healthy and wise, plus 15 pens just in case, and headed out blissfully to see Levon Helm, Rick Danko, Bob Weir, Bruce Hornsby, Crosby, Stills & you get the idea.

As I walked over to the South Stage I was thinking how I'd seen some slippage on their strict "no drugs" rule earlier in the morning; and how there may have been some minor digressions on the "no alcohol" rule as a breakfast eye-opener; and I think saw people cooking on some "open grills" over lunch; and I may have seen one or two people using "camcorders" during the afternoon; and I think there were actually some "fireworks" around dinnertime; and I know I tripped over some "metal tent stakes" at night; but you'll be relieved to know the "no pets" rule was strictly enforced all weekend.

* * *

And as I walked onto the South Stage field around 3 PM, the exotic Senegalese songbird Youssou N'Dour was singing and swooping above the colorful pollen garden of people in his rainbow plumage of robes. Singing in half-Senegalese and half-English, he was trance-dancing around the stage like a possessed shaman trying to save our souls, and it appeared to be working. He was covering Dylan's *Chimes of Freedom* the second act so far to be covering a tune by somebody else who would later be playing Woodstock. (Cocker with Traffic; Youssou with Dylan.)

I don't mean to praise every act I saw up the wazoo like some *Entertainment Tonight!* lather brush, but every singer so far, namely Sheryl, Joe, and now Youssou, was giving the performance of a lifetime, perhaps surprising even the artists themselves, and this was actually going to continue throughout the whole weekend. If you want complaints just to prove I don't see the Whole Earth Cavalcade through rosé bottle eyes, Cypress Hill sounded more like a Toxic Spill, Traffic wasn't exactly flowing on Sunday, and Bob Weir was no Grateful Dead. Some wrong chords were struck in the muck over the weekend but why fan the poop when bulbs were a poppin' all over the garden?

The South Field had a perfect natural dip right in front of the stage that held about 10,000 people in a circular mosh-pit saucer. You could easily walk its rim because all the people who wanted to see a particular band would gravitate down into the bowl leaving the rest of the field free to wander. It was a naturally perfect design that kept the moshers pummeling themselves at will, the rest safely on the circular observation deck.

Once again, however, I opted for the ease and comfort of the V.I.P. bleachers. And once again, there were all these straight reporter types from I don't know, Utah or England or something sitting there with their hands crossed watching that lovely African chap, when up bounds I two planks at a time to the very last row of the bleachers and heaven forbid pop a frosty. Much to my surprise, I stood out.

Then a funny thing happened right after Youssou N'Dour — oh, you're not going to believe it! — It started to rain! Yup.

Okay, a lot of other people didn't find it funny either. You have to have a certain dry perspective, which I immediately acquired by climbing underneath the bleachers and watching the *Salt Lake Gazette* geeks go flapping off down the quickly-flooding road holding pizza cartons over their heads like Chinese hats that flapped when they ran, and tinted their hair with the sweet scent of pizza juice.

In fact the rain became my favorite part of the whole weekend. Allow me to tell you in excruciating detail about every drop that fell on the site that day:

It all began when I was nine. It was a crispy spring day and I was over at a friend's house and there by their record player was a copy of her parents' 3-disk fold-out Woodstock album, and I sat there for hours staring into the pictures. I studied the faces of every person in the crowd and imagined I knew them. I'd talk to each one to get to know what they'd seen. As they'd turn their head the whole field would open up to me and I could see beyond the frames of the picture. I'd see the field curving down to the stage, and all those people that seemed so bizarre to this wee Winnipeger who couldn't believe there were real human beings who dressed in those beads and paisley and hair styles. And you could tell it went on for miles. And then — oh my God — *there's a movie*!?! These pictures <u>can</u> talk?!

The next thing I knew, they're having *another one?!* And I was there! And it was starting to rain!

I hung out under the bleachers so contentedly smoking and drinking and yakking up a rain storm. A young couple from Wisconsin fell in and said they'd just walked in the main gate and there wasn't a single person manning it. It was only 4:00 on Saturday afternoon and I couldn't believe these experienced promoters would be losing control of the perimeter so completely, so early. But every traveler had the same story. If there was no security when conditions were perfect, what was it going to be like after this rain?

As soon as the drizzling let up to a light mist I calmly, knowingly, bid farewell to my under-bleacher brethren and headed out to stake my early claim on some nice firm farmland in front of the stage for The Band. The Band at Woodstock — their historic hometown since before this all began. There were even people in the crowd wearing special shirts for this performance: "Spirit of Big Pink — The Band & Special Guests, August 13th, 1994, Saugerties"

Crossing the newly slick mud was like running across a hockey rink in bowling shoes. Being a penguin from the tundra, I was very experienced at this and skated gracefully over the sloppy brown rink, breezing past all the ill-balanced Yankees who stared in awe at my Gretzky-like shushing. Finally, I slid into home plate, the most perfect spot in the universe, hovering on the edge of the giant saucer — directly in front of the stage, clear view, dancing room, and tons of cool people because, after all — this was The Band!

And in keeping with this Canadian theme of ice skating and rural Maple Leaf music, along comes Neil Young cranking over the P.A. for the first and only time all weekend! Father Grunge Factors In — via tape but at least the Winnipeger's voice carried over the fields of Woodstock once.

The squeegee guys were frantically clearing the rain off the stage while Wavy Gravy interviewed the moshers in the front row about the major issues of the day from his security ledge along the front of the stage. Wavy fell for the old "Primus Sucks" routine, kind of your 90s version of "Live Dead" with its fans stealing the expression from the band's detractors and using it to mean the opposite of what it said. They even sold "Primus Sucks" T-shirts as a joke.

Standing next to me on the saucer rim hillette was a local couple from Saugerties. She taught music at the elementary school, and he was an assistant engineer at a recording studio, which is something the region is known for. As opposed to, say, bike shops. As an example of what kind of a weekend I was having, he'd just finished working on The Band's latest album. No, *you* won't be any fun to stand beside during their show or anything. "Color-man report to the booth."

I couldn't believe I had a real live local music expert from Saugerties on my hands, so I immediately began pumping him with questions about the local lore. Of course the whole reason the town of Saugerties (or is that the village?) is even placed on state maps is because of one "pink house seated in the sun of Overlook Mountain in West Saugerties, New York." Its exact location has been kept a deep secret despite a quarter-century of prophet seekers combing the woods at night. It was one of Dylan's hideouts during his Motorcycle-Accident Secluded Blue Period. In fact it was the very place where he and some pickers he called "the band" played music while he recuperated, and they managed to redirect the river's flow of rock 'n' roll in the process. From these sessions, Dylan later released *The Basement Tapes*, while The Band simply made *Music From Big Pink*.

While we were talking, and I didn't want to admit it at the time, but I'd noticed the school teacher's hair was getting increasingly wet as we'd been talkin . . . and I'd been doing a Grade A job of denying it. "It's always been that wet. She must have gotten caught in the rain before. Yeah, that's it." (hint: *No it wasn't.*)

Somewhere along the line that fine young post-rain mist fattened up into something that began to resemble a rain-like substance. *"But everything's going so well. It won't rain. That's just a light overcast. You can practically see the sun. There's no way it's going to rain. This'll let up any second. It's just . . . a light . . . It's fuckin' pouring!"* I screamed, as I sprinted across the field like a cat in a sprinkler to a pile of garbage bags and dove underneath them. Or at least that's what I wanted to do. But since I wasn't a furry little cat but a big wet man desperately trying to save himself from becoming a total washout, I scooped an armful of government-issue People's Army Trashbag Raincoats and dashed back to our sacred hillette on the rim of the mosh bowl.

The rains had come!

We quickly poked head holes in the ends of our bags and pulled them over ourselves like giant condoms. The whole field became a dish of green & black jumping beans with white beanie nipples on top. I tore two tiny hand-holes at elbow-height like a doctor using a radiation machine so I could stick my hands out only when I needed to. There was a chance I may have slightly misjudged my brilliant exit from under the bleachers. Of course we all knew it was going to stop any second. And getting worse wasn't even a consideration. (!)

But just then, out of the very mud below us, we witnessed — the Birth of The Mud People!

Running down the center of the concert bowl was the field's natural drainage wash carrying water to — you guessed it — the sunken saucer mosh pit right in front of the stage. This became the lake, and our hillette became waterfront property to watch The Woodstock Players reenactment of Darwin's *Origin of Species*, as the Mud Fetuses crawled and wiggling to life out of the water before us in that first dramatic scene of history.

I'm sure you've seen pictures of the reptilian mud people by now. They looked like the creatures from the end of the river in *Apocalypse Now*, or those life-sized bronze statues by Seward Johnson. They looked like moving replicas of humans, except they were the uniform color of unglazed clay. The clay. You could smell it. That sloppy mess you used to make in art class turned into people! *That's* why the bodies looked so sexy — reliving the *Ghost*-reflecting rush of sliding your fingers through wet pottery . . . mmmmmm . . .

While the Saugerties couple and I were watching the birth of a nation, we hadn't noticed it had started to rain a little harder. Without saying anything we pulled the garbage bags up over our three heads, then pulled the tops out over our faces, creating a plastic visor roof over our eyes. And there we were, three little porches sitting on the hill near the lake, looking out at the rain in vain. Any fool knew it was time for a smoke.

Hey I got it! Why don't we wait for the most adverse conditions possible, like a gale storm in an open field, then try to fill up a pipe and keep it dry and light it all under a plastic flapping porch roof stretching maybe four inches in front of your face. Of course we pulled it off. And as you know, achieving anything under adverse conditions only elevates the high of elation. And with herbal kindness, the chemicals your body's already secreting to fight off the adversity are suddenly boosted by the feelgood breezes, so instead of the natural endorphin explosions just making you warm they're suddenly getting a huge push from behind and are saying, "Wow! Not only am I going to make you warm, Mr. Bloodstream, I'm going to make you *tingle!*"

Of course the rain had to hit during the most complicated set-change of the entire weekend. The Band had a full horn section complete with music stands, and a half a dozen guest artists all with different amps and set-ups, and meanwhile this twisted typhoon was blowing rain sideways across the stage like you were driving into it on the highway.

Think of the '69 site they threw together in three weeks! If things are slightly delayed here, imagine it then?! I was marveling at the modern steel and tarp superstage, when all of a sudden KA-PLOOSH!! — a huge part of the stage roof collapsed and an enormous boat-sized bucket of water dropped on a bunch of cameramen and keyboard equipment like an unexpected typhoon wave. There was a collective gasp from the audience as the flood washed all the dry camerapeople right off the stage.

I couldn't help thinking of John Scher's well-publicized comment before the show: "Don't worry, it won't rain." I don't know why, but I sort of believed him. What an idiot. It always rains in the Catskills in August.

But the most essential fact of the whole entire story (as Kerouac's friend Henri Cru always said) was that it poured. In order to keep any semblance of dryness in this ever-increasing mud field you had to squat down until your bag piece touched the earth, and you became this ball inside your bag, with your porch beak sticking out so you could still keep an eye on all the people taking their clothes off.

What began as rain became a monsoon. If you were driving you'd pull over. If you were walking you'd drown. Exposed flesh was soaked in a New York second. Your head hurt like hailstones – the steady thumpity-thumpity-thump of fat raindrops rapping the crown of your skull like a thousand piano hammers being played by Cecil Taylor. It was the kind of rain where you have absolutely no idea.

This went on for another day or two and then everyone packed up and went home.

The End

Ha-ha. Only kidding.

But the rain went on for days, including an entire week in the next hour alone.

It was still drizzling by the time The Band took the stage around 4:30, and it completely stopped not long afterwards. Amazing how fast things can turn around isn't it? Everyone began taking off their garbage bags, and a lot of the girls didn't stop there. Once people and their outfits had been through the mud bath, the Inhibitions Committee begin loosening its restrictions.

My newfound local Band-Buddies and I were already singing, *"When I get off of this mountain, You know where I wanna go,"* we were so confident they were going to open with *Up On Cripple Creek* just like *The Last Waltz*. But nooooooo. It seemed they were doing everything they could to steer away from any allusions to their old guitar player, including evoking his *Last Waltz*. But other than the set list which mirrored their live *Rock of Ages* album, this show was still a *Last Waltz* redux: huge horn section, multi-camera shoot, and a string of special guests expounding upon the architecture of rock 'n' roll. It was American music at its finest, played mostly by Canadians. Except, of course, for Levon, and Jim Weider, the local Woodstock guitarist they picked to fill Robbie's strings back in '83, and who played a prove-it show. And ironically, his brilliant guitar playing only made it more like *The Last Waltz*.

Woodstock's officially ridiculous ubiquitous

Wavy Gravy was running back and forth across the stage sprinkling "no rain" dust to encourage the growing sunshine daydream, and then blowing bubbles to prove it was working. My spider sense was tingling: The rain, The Band, Wavy, a farmer's muddy field in the Catskills in August . . . I was starting to have flashbacks to something I was never at.

Then the backdrop scrims behind the stage opened up and suddenly you could see over the musicians to the rolling trees of the wind-weaving farmland behind. The fresh breeze that was rippling the stage dressings was the same driving force behind pushing our storm clouds away. What once delivered our shower was now blow-drying our hair and combing our trees. Mother Nature, another popular sixties act, happily took over the lighting, the backdrop, the air conditioning, and the show.

After their rainy day overture and several new tunes, they finally let us in on *It Makes No Difference*, Robbie's metaphor masterpiece of lost love, and the best song Robbie ever wrote for Rick's voice. And this afternoon the chorus about the sun not shining and the rain falling went over even better than usual. Every time we heard it, a roar rose from the front of the crowd that rumbled all the way back like rolling thunder. The rain had bonded us, and now it was obvious. It ruined our hairdos, soaked our clothes, muddied our shoes, shook us up, and loosened our control, the truth only sinking in as our feet did more to the railroad red earth. For the first time the audience had its common obstacle and became a unified force.

The effort involved in being here had bonded us this morning; but the downpours raised it to a whole other level by this afternoon. As we stood soaking wet in those rivers of mud we knew for the first time we were all crazy together and altogether crazy. When Joe Cocker started us off on the long hike up this very strange hill we were still in our street clothes and didn't know one another very well. But now, after being together a while, the rains became the unifying rapids that bonded us for more than a weekend. This was a helluva big raft, and we were definitely all on it together.

Then right there when you weren't expecting it they hit us upside the head with *Don't Do It*, with its refrain, "I'm trying to do my best, I'm trying to do my best," with horns blaring like Gabriel's trumpets. Everyone was suddenly shaking in the mud like an electric current shocking the eclectic circus. Flickering patches of direct sunlight were forcing their way through the clouds for the first time and highlighting dancers like *Bandstand* spotlights.

The rain also gave birth to the toplessness in both genders, which was blossoming all over the garden. Girls convinced their boyfriends to hoist them on their shoulders and they'd proceed to shake off years of suppression. Swinging around in front of both stages was a boom crane with a rotating camera, and whenever it swept anywhere near one of the New

Exhibitionists, she would smile, wave, and shake her assets.

Another Woodstock Lesson: Women definitely have a much greater tendency towards public exhibitionism than men do.

What men *will* do is dive on top of their friends' heads and get pushed around. Since both of these nearly-naked behaviors took hold simultaneously at Woodstock, and both occur above head level, as you looked above the crowd in any direction all you could see floating over this bobbing sea was bouncing flesh.

And then somewhere in here, Sir Levon of Honkdom finally wound-up his Arkansas spring and twanged our tootle with *Up On Cripple Creek* about an hour away from our opening prediction but perfectly preserved in his backwoods still. They coupled it with *The Night They Drove Old Dixie Down* for one of the sweetest back-to-backs of the weekend.

Woodstock '69 was my most studied event of this century, just as the Civil War was for the last, and suddenly here were the two richest stories over two centuries of American history coming together before me. As Woodstock's own locals The Band sang about America's great drama starring Robert E. Lee and the fall of Richmond, all the scattered colors of our regiment's flags, firing canons, uniforms of blue, grey and tie-die came swooping together from the periphery of memory into a single history coalescing into one, the part of the story where all the stories come together, right now, over here.

As I was hearing Levon's Southern accent singing of the day the Confederacy fell, I could hear the galloping drumbeat hoofs, the steady stomp of the marching army, and felt the breeze of revolution blowin' over the land. I don't mind chopping wood, and I don't care if the money's no good, but I swear by the Woodstock mud below my feet, that I wasn't sure which past life I was reliving as time as I knew it had long-since slid down the hill into the mosh pit.

A century later as I drifted back from war, a Band was playing . . . trumpets were blaring . . . we must have won, I thought, because arms were flailing, girls were singing, music was playing, and a party was on!

Up on stage it became obvious even though Levon sang the hits, he was no longer at the Helm. Hidden away behind his drums, and with Garth walled in behind his keyboards, The Weight of The Band had fallen to the only mobile instrument in the group – Rick Danko and his bass. Out there in front of all the moshers, Rick was bouncing around gamely trying to carry the show like a traditional bandleader who doesn't take any solos but directs the audience's attention to those who do. Who would have thunk oh those many waltz's ago that it would be Rick leading the Band through their big All-Star Woodstock Review.

First he introduced Roger McGuinn, who did not sing *Mr. Tambourine Man*! He sang *Knockin' On Heaven's Door* which is like – What's the deal with that song anyway? We're in Dylan's hometown; McGuinn recorded his greatest song as The Byrds' first hit which put Dylan in the pop mainstream; it was McGuinn's voice that sang the anthem of the generation that *became* Woodstock; he was playing with Dylan's old Band; only about half the world was watching — and he chose the most simplistic, commonly played non-Masterpiece in the Jokerman's stacked deck. But then, Roger's been living in Florida for many years now.

Jorma Kaukonen and Jack Casady from the Airplane and Hot Tuna came out and did they play *Keep Your Lamps Trimmed And Burnin'?* Nooooo. Jorma plays some acoustic guitar blues flamenco somethingorother that had the Jormaheads whooping it up and the rest of us going, "What the hell is this?"

Then out bounded the perpetually confused-looking Bruce Hornsby, the guy who can play the piano in seven different languages and who joined the Grateful Dead along with Vince Welnick after Brent Mydland died when they became The Magnificent Seven for a while. Now here he was, the Horny Bee, back, joining chords with Jorma and Jack and the grateful Band, and all with a horn section that could blow over a barn at a hundred paces for what turns into The Band's Greatest Hits portion of the program, kicking off with their heaviest song . . . *THE WEIGHT* !

Great tune but weird choice for Hornsby to open with. Besides the desperation and finality of its characters, there's an even darker subtext: When Mydland died following the summer 1990 Dead tour, the final encore he sang the final night he played was *The Weight*. And since each band member takes a different verse, the last line of the last verse of the last song Brent Mydland ever sang before he died was, "I gotta go but my friend can stick around."

Of course it became "friends can stick around," and when The Dead finally played it for the first time after Brent died — and everyone knew there at Madison Square Garden where I was among the assembled — the new kid Hornsby took Brent's part and added the "s" when he sang the line.

The song was haunting the day it was written, but this afternoon with Bruce back again singing the same song, the same verse, and the same damn line, it sent shivers up an already wet spine. Circles were converging like a Spirograph all over the farm, and I was looking at the hand that was drawing it.

Then right on schedule the *Mystery Train* came rolling in, evoking the spirit of Paul Butterfield blowing harp in the twilight along the wind-howling ghost tracks of America. Butterfield, who died of overuse in 1990, used to play such a rollicking blues harmonica on this song that he actually *became* the train. And every time this song is played a little of the Butterfield Express comes back.

Then the all-stars vamoosed and left The Band to their original quintet devises, and they immediately cracked open *Stage Fright*, their ode to the price that fame extracts. Janis, Jimi, Pigpen, Keith Moon, Paul Butterfield, and The Band's own Richard Manuel were unable to make the reunion due to prior commitments with the pain-killers of life on the stage.

Then that stage freight ran directly into *Ophelia* like two old friends on the street, and Levon began honking so loud the geese were landing. There were saxes blaring, hips shaking, history making — dancing to The Band at Woodstock, who by the way were playing a <u>much</u> livelier set than '69. In fact, as Danko himself said directly, "I just have to say I was at both Woodstocks, and this one's a whole lot better than the first one."

CHAAAA! ☺

Then as if this weren't enough to satisfy a hungry man, the calliope began *Life Is A Carnival*, which in terms of Mantras To Live By, is pretty much mine.

And it seemed to be working. Joe Cocker → biking the site → Youssou N'Dour → some vague rain-like mist → *Mystery Train* → *Stage Fright* → *Ophelia* → *Life Is A Carnival*. Then just when it felt our spirit collectors could hold no more butterflies of bliss, they shook us up with a little *Willie and the Hand Jive*, the Johnny Otis song (via Clapton), with Hornsby on lead everything.

Then Danko took the mic on what used to be Richard Manuel's plea for help, *The Shape I'm In*, but which is sadly now too late.

Richard Manuel hung himself by wrapping his belt around his neck in the shower stall of his Florida motel room after a show in 1986. The Band had been back on the road for the first time since *The Last Waltz*, but were ten years out of the loop and playing small clubs instead of the biggest rooms in town. It was a far drop from the top where they lived for so long. I talked to Richard in Greenwich Village after a great set at Folk City a month before he died and he seemed really down and out and frail and gaunt and small and far away like he didn't want to be here. And I thought it was just Folk City.

I remember it so well because I was facing the abyss myself at the time. Like Richard, I wanted the pain to end. When he succumbed to the demons later that spring, instead of joining him, I realized – "Well *that's* not the answer. He gave up when he shouldn't have."

The battlefield takes too many of the best ones anyway. If any of us up and desert, we're just abandoning the rest of us. I understood why he was heading that way because I was one step behind him. He showed me how close to the edge I was, and how final it is when you go over it. That was as close as I ever got, and I never went back.

More than any other teaching, it was his death that showed me we're one life force, and taking away one is like losing part of yourself. Heart attacks, blood clots, cancer & guns kill too many of the best we have anyway, so taking out yourself doesn't seem fair to the rest of us. Life may not seem worth it sometimes, but if you took you out of the picture, the world wouldn't be nearly as good. Even keyboard players in small-club bands in Florida make a huge difference and don't even know it.

He was up in those billowing white clouds, playing along, and his wide beaked smile made a rainbow that covered the site. The heavens cast her smiling arc, and Richard cast his spell. It was nice to know you get to come home again.

Danko said, "Thank you very much," and they left the stage, their classic set at Woodstock complete.

Perhaps we should take a little break here.

If you could just put the book down and go do something in silence, that would be really good. Maybe grab some popcorn. Put on some coffee. Feed the cats. Twist a fern. But don't utter a sound till you're done. (Buddha's 4-20)

I'm serious!

Out of the drift of echoing cheers you could imagine somewhere in the distance a whirling church organ beginning to rise above the falling tide of applause and carry us off to an old-time Baptist service down some muddy bayou backroad. A possessed Thelonious Hieronymus Bach was sending haunting waves out from the stage and rolling across the 70-acre southern mini-field, every one of us glued, perplexed, uncertain, frozen in reverence and waiting for *Amazing Grace*.

Until finally it turned out to be the distinguished Doctor Garth blessing us with his afternoon benediction from his Hammond before the rest of The Band came back out to cure our *Chest Fever*.

It was around 6:00 when Rick "It's My Band" Danko told us, "We got one more guest for ya," the point in *The Last Waltz* where Robbie introduced Bob Dylan, but the Bob in '94 was Weir of the Grateful Dead. You can read into that what you want, and you'd probably be right.

Weir walked out with his bassist Rob Wasserman to the biggest applause of the day after Joe Cocker, and the sides of the stage immediately filled in with the curious, the connected and the nearly Dead. There was such a surging undercurrent of Grateful Dead energy pumping throughout the whole festival that the slightest rumble brought the volcano to eruption. The regular stage-crashing schmoozaholics got unexpectedly and humorously covered in flying Prankster dust.

Here, finally, was the San Francisco wing of The Party weighing in at the Eastern fete, except that it was Bobby, the only Grateful Designate who wears collared polo shirts and sometimes looks more like a narc than a Beatle. But he's a good man who actually brings more Deadheads to good causes, and more straight-streets to good music, than any five other band members I can think of.

This whole event was taking on serious flashbacks of Clinton's Inauguration last year: Me and Ranger in the KarmaCoupe Cabin living on the streets of D.C. a few hundred feet from the White House for the entire Inaugural week, skip-boppin' bee-bee's in the land of the free-be's, wailing with hundreds of thousands in the chorus for change. So many performers in common, both there and here, both Bobs Dylan and Weir, and Melissa Etheridge, Stephen Stills, Blues Traveler, Salt-N-Pepa – all playing outdoors non-stop for days on multiple stages with giant video screens, swooping camera booms, historic pageantry, and a rainbow coalition of dancing people. We must be doing something right if the inauguration of a President has the same lineup as Woodstock.

And it makes you wonder: If you were lying on the grass and smoking some of the good stuff with your friends in 1969 and said, "Imagine a time where it was like, *Dylan* playing at the White House instead of some opera singer? And then say, Jerry or Bob shows up on the Mall for the Inauguration, right?!" People would have thought you were out of your mind even by the standards of the day.

"Yeah right. Dylan doesn't show up at Woodstock but he'll play at an inauguration! Sure. And someday the President'll be a sax-playing Deadhead. Have another hit."

But it's true, it's true! Thank you Dreamers. "Optimists pick up your pass to heaven!" If the impossible 25 years ago can be reality today, anything is possible tomorrow.

Back in something resembling real time, everything had been going so smooth & normal it was clearly time for the Dead to come out and screw things up. Or in particular, Bob Weird, who's stage act includes no words or gestures yet taking roughly a week to re-tune his guitar between every song. The Dead's lack of having grown into anything even vaguely resembling professional entertainers after almost 30 years is astonishing. Everyone from kids to older people were looking at each other like Rosanne was singing the national anthem, and a buzz began to rumble through this non-Dead audience asking the musical question, "What the hell's going on, and who's on first?"

"The Who's not playing," I heard her husband say.

"I don't want to know who's *not* playing."

"Exactly."

"But, who's on next?"

"The Who's not here."

"But what's on after this?"

"The Band."

"Yeah, that's what I want to know."

"You got it."

"I got what? Are you going to make me guess who?"

"Now don't go bringing them into this."

"Bring *Who* into it?"

"I told you – they're not here."

"But what's the band on after this?"

"The Band's on after this."

"That's what I want to know."

"And that's what I'm telling you."

"Who? Who's on after this?"

"The Who's not here."

"Oh, this is beat."

"No, this is Dead."

"I just want to know which band is playing next."

"The Band."

"Exactly."

"Then you know."

"What do I know?"

"The Band's name."

"I don't know nuthin'. What's their name?"

"The Band."

"Yes."

"Yes is definitely not here."

And this went on for several hours until sometime Wednesday afternoon Weir finished tuning up and unfortunately began playing *Fever*. Picture

Glen Campbell doing Aretha Franklin's *Respect* and you'd have some idea. Most Deadheads were dancing like St. Stephen had opened the gates to heavens, while the rest of the audience broke into discussion groups.

Weir further punished the envelope with that rancid relative *Eternity* (named for how long the song goes on for), which was followed by Rob Wasserman playing a bass solo until about Thanksgiving of (*I Can't Get No) Satisfaction*, after which he promptly fell off the stage and broke his arm. Seriously.

Finally Bobby brought "Cousin Bruce" back out for *Throwing Stones*, the first actual Dead song of Woodstock, and the volcano erupted again — which just goes to show — with only a pair of Bob & Bruces doing a smidgen of the most over-played Dead song of the decade, the entire field of dancing bones began shaking faster than the politicians throwing stones.

Weir followed his prophesy of frenzy with *Easy Answers*, which, of course, was incorrect. Just when he could have sparked the torch of a global inferno on the pay-per-view by treating non-Deadheads to a tasty *Playin' In The Band*, or a polyrhythmic *Sugar Magnolia*, or a poetic *Jack Straw* duet with Cousin Bruce, he bumbled through an unintelligible fourth-string castaway. Uuuuu and it makes me wonder.

Thankfully to all things that are good in the universe The Band returned with their all-star lineup and saved the day. The Bruce 'n' Bob Show was rejoined by McGuinn, Jorma, Levon, Garth, Rick, and a smokin' horn section that kicked into *I Don't Want To Hang Up My Rock 'n' Roll Shoes*, like the climax of *Rock of Ages*. Except this time it was The Jefferson Dead Byrds Band. And they never did <u>that</u> in '69.

Levon summed up our lives rather nicely at this point:

> "Some might say it's the devil in my soul;
> But that's a bunch of shit, I just wanna rock 'n' roll."

Twirling hippie-skirts billowed like a ballroom and flailing arms spun like ballerinas all over the dance-floor field in a chorus-howling frenzy:

> "They say that rock 'n' roll will soon fade away —
> I just wanna tell you rock 'n' roll is here to stay."

Which may be true, but I wasn't. Suddenly it was 6:30 and Crosby, Stills & Nash were due on the North Stage in 15 minutes. Holy Cats! There was another dream to catch one field over. It was time to leave the hip, mellow, older audience, and rejoin the North Field's Generation X moshing mass.

As I walked out the backstage road connecting the two stages, Bobby led The Band through a funky, hiccuppy *Take Me To The River*, and I probably wouldn't be walking away from Bob Weir playing with The Band at Woodstock, if I wasn't heading for Crosby, Stills & Nash singing *Woodstock* at Woodstock.

I paused at a sacred point on the road, where the energy of the two stages came together, where the sound of one was ending and the sounds of the other beckoning, crackling together like opposing energy forces in a gravitational pushmi-pullyu. Together, apart, together, apart. Like the Continental Divide, it was one way or the other baby, the dividing line between two very different fates — between thousands of different potential encounters. It was the most amazing spot on the site in many ways, because you could see, hear and feel both of these enormous life-forces at the same time. Ten feet in either direction and you were completely immersed in that stage's sound and aura. Ten feet the other way a totally different sound feeling heart beat. Individual human energy fields slid past, each coming from one sphere and moving to another – crossing the musical border through leprechaun immigration.

Suddenly I could hear a band playing on the North Stage — and they didn't sound like Melissa Etheridge.

Yikes!

Sure enough, CSN had come on <u>early</u>! I flashed a party-dance parting glance to the raging Dead Byrds' jam and headed off for the bread & butter of rock 'n' roll, the harmonies of Crosby, Stills & Nash who had already begun their songbook of hits.

But something had changed at the festival.

It was my first time back at the main stage since the rain, and everything was a lot wetter than before. And darker. But the people were even nicer somehow. Everything had become . . . *sillier.* People were wearing garbage bags as clothing, make-up was streaking, and everybody was just slopping happily along in the brown slurpee earth, all washed up in the same boat and laughing.

While I was over at the old fogies' show on the South Stage, apparently about a half a million youngsters had gathered in the living room. But frankly none of them were paying the slightest bit of attention to the stage. It turns out CSN had been scheduled, in effect, as the opening act for Nine Inch Nails, Metallica and Aerosmith who were slated to follow and close the North Stage for Saturday night. Not exactly a CSN crowd.

Who should they have followed? Hmmm, let's see, what other Band was ending around this time? Perhaps one with an all-star jam of musicians already gathered and most of whom had played with CSN on and off for about 25 years. No that wouldn't work at all. I know, let's put them on right before Nine Inch Nails Across A Chalkboard!

I pictured all the dancing Deadheads I just left at the renegade South Stage, then looked across this swarm of Saturday night loogans waiting for The Moshing Hour. It seemed so sad all those Band fans who loved CSN were not making this logical segue. Instead of playing in front of a hundred-thousand folk-rock harmony-loving first-Woodstock fans, CSN were singing to a million moshers who didn't give a flying fuck off. But with thirty bands and two stages it was one of only two scheduling conflict snafus all weekend, so there was really nothing left to do but smile, smile, smile. (The other being Dylan & Santana at the same time of day tomorrow).

But each of these million moshers came with a tent, and you would walk and walk and walk and get nowhere cause you were always zigzagging and sidestepping over tent corners and between people and weaving like a snake through the grass, slithering between the human blades until you ran into another snake slithering in the same direction and then a bunch would join together and weave, and if you pulled the camera up you'd see little water snakes weaving everywhere through the flowing sea of people.

As I was slithering under the setting sun that had scattershot a spectrum of oranges across the sky, I overheard someone say that John Sebastian had introduced CSN, but I don't know how they'd know from back here. This was when CSN stood for Can't See Nuthin. Faintly in the distance you could hear a train, which by my watch was the *Marrakesh Express*, and I wanted on.

So I kept walking for a week or two until I found a place to stand in a little pocket between some tents and fell in with a group of college kids from New Paltz. Standing among them was the most beautiful girl in the world. Or so I thought when I was 15. Her name was Alison and she lived down the street. We had a crush on each other but neither ever had the courage to say anything. She emblazoned an image of beauty in my mind that never went away, and now suddenly she was standing right in front of me, living and breathing, maybe 22-years-old, same smile, same swirling ocean-green eyes, same confidence in movement but gentleness in intent.

And you guessed it — I couldn't talk to her this time either. Not even close. I'd just look at her and my mind would start churning, "That's the most beautiful girl in the world, that's the most beautiful girl in the world, oh my God, oh my God," over and over, and my bottom lip would droop open like Bubba in Gump and several minutes would pass before I'd realize I was standing right in front of her with this dumb blank expression on my face saying nothing. Nobody noticed or anything. Least of all her.

I heard one of the group whisper, "Hey, that guy likes Nicki," and they all smiled. Oh, is it obvious?

This can't happen in life. The past cannot come back or be repeated. Yet here it was. Alison – and Woodstock – in the flesh. The first two loves come back at once. She was my girl as much as I had one back in the Woodstock reunion days in Winnipeg, and now here she was in person at the real thing. First my oldest friend then my oldest love show up at my oldest dream, which was rapidly becoming more real all around me.

* * *

Graham Nash broke things up nicely in the middle of their set to make a special tribute to recently late-great Bill Graham, my real-life mentor, one-time employer, and the man who won Best Supporting Activist at the first Woodstock. Unfortunately now gone to the great gig in the sky, but John Scher, this show's co-promoter along with Michael Lang, was one of Bill's apostles and became his de facto east coast legacy. Once again, just like Alison, Robbie, Richard, Butterfield, and Lennon, all these spirits were making the scene using surrogates to summon their essence.

Then Nash stepped into Lennon's *In My Life* for Bill, once again bringing The Beatles into the house.

I scanned down my Itinerary of things to do:

· See Crosby, Stills& Nash singing a Beatles' song for Bill Graham at Woodstock.

Check.

Besides being yet another juicy John gem, the last verse about never losing your love for those who came before hit hauntingly home for Bill, for Woodstock, and for all the missing voices.

Then Nash said, "This song is as true now as when it was written," and all the Butthead scholars around me starting howling "Woodstock" again, but the boys had *Long Time Gone* in mind, Crosby's brilliant call to action that appropriately opened the *Woodstock* movie. And when he screamed, "Speak out against the madness," it wasn't about dieting.

As darkness settled over the site, the huge movie screens became even more dominant by showing off the most advanced digital video effects any of us had ever seen. They could stretch parts of moving images out and hold them on the screen while the musician continued to erase or overlap his own images in a continuous colorful wash that made Grateful Dead shows look like the old Indian head test pattern. Parts of the moving musicians' images became electrified in neon light, while the rest of the screen would fill with pastel brush strokes, all of it incorporating the live action on stage. It was improvised movie making in real time with a great live soundtrack.

And into this surreal swirling picture-scape CSN wove their trance-like *Deja Vu*, with its refrain, "We have all been here before," and I thought, "Boy, you're not kidding!" The song unfolds slowly like a Gregorian Chant, repeating its chorus and weaving its ageless chest-thumping psychedelic riff through a half-million hearts at once. Then John Sebastian slowly strolls out from the side of the stage and blew a soulful harp solo that stilled even the moshers. He became the final spice in the potion that ignited the crowd into chanting as a whole: "We have all been here before. We have all been here before." And the sweet music permeated everything, shimmering across the shy smiles of loners, glittering in the wide eyes of the young, and silencing the breath of the loud, as the whole crowd began humming in harmony.

After all the stupid pre-show security bullshit and Pepsi-blather that prevented so many people from coming, it was becoming inescapably obvious that the unthinkable was happening: This *was* Woodstock. Everywhere you looked, there was only one thing this picture reminded you of.

There wasn't one single corporate logo visible from anywhere on the field. There was enough rain to capsize the Titanic. A half-million people were on a farm in the mud listening to Crosby, Stills & Nash. There was no cement, no rules, no police and a sound system that could be heard in Canada. I was expecting to spend the day in Bethel because this was supposed to be the yucky yuppie corporate greedfest. But something totally unexpected was happening. And that was the biggest truth of the day. As Rick Danko kept saying over and over in my head, "This is a whole lot better than the first one."

The song *Southern Cross* must be CSN's MTV hit or something because as soon as it started all the newbies suddenly recognized who was playing and tuned in. Don't ask me. At least they weren't calling out "*Woodstock*" again.

Seeing as my favorite Crosby was David, I was pleased they played his *Wooden Ships*, an oddball entry that was part of a longer opus he was writing in the '60s, and which, incidentally, they played at the original festival and is on that triple album. Apparently I started rocking 'n' thrashing 'n' dancing furly weird cause I freaked the New Paltz freshmen right out of there. "Oh-oh," I'm sure I heard one of them say. "The old guy's dancing. Looks like he's having an epileptic fit, dude. Let's blow."

Then to add to my Cockerian spasathon, they played a rockin' pneumonia shall-we-say e-long-ated *Carry On.* It had become pretty much the Greatest Hits Revue for an hour and a half, except by this part of the program a few more of us were getting physically involved. It became a body thing, a feeling, brainless, unabashed dancing thing. At one point, when they all sang the line, "The sky is clearing, and the night is coming on," there was a rolling thunder of cheering that started at the stage and cracked into lightning as it passed overhead. Gale storms of blowing rock 'n' roll seerdom crossed the now electrified masses. Get a grip in the mud, we're sinkin' fast!

Then with the running rush of "the night is coming on," they finally began their *Woodstock* climax.

When I was screaming the song out the van windows on the way up I had no idea if I'd ever see CSN, or catch this song, but here it was, going down at Woodstock.

The field became a Mardi Gras of whoops and howls and skin-slapping joy at every beat. The whole crowd of shaved-head moshers and grey-haired hippies and little kids were singing all the words as one, growing louder and louder until the whole 500,000 peaked: *"By the time we got to Woodstock, we were half a million strong,"* and a tingling roar rose through the ecstatic crowd and obliterated the rest of the verse. Tears rolled down singing cheeks. Lights illuminated a phat mist rising above the crowd. Beaming faces were singing their hearts out. We *had* got to Woodstock, through the web of bad press, the physical and psychic roadblocks, the mud and the mayhem, yet each of us was here. It was a moment of pure nirvana with so many people being so happy in one place at one time.

In a way, this was the song and the moment that a lot of us came for. Joni Mitchell penned the anthem while watching the first news reports come over the TV while she was alone in her hotel room in Manhattan in 1969. As she put it, "I wasn't there. Crosby, Stills, Nash and myself all went out to the airport. Woodstock had been declared a national disaster area, so we were told we couldn't get in or get out. I had to do *The Dick Cavett Show* the following day, so I left the boys there, thinking they were going someplace else. But they rented a helicopter. I felt left out. I really felt like 'The Girl.' The Girl couldn't go, but the Boys could. I watched everything on TV. But I don't know if I would have written the song *Woodstock* if I had gone. I was the fan that couldn't go."

The song's been sung in every language in every country around the world and transformed the original concert from a big event to a state of mind. It could never have actually been performed at Woodstock, of course, yet it has evoked the feeling every time its been played since. And for one magic moment the song came home.

As an encore, they brought out a cake and the half-a-million strong sang David Crosby *Happy Birthday*.

"Yeah, sure. And then some guy turned water into wine." No really, it happened. Crosby played *Woodstock* at Woodstock, on his birthday weekend!

In keeping with the philosophy of securing Divine Moments, I grabbed my piece of the metaphorical cake and left the building. A group called Nine Inch Nails (named because that's what it feels like is being hammered into your skull when you hear them) was coming on next, and I wanted to be on about Mars for that.

While the departing CSN fans clogged the exits, there was this blissful feeling again that we'd all been here before, that we'd all been to see the Magic Fairy and she'd tapped us with her wand. Everyone was bopping along in silence with silly-big grins on their faces. This may be where the acid rumors got started, I don't know.

Nor do I know what I did after that. I was so stunned by having shared that one Woodstock moment with so many that nothing else was real. I remember trying not to run into anything but just keep moving with the flow in any direction as long as it didn't pop the beautiful tranquility balloon. How often do you net one of these in your life? And it seemed like there had been so many of them already in one day. "By the time we got to Woodstock, we were half-a-million strong," I kept singing in a whisper along with everyone else, looking bleary-eyed at the passing angels of the Saturday night.

The refrain became emblazoned into a physical trophy on a shelf simply by repeating it. Magic was evoked at the snap of your fingers. It's what we live for in a way, mashing the fruits of the search in your face and getting covered in the juice until it drips down your chin in crazy-pure joy.

So I let the Adventure Card sink in as I walked around the backstage area, blindly avoided the bees buzzing about on business. When I came to I was in the Media Tent sitting cockeyed on one of the folding chairs, and there was some punk rock guy all covered in mud on the TV screaming into a microphone. I'll never understand why anyone listens to people scream at them. I wondered if kids had it so good these days they actually paid to have people scream at them. In my time we used to avoid that sort of thing.

Clearly out-ranked generationally, I retreated to the KarmaCoupe to let the visions of Woodstock dance in my brain and was asleep within seconds of the steel door slamming.

* * *

"Rain. It's raining on the cottage roof. I love rain at the cottage. I should go sit on the porch." I opened my eyes but only saw dark night blacking out van windows. "Oh yeah," I realized. "It's raining at *Woodstock*. I love Woodstock. This is great." I closed my eyes again.

* * *

Suddenly the pounding of the rain on the roof stopped and I woke up. "A voice? Announcements from the stage at this hour? It's still dark out." I sat up and rolled down the window. It sounded like John Scher babbling away in some distant echo chamber I was still too asleep to decipher.

Then some band came on. "How could a band be *starting* now? This doesn't make any sense. All there was left was Metallica and Aerosmith when I went to sleep. This definitely isn't Metallica, and it sure doesn't sound like Aerosmith."

But being the dedicated dream-catcher I am, I immediately began preparing for the next installment. The roof-pounding rain had eased up, but the wet seat where I'd left the window open a breathable crack suggested I needed the portable rain poncho for the first time. This was suddenly a job for – All-Weatherman! Neither rain nor sleet nor zoom a'loom shall keep this Card collector from his appointed Adventures.

Suddenly I heard a familiar voice from the stage: "We were supposed to play Saturday night. This is fuckin' Sunday morning!"

"Definitely Steve Tyler," I smiled. "This is gonna be *great!*"

I bolted out to the field and discovered the following: I'd slept through Nine Inch Nails and Metallica; there was a hell of a lot more water on the ground; half the people had gone home leaving the field half-empty; it was around 2 AM — and Aerosmith had just hit the stage.

"Happy camper" took on a whole new literal meaning. I'd just had a four hour nap, avoided the worst brain-pain music of the weekend, and was pit-stop fresh for the climax of Saturday night at Woodstock. Plus, I was dry as a cotton ball on a radiator as I walked into that mud-soaked beer-soaked rain-soaked field of stoned survivors looking like refugees from a Midwestern flood.

Here we were 14 hours after Joe Cocker kicked things off on the same stage, and now Steven Tyler was sprinting end-to-end and putting on one heck of a show. At least the kids were getting their plastic Woodstock scrip's worth. I know I was.

Apparently Aerosmith have been making hit songs in the years since I was a fan of theirs in the seventies. All of a sudden I realized they'd been playing the soundtrack to my life for the last 15 years, as the songs I'd been hearing in clubs 'n' cabs 'n' delis 'n' things — *Cryin', Janie's Got A Gun, Love In An*

Elevator, Dude Looks Like A Lady — were now playing from the stage like a *This Is Your Life* weekend.

As I roamed the open spaces, "Life, liberty, and the pursuit of happiness" were all being celebrated at ear-splitting volume all over this hot August farm. In the midst of all the oozing, frothing sex, mud & freedom, Tyler was encouraging the topless girls. "Undress yourself. Express yourself," he'd scream in that crazy-high voice of his, and a dozen new shirts flew through the misty concert air. Breasts were so pervasive they almost became natural. And just as I was getting acclimatized to the sea of skin, it suddenly hit me why they were called Generation "X". Slow or what, eh?

Steve Tyler is The Brilliant Goof hosting this idiot-rock entertainment-schlock generation. Ever notice how most rock stars always run around *trying* to be cool? You have to goof on it if it's going to be real, and Tyler openly makes fun of the genre at the same time he masters it. I was so proud of these guys somehow. They harked back to when I first discovered rock 'n' roll, and now here they were closing Saturday night at Woodstock and hitting it clean out of the park.

Years earlier they'd really hit the bottom. I remember bumping into Tyler in Washington Square Park when he was looking to score. In fact I think he even got busted there in some round-up of the desperate. He'd become known in the business as a scammer of whatever free schmack he could scrounge. Which is okay. Nothing wrong with falling. Most do.

But not many climb back out.

I thought before this weekend how pathetic it was that the Jefferson Airplane had the top headlining slot to close the Saturday night (Sunday morning) of the first Woodstock, and this time they had *Aerosmith* of all watered-down choices! "If that isn't emblematic of how far we've fallen I don't know what is," I thought.

But *y'know* . . . These Aerosmith guys with their double album package of hits spanning 20 years were putting on an outrageously great show. I don't take too kindly to music I don't take too kindly to, and I was not prepared to like these old retreads who were booked to steal the thunder from *my* eternal Woodstock memories. No siree. But what a blow out! I don't think I really want to see how the Airplane's performance would stack up against Aerosmith if you know what I mean. It was kind of spooky in that way. Could things actually *be better* now?

It was Saturday night in America, 1994, and Aerosmith is exactly who should be playing.

* * *

Utilizing the nocturnal openness of the rain-evacuated field, I naturally performed one of my standard, circular, cover-absolutely-everything explorative reconnaissance mapping expeditions.

Squwelph squwelph squwelph, I galooshed. Kerrr-plooff. "Just keep it below the bootline and you're fine," I concentrated, trying to learn how to walk in a world made of pudding. Ker-ploosh ker-ploosh ker-plunk.

After miles of surfing like a spoon over tapioca, I came upon The Great River of Mud that cut through the center of our nation. It was a dense chocolate shake, 30 feet across — watery along its shores and deceptively deep in the middle. Just like on the South Field, the gathering water began on the rise at the back and gradually ran all the way down the natural amphitheater to the mosh pit stage front. By this time, the mudpeople had developed a series of sports involving the natural wonder, and at this hour they were practicing the ever-popular, Long-Distance Dive & Slide Competition, where human seals sprinted, back-flipped and slid for miles down the hill towards the stage. "Mudslide" took on a whole new meaning.

If you see aerial photographs of the site, you can tell the post-Saturday afternoon rain shots by the wide dark river that splits the crowd down the middle. And I mean in more ways than geography. Our world had changed today. The Family Tree of Woodstock had forked at the mud in the road, and we now had two different strains, related but very different. There were the tribal gorillas for whom mud meant freedom, earth and happiness and who clearly had some primal edge over the rest of us. While we, on the other hand, weren't eating dirt. There were those who just orgasmically threw aside everything they'd carried with them and pursued the pleasure of the experience, and those who carried cameras, wallets, or their dignity, and didn't want any of them to get wet. It was the flopping aquatic waterpeople, and the upright dancing landlubbers. Dark ones and light ones. Earth people verses air people.

In my search for somewhere remotely dry to stand I found the shale-surrounded water hitch in the bullseye center of the field. It was perfect diamond-hard ground to soak up the energy but not the water from the encroaching sea of life.

And there, THERE above it all, standing on the 20 foot square frame was the California bikeman from the JamesWorld! YES! The cosmic connection. The pulling together of two out of a million lottery winners. The knowing look — deep piercing eye-lock — without saying a word — YES! Ear to ear grins on both of us. Him up on the wooden mountain dancing over the masses, me prowling the trenches. YES! Inner Connection. His ecstatic face. Mine beaming back. Man! Like two brothers across a battlefield we stared at each other, smoke wafting between us, silent but for the hundred-thousand muskets going off all around us. Then we both smiled again at the same time, nodding to the field, nodding to the people, nodding to each other in recognition that this was all so far beyond anything we ever imagined when we saw each other on Friday. *"What the hell has happened?"* our dropped-jaws mouthed. "Did you expect this?" Everything in the world had been so normal when we last saw each other, and now we both looked like airplane wreckage survivors coming out of the jungle.

After a lengthy solidification of spirits, I turned my attention back to assessing the Adventure at hand, namely, crossing The Great River of Mud. I studied my fellow commuters as they tried to negotiate this surreal-field. "Survey like Grant, then cross like Custer," I said to my troops as I strategically plotted the quickest route across the impediment. Unfortunately the optical survey results were yielding the following pattern: an explorer-person would be tentatively walking across the river just fine until suddenly ker-S'PLOOSH — down to their knees they'd drop in some hole.

"Forget the Yankee generals dude, its time to revert to your Canadianism," I realized. We know walking on water is possible. Done it a million times. Even partially frozen, or not even frozen, Canadians learn to do it from infancy. And okay, since you've read this far and put up with so much I'll share this little insider's tidbit but don't say where you got it: Hold this page up to a mirror and play it backward:

run really fast.

It's possible to run across rivers as long as you're light and fast: With a little warm-up you just run so fast you barely touch your foot to the surface for a split-second then pick it up again, never leaving your foot anywhere long enough to sink beneath the surface, but tapping the hard surface of the water to keep you going. It's kind of the same way a flat rock skips over a flat lake. With just a little momentum you can skim the surface of a river and get to the other side. And so it was that Dudley Doobie crossed the Mighty St. Lawrence like so many times before.

And then, just when I was thinking all Aerosmith ever played anymore were these new hits – *finally* they broke into an extremely psychedelic *Sweet Emotion*, a song we used to listen to back when we first learned to run on water. Don't tell me you can't go home again. This whole damn weekend was proof you can! I'd crossed not only a river but a threshold into a part of my past I had never lived: Aerosmith playing the songs I knew by rote but had forgotten completely – at an altogether familiar event I had never been to. Was this a dream, or do they simply come true?

Holy toast, I'm crackin' the eggs, there's mud-covered babes, blanket-wrapped snugglers and drug-dealing smugglers, and a quarter-million happy campers who survived a noon-till-now stretch of rock 'n' roll through a pouring rainstorm in a farmer's field and were still here to honk about it. I was in love.

There may have been that moment when Crosby, Stills & Nash were singing *Woodstock* that bonded the half-million strangers at one point, but this was another: The All-Night Survivors, the rock 'n' roll hard-core who were still toasting the air and proud to be there. *This* was a rock 'n' roll acid test, and it didn't matter what drugs or not it took to get here, as long as you could Be Here Now. And the hundred thousand who'd stuck it out were guaranteed induction into the Rock 'n' Roll Fan's Hall of Fame, located in Woodstock, New York, State of Mind.

Over at the V.I.P. bleachers once again, I climbed the slippery slats of the rickety benches for the sunset of music on Saturday night at Woodstock. And you can bet I put that in my pipe and smoked it. From the half-empty bleachers you could see all the way across the dark sea of people to the jagged horizon. And it was so late at night there was a real sense that you were breaking the rules even for Woodstock.

The Tyler-Jaggerman was running up and down the stage while close-ups from the sixteen cameras were flashing on the giant video screens which were continually streaming down both sides of the stage like a psychedelic waterfall.

I was at peace. I was at home. I was sitting down! For the first time in a long time I had a seat! I settled in nicely on the wide, open bench, took a heavy load off my hiking boots, cracked my second frosty cold one, and Aerosmith promptly said goodnight. "Yeah, I knew that," I said.

But just then the beautiful rolling sea of mud people suddenly burst into a city of lights as each one of the temples raised a flame to the sky. 50 stadiums of fans spread out to the horizon, all aglow with camping candles and all-weather lighters in a giant tribal ceremony.

And then out of the fan-roaring light-twinkling darkness I heard Tyler's voice say, "This one's for John Lennon. He'd play it if he were here." My mouth dropped open and the band popped open *Come Together*, John's gentle plea to we masses.

A) Surprising. B) Holy Cats. C) what I mean? D) Can you believe it? E) Aerosmith covering *The Beatles?* F) Just about my favorite John Lennon Beatles song. G) Whiz. H) <u>Another</u> Beatles's tune? I) was duly impressed and promptly fired-up a J) passing it along the row of my fellow mudniks, thinking, "K) this is amazing. I'm so L) ivated above the crowd right now I feel like Dorothy spinning in the sky and calling out to Auntie M). There is N) O) way I'm ever going back to earth," I'm thinking. Only thing was, suddenly I had to take a P) and could see from here the Q) was like around the bleachers. "Oh no, R) you kidding? Now I have to do that S) kimo thing & hold it till spring, T) hee." But I can tell U) right now, I was getting pretty swept up in the sweet emotion of the thing, riding out the Utopian Day in the V) I.P. bleachers, toasting the air, sharing a bone under a shimmering dome, images splintering into prisms of dancing Picassos, double me, W) fracturing pictures and splitting atoms into 3-D magic eye images floating in X) tacy. When the heavens open, I don't ask Y) I just report back what I Z).

Besides the blinding kaleidoscopic fractals, did you notice that every band we saw on the North Stage except the Native Americans on Friday morning have played a Beatles tune?

Sheryl Crow: *I've Got A Feeling* (the John part)

Joe Cocker: *With A Little Help From My Friends*
CSN: *In My Life*
Aerosmith: *Come Together*

And all with a heavy slant towards John might I point out.

True Digressions: You know that house I went over to when I was 9 and saw the album cover of *Woodstock* that kicked off this whole adventure? Well that same stereo had *The White Album* by The Beatles with its 8-by-10 glossy of each musician. That picture of John Lennon changed my life — even before I knew who he was. Something about how his hair hung around his face touched me, something about the peaceful way he just *was* changed me. And I've had long hair and a penchant for peace ever since.

Then I heard his music and moved to New York City.

How could so many of the main characters in my life suddenly be showing up and acting out some sort of ensemble drama of the building blocks that got me here? My oldest friend in the world is here somewhere. John Lennon, Woodstock, Winnipeg, Alison, Richard Manuel, The Dead, Bill Graham, John Scher, Michael Lang, the Clinton Inaugural . . . All the High Lights of my Northern Lights were shining in the same sky over this magic field.

Get outta town! This didn't happen. Aerosmith didn't start playing Lennon as soon as you got to the bleachers overlooking the field. No way. Like

Woodstock would ever happen again.

Come together.

Check.

From the blinding bliss of that fantasy field rose the opening guitar lick from *Dream On*, the greatest rock 'n' roll song ever written. Or so it seemed at that moment. This was Alison's and my song, and I've carefully locked it in a time capsule I cannot open. But suddenly I was face-to-face with all those steps untaken, and all those words unsaid. First she was here in body, and now in song — and there's no getting out of it.

Obviously one of those spirit flow hurricane's was howling over the site. Why did I sleep through Metallica but wake up just as Aerosmith was hitting the stage? Why didn't they play this at any other point in the set instead of right when I get to the home-base big-picture bleachers?

When the wind's blowing this hard I try to recognize it and get my sail up as soon as it rises so I can ride it for as long as possible. Once on, catch the breeze, GO with the flow, ride the wave, channel the Chi, grab the tow rope, roll the dice, play the game, feel the tingle, throttle down. Do anything and everything. Do the thing you're supposed to do, you know to do, you feel to do. Do what you're afraid to do. You'll succeed at whatever you try during these times.

When the wind's against me and everything's going wrong, I lay low, batten down the hatches and don't take chances. I keep working fast and hard on whatever needs doing so I get as much done during the shitty time as possible. That way, when the anti-flow, bad luck streak is over, the chores are done and I can sail again free and easy. It's a great way of beating the devil – by secretly being productive behind closed doors while he's raging and not raising your head till it's over. Or, as Matisse says, "Work cures everything."

When it's bad, get the hell out of there; When it's good, wail like a 'Trane solo for as long as you have the wind.

And here tonight were Aerosmith playing the sad minor-key memory of two children cracking love's door and peeking through for the first time, but too scared to cross the threshold. We both saw the cozy fire, the soft flickering light and could feel its warmth, but were too scared to leave the playground just yet. We each went home and cried. Maybe we'd have to find somewhere less hot to start.

Learning from fools and sages . . . tears were streaming down my cheeks and I had trouble breathing. My first sweetheart was suddenly in that field before me. We never saw each other again, until now through twinkling splashes of teary light. This shouldn't be happening. I was leaning against the white picket fence on Grosvenor Street talking with her. Everyone else had gone home, it was late, it was summer, and it was just us. It was after the big dance when all the eyes were on us, when it was supposed to happen. She liked me. I liked her. But I just said, "Good night," and walked away, walked away from it all. Oh Great Spirit, give me that one more shot at that moment of life.

But missed bliss is never given a second chance.

And yet somehow here I was at something that happened in 1969, with my first love from childhood, all alive again before me.

I was dizzy, confused about what was memory or real or imagined – watching fuzzy colors and blurry memories meld with the present. I tried to open my eyes but it was like looking in the mirror in the shower. I couldn't see a thing, but I knew I was there.

The bleachers bounced like a diving board, and I just let the lovelight shine.

Let it shine. Let it shine, shine, shine.

Had I dreamed until my dreams came true? Was this happening or am I about to wake up on a waterbed?

* * *

Somewhere in the distance – music. Loud. Shaking. Bouncing diving board.

As I faded back in, a rock band was playing a song that seemed to be called *Living On The Edge* and I smiled, then choked with laughter. *Of course.*

I knew this all would be ending soon so I better get up and enjoy it. So I climbed to the top row of the bleachers to stand with all the singing swinging shirtless yahoos as the band kicked into *Walk This Way* to close the show, the day, and the night.

15 hours of rock 'n' roll came rolling up into one final triumphant cheer as we thanked not only them but everyone else who had rocked our foundations all day.

And just then one of those crisp country nighttime breezes started blowing over the crowd and caught us bleacher-high surfers right off our perch. But there was something sacred and healing about that farm-cured air. It circulated the scents and magic molecules of a pretty special gathering to all who were there and beyond. The closing of Saturday night at Woodstock was only going to happen once or twice in 50 years, and this was its chemical make-up. Mother nature's lion rose and joined with a hundred thousand of her most enthusiastic cubs, chilling the bones and raising the spirits.

Even after they said goodnight and turned on the house lights everyone just stood there cheering and cheering and cheering. Then all of a sudden above the stage two wiggling white flares shot up like sperm cells towards the heavens. They hovered at their peak in the black sky, then suddenly exploded into fireworks!!

KA'BANG! KA'BANG! Huge white explosions began sounding and dripping white firelight over the stage. Fireworks! *I love fireworks!* They had fireworks at Clinton's Inaugural right after his big speech at the Lincoln Memorial when Dylan played, like a simulated Civil War battle in the air.

That's what I love about fireworks, it's like a peaceful war — a celebration that we aren't having a war. To get the public's ya-ya's out on gunfire, we stage these simulated bomb blasts where nobody gets hurt but we get to oo and ahh at the big Ka-Pows. Like on the Fourth of July — we're faking a war. It's an imaginary battle that we drive to a park to watch. I think it's great. Wars seem so safe on TV, but when you hear the bombs bursting in air above you, and feel the ground shake below, a battlefield didn't seem so romantic anymore.

wwzzz — CRRRACKKK wwzzz — KA'BAMMM wwzzz — POOFFF Hot snorkin' zammies! — KA' BOOOOM !!!

And you're not going to believe this part, but the giant video drive-in movie screens were filming the fireworks and broadcasting them right beneath the actual explosions. BUT they weren't just doing that, they were also using the digitized computer animation to freeze-frame explosions in succession so each one would splash a different color on the screen until another would explode and cover part of it like continuous balloons of paint smacking a canvas, while the real image was exploding right above it. It was full color Pollocks, God-size and digitally enhanced — simultaneous dissolving slow-motion explosions in brilliant color splashing in our faces while sonic booms cracked the air above. Then they sent up the fireworks that dropped slow dripping flames and the video screens captured each streaking image in a different color of dripping psychedelic rain. And flashing between the explosions were shots of topless girls dancing on shoulders while new fireworks slowly exploded all over them and eventually wiped their dancing image from the screen.

The entire farm was lit up under a hovering cloud of smoke that reflected the light of the explosions. I could see all the way past the South Stage to the row of houses along Route 212 and wondered what the old farmers were thinking of <u>this</u>. "If they weren't awake before, they're awake now!" I smiled.

Clinton, Woodstock, Civil War, the Statue of Liberty, America, July Fourth, celebration, cascading completion of life cycle.

Thank you God. Thank you Spirit. Thank you Earth.

* * *

Now the music was done and the secret doors of the tranquil night were opening — and I was the most rested guy on the site!

I rubbed my hands together like the diabolical scientist I was, about to pull the switch. "What do we conquer now?" I pondered. "Ha-ha ha-ha ha." Everyone who'd watched Aerosmith must have been true fans and not simply still-standing loogans, because as soon as the music was over they all went to sleep. In fact, I was all alone chang-changing down the middle of that old ghost town main street once again.

What magic spell shall we weave over this haunted bayou tonight? Eerie silence. Spooky wooky. Foggy mountain high. Time to go undercover. To seek out strange new tents, new campgrounds, to boldly go where we were not supposed to.

I continued Buddhisticly quiet along Main Street, using the force and skipping the light fandango, until I came upon a child of a guard sitting in a chair watching me for longer than I care to know. "Walk like you belong here," I quickly ordered myself. "Be proud, be real. Think fast. Be clear. Be clear," I scrambled through my fumbling mind.

"Press isn't allowed back here."

"I was interviewing Country Joe McDonald today and I think I left my tape deck in there," I said pointing to a row of tents I'd seen people hanging in earlier.

"Sorry, you're not allowed."

"Listen, I've been up looking for this thing for hours and if it's not back here, I'm screwed."

The young local guy, who was just as jazzed to be here as I was, looked me up and down then finally smiled and said, "Okay. Have fun."

Holy Cats! For the first time I was coasting down the hill into the heart of the beast. Tour buses and semi-trailers were parked along the ridge side of the road overlooking the field. On the other side was the row of dressing room tents for the artists. "Right place, wrong time," I thought, as I noted the map and Itinerary for tomorrow.

It was clearly time to disappear to some babbling brook, some private nook, some party that shook, whatever it took. I blew out of the high security Pentagon Zone for the more general backstage. "What I need to find is some sort of a . . ." suddenly appeared a mirage of lights, of TVs that were on, and insomniacs that were gone. "The Häagen-Dazs Tent!"

The on-site ice cream party center was equipped with your thousand dollar Bose speakers in all four corners so every instrument was crystal clear even though the volume was low. A half-dozen dudes in their early twenties were slouched in chairs in various degrees of consciousness. One of them was concentrating very hard on drawing the number "1" on his laminate with a thick black felt because it could increase his level of schmoozathon participation.

"What's on?" I asked the wildest eyes, nodding

to the screens.

"Melissa Etheridge this afternoon from the pay-per-view," he mumbled under shoulder-length dreads.

"Having a good time so far?" I asked.

"Oh *yeah*. Did you see all the looting after it rained?" he asked, his face coming somewhat to life.

"What?"

"The food riots. You didn't see it? Oh man," he said, laughing. "People stormed the food stands near the stage. It was phat."

"No way!"

"Way," he said. "They climbed right over the walls. They didn't want to wait in line I guess," he laughed. "They were just stuffing hamburgers in their pockets and throwing sodas out to people. It got pretty hairy," he paused. "But it was kind of funny in a way," he said as a bigger laugh broke out. "They're charging too much, man," and a few of the sedate buds woke themselves laughing.

"People stormed the food stands?" I said, still in disbelief.

"Right over the walls," he was barely able to get it out. "There was nothing they could do — no security anywhere. It was like when they threw the beer cans from the stage in the movie. Only this was those food stands, and it was hamburgers," he said, mimicking a quarterback throwing long, prompting a new round of buddy laughter.

"Well, here's to riot-free tomorrows," I said,

raising my beer to the group, then went and found myself a seat in the Bose Pleasuredome. It'd been a long day and was time to pop the feet open and put up my Heinekens – and all within eyesight of Melissa Etheridge filling the tent with the songs & spirit of Janis – yet another evocative Clinton Inaugural alumnae. She was *killing* and certainly would have been my first pick except she was the same time The Band were celebrating *The Last Waltz II* on the South Stage, and a full house beats one pearly queen.

Slowly I began to notice there were people sleeping all around me. Under the tables, *on* the tables, behind the fridge, couples entwined, and guys with no sleeping bags in embryonic curls on the plywood with their hands tucked between their knees. There must have been 50 motionless people having varying success at sleep on Saturday night, compliments of the Häagen-Dazs Shelter.

I pictured the ghost town site waiting outside and all the possibilities while it was still so peacefully quiet and dark, so I dropped my feet, raised my cold one like the Statue of Liberty's torch to toast these campers' effort, and pushed off into the night for one final round of Adventure Card collecting before the dawn.

I wafted back into the fog, among the quiet tents, the wet fields, the basketball courts they'd built for the crew and a volleyball field that had been converted into a water polo ground starting at about 4:00 today. The rumbly brown gravel underboot was the only sound breaking the pre-dawn silence. Tents lay motionless on every dewy patch of grass. I felt like I'd stopped time and could walk around people without them seeing me because no person or thing was moving.

Suddenly a mirage of old ruins weaved into focus – the walls of a small stone settler's house still standing with windows like mysterious dark eyes luring me in. "Ruins? Ruins? What in the name of archeological cave-digging Tom Sawyer heaven is _this_?" — yet another tangible history ring on the site: thick stone walls held a splintered door frame while crumbling wooden beams sketched a roof. Wooden window frames had rotted through long ago to the crumbling, soft, wind-rounded stone beneath. Trees and weeds were growing up where people once did, covering the floor where they'd walk, cook and make love, all within the four stone walls against the elements — and you could still feel them here no matter how much time had past.

I sat on a windowsill to soak up the energy and let the history seep in. I had a perfect view through the trees of the back of the stage. "Boy, they were just 200 years early for some excellent seats!"

Commemorative Bowls were made for moments like this — the celebration of uncovering uncharted history in the secret places of earth, like churches on cliffsides by oceans at sunset. Ghosts and poets and dancers and vixens skip through the ruins like flickers of light, friendly eyes flashing like lovers at night, the dark is alive and glowing bright, the heavens dance with the Northern Lights.

My body melted further and further into the revolutionary masonry — stretching across two centuries of man's work, listening to Mother Nature breathe at the heart of Woodstock — nothing moving — silent bones on ancient stones — not alone.

Like the gathering fog, I was suddenly swept up in a rolling cloud of memory. "I've been here before!" I whispered. "When Phil and I explored the site back in April. We drove along that road there past the barn, and followed it all the way to the end of that lane," I realized, looking up the road that led through the backstage area. "On the way out, he wouldn't stop because of all the `No Trespassing' signs, but when we spotted these ruins I made him pull over," I said out loud, as a real-life deja vu began growing goosebumps all over my chilly body.

"He stayed in the car and I ran through those trees and stood right on that little hump," I mumbled, as the memories tumbled into place. "I looked into the field and imagined it being filled with people as though it was the concert bowl — but it's only the bus stop! No wonder I didn't recognize it," I whispered, as I looked around at the crumbling fortress.

I stayed motionless on the windowsill for fear of breaking the spell of whatever was happening. "These are the same stones I touched when I first came here. I'm standing where I started," my mind began clicking ... "You come to where you began, but with a different perspective. You're brought to the places you're meant to be. Where you are is where you're meant to be. And where you're going tomorrow is where you're supposed to be going." I pulled out Sunday's Itinerary to see what it said, but then put it back away without looking.

While simultaneously reliving my first visit and opening my present, the obvious commonality was that I was alone in both pictures. Phil didn't get out of his car then, and only one person I knew from the outside world left their homemade prisons for the big show this weekend. I've seen the best minds of my generation destroyed by mortgages, starving hysterical grumpy, dragging themselves through their corporate hallways at dawn looking for their next angry fix. Where were all those happy hopeful spirits who once rode together, danced together, tripped together, slept? The bandmates and bud lovers, schoolmates and blood brothers, gone – like they were never here at all. But if I was the last soldier still out in the rain still riding the train and only questionably sane, at least I was going to rally the spirits for one final charge.

Oh spirits who rode the road beside me, guiding, protecting — oh God, oh you twisted Twain of all heaven and earth, stand by me now, don't fade to mist before me you saint of freedom, you yarn-spinning bard of road river song. Oh Father Jack, oh Kerouac, I see you smiling, quiet in corner, pencil in hand, thinking of Neal, sketching like mad. Oh Walt, oh Captain my Captain, your song, *my* song rings from the towers of the worlds that don't sleep, as we wander the roads at night, and you tell me to close my eyes and write. Oh General Grant, my General guide, I've led the troops with you inside; I've lived on the courage you drank, and when I get home from battle it's you I thank. Oh Sam and Tom and Benny frankly, and all the boys from Bosston to Pencilvania who ever pushed the button of a bozo in power — I summon you now like all those nights before, cuz I know you'll show and bring old Four-Score. Oh Abbie and Janis and Jesus and John, your bodies are missing but you ain't gone. I feel you now taking over my soul, even playing the beat of this little roll; keeping it going just to prove you're here, so I won't mix your presence with a night of beer. Thanks for the fun and thanks for the ride; I've got you forever on the track inside.

It's you I've been dancing with all along.

If it took a rendezvous with no one at high midnight at ancient ruins in the middle of the Woodstockian jungle to prove that not only was there *Nobody Left To Run With Anymore* (as Gregg Allman sang it) but that I was running solo with the spirits to begin with, then this long strange Adventure had reaped another gemstone.

The old friends I missed were just pedestrians standing beside me at some crossroad long ago. We all had different destinations in mind and nothing more in common than being caught at a light. We shared part of a path, exchanged some baggage, then continued on to completely different places. Now here I was blissfully standing at a new intersection with a half-million people going my way. And the light was about to change on a lot more than the day.

To usher it in, the horizon was just beginning to crack its baby blue whisper. Clouds of thick Hudson Valley fog lingered between the trees. Evidence of epiphanies and destruction lay everywhere. Not a dog barked. Not a hammer hammed. Not a bacon baked. Only the cheek-feather stillness as the whole earth held its breath just before the dawn of a climax of history.

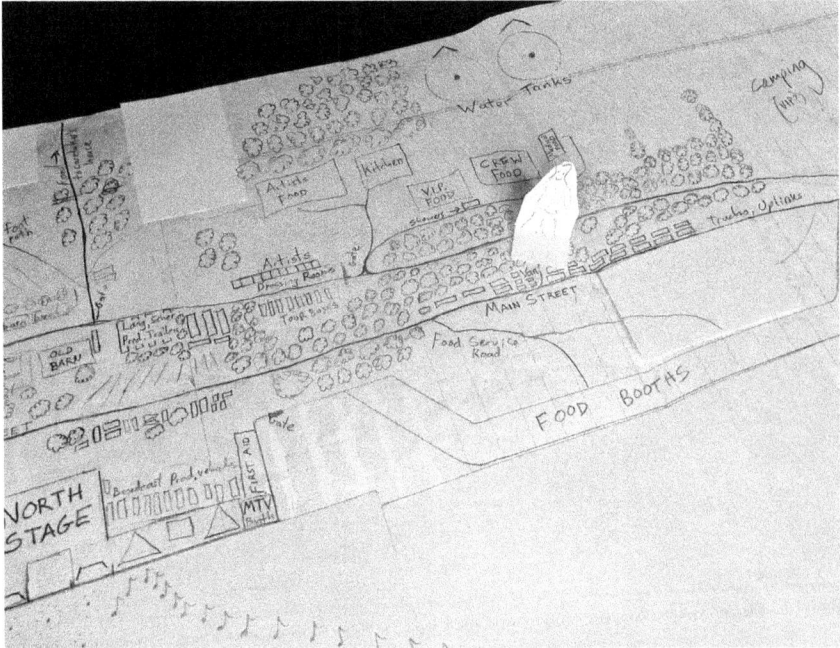

My hand-drawn map of the site that I made to help me
visualize it while writing the book.
Then I created a little man out of a post-it so I could place him
wherever I was while I wrote that part.
It helped ground me in a physical place while I created what
you're experiencing now.
If you look just below his feet you might be able to see the
word "Van" — that's where the KarmaCoupe was parked.

Sunday

Knock-knock-knock.

Rap-rap-rap.

"Hey All Star guy! You in there?" Rap-rap-rap.

"Shit," I mumbled as my happy dreamscape began to dissolve into a loaded van for one. I kicked at the knotted sleeping bag locking my legs and crawled up to the steamy window. Outside a dripping head and yellow raincoat was yelling at me.

"You gotta move your van!" the rainy blur yelled. "We need to get a vehicle in here. Our cameras are getting soaked and we need dry space."

"Holy-fuckin'-no-way," I'm thinking. "Nightmare NIGHTMARE nightmare," began flashing like a neon warning light. "Severe attack. Severe attack. All hands on deck."

The moment I popped the hatch to talk to the wet-head the ship got flooded. It was like a gale at sea and the First Mate was about to get blown overboard. "Ya gotta pull out, ya gotta pull out," he kept yelling through the storm. There was some guy standing under their flapping tarp with car keys in his hand and dancing like he had to go to the bathroom. "Hey, that's the same little runt who was bugging me for pot yesterday," I realized. "Now he's trying to get me to move, the leech. My perfect spot! Ahhhhhhhhh."

"There's mud slides — the roads are closed — everything's falling apart. You gotta move so we can get our other van in here," Mr. Goodnews was hollering through the gushing crack in my window while I — Holy smokes! — scrambled for options.

I threw on my raincoat and climbed out to join him so at least I wouldn't be sitting at the ignition. I knew if I started the van up I was doomed.

I plopped my morning boots down onto the earth and promptly sunk like an anvil in a swamp. Even the ground that had stayed solid until the very end was now a sponge. It didn't look like I'd be able to move and even if I did the van would just slide down the hill. Up the hill from our position ran the fiber optic cables that couldn't be crossed by a vehicle. And by this point every other square foot of land was covered with equipment cases, cars, trailers, and tents.

"What about here? What about there?" I kept stalling for time and trying to find an option and hoping it would stop raining or something. "Just don't give in," I kept thinking. "Just keep dancing and looking for an opening."

"What's that?" Suddenly there was a hole!

While we were standing there, one of the three other support vans nearby had pulled out! Holy cats! The dripping raincoat sailor skated over to hold it while I jumped in like a mud splash to the front seat and fired up the gasless wonder and oh god I won't even go into how hard it was to back up in a mud slide with about as much room as a Manhattan studio apartment while you're hung-over and your life's on the line. But just before I died, I was re-parked and the nightmare was over.

"What just happened?" I wondered, as a bead of rain dropped off my nose. "Two seconds ago I was sneaking through abandoned buildings in my dreams — then I had to move. Now I don't. Too quick. Heart racing. Too close," I was thinking out loud, my wet hands still glued to the steering wheel in terror.

The windows were steamed like a lover's lane. I wiped part of it clear and water was pouring off the roof like a river. The cameraman's car was spinning its way up the hill behind me, shooting mud backwards like a cannon as it shushed. Sentence fragments began penetrating the morning fog. "Mud slides," "roads closed," "disaster," began sinking in (as it were).

I leapt out of the van and into the void. "Did you say the roads are out?"

"Yeah," Andy yelled, as he ran camera gear from the tarp to his new dry trunk. "There's been mud slides in places and roads are washed out. Shuttle buses are stuck all over the place and they can't even get tow trucks to them. Everything that's heavy is just sinking," he said as I looked at my half-covered feet in the puddled earth. "Nobody's getting in or out for a long time," he said. "Make yourself comfortable. This is a disaster area." Deja bad-view.

It was nine in the morning. Spotlights were illuminating the pouring rain and the washed-out damage all over the field. This wasn't a sprinkle, it was a deluge. The sun had been up for hours but it was still scary dark, like you wanted to crawl back inside the cottage with extra blankets and a stack of good books and nothing to do. Unfortunately there were about 7,000 more bands scheduled.

After surveying the battlefield, this General went back in his tent to plot the next move. In all truthfulness, this wasn't funny. For the first time all weekend a vague sense of concern began to seep into Adventureman's Edge City.

"If the roads are down and no food's getting in, there could actually be a problem," I realized, as visions of looters climbing over the food stands flashed through my brain. "If they stormed the booths yesterday, what's going to happen when it gets worse? This could get rather unpleasant. And if things get one degree weirder, like we lose electricity or something, the town stores would be the next thing to be looted."

"I have to get to the Cent-Com Media Tent," the General concluded. Things sounded bad, but all I had to go on was these New York-1 News guys who were always full of disaster reports. But it was their job. "Because this is Woodstock. And you live here."

Before I left the cottage, though, I decided to spin the shower trailer lottery wheel one last time and and found by Sunday morning the showers weren't much of a secret anymore. In fact the sacred savior water trailer had become a fully blown-out war zone with mud and bottles covering the floor. Freaky African voodoo men with beads and pendants and dread-locks stood stark naked in their hardbody blackness. Fat women were complaining about how dirty it was and how no one was doing their fair share. Biker dudes and biker babes were being loud, crude and rude all at the same time. And scrawny little pale-faced writers were sneaking in between them undetected.

I carefully hung my backpack on a chink of metal sticking out of the air vent grate near my stall. The floor was such a sick soup of mud and goop if you dropped anything in a split second it would dissolve into fibre shavings. You didn't want to go near that floor, or at least I didn't. And it was a little difficult to pull your foot up and drop it through a pant leg in a one-legged balancing act in a swamp where the penalty of slippage was death.

On the way back to the Coupe I stopped at the top of Guerrilla Ridge and surveyed the hazy morning field. The usually vibrant colors of the slippery plastic tents were washed out by the rain, and some degree of mud was now covering everything on site. The fluffy white sky was heavy and hanging low. A foggy, misty haze was blowing across the field alternatingly obliterating the view, then opening new vistas. The tents weren't as tightly packed together as yesterday, like perhaps we'd had a few desertions. The weather had been flipping between flash downpours and constant drizzling, and it looked like it had finally taken its toll.

As I was throwing everything you'd need to start a new colony into my day-pack to reconnoiter the Media Tent, I heard the morning stage announcements begin with John Scher and his patently uncool and regularly repeated request for everyone to *pleeeease* move their tents to the back. If there was one thing that didn't hold a candle in the rain to the original festival, it was the boring stage announcements.

"Don't take the bad antacid." Ha-ha, get it? I ran from the field whenever they'd start. The music was exciting, the scene was fun, but every good drink needs a twist, and they forget to schedule in freeform chaos. Where was the Robin Williams, Dan Aykroyd, Whoopi, Pee Wee, Seinfeld, Keillor or Kesey? The noticeable absence of Preachers of the Pranksterhood turned the breaks into a bad PBS pledge-weeks.

But TODAY, needles to say in all holy excellantness, suddenly I heard Wavy Gravy start doing his rap. In fact he said, "What we have in mind is breakfast in bed for 400,000," exactly how he christened Sunday morning in '69! I had my head in the van trying to rainproof the gunpowder when all of a sudden I heard, "Gimme an F."

"What, for `Flashback'? What the hell's going on? That sounded like Country Joe!" I thought. "Weird."

"Gimme a 'U'!"

"I did! I did hear Country Joe!"

I slid the van door closed with a bang just like my day started. I always thought Country Joe McDonald embodied the ethos of Woodstock more than anyone else, and in fact when I later staged my own Woodstock at NYU in November '82, I booked Joe as the centerpiece and surrounded him with Rick Danko, Paul Butterfield, the Joshua Light Show, San Francisco Lightworks, magicians, jugglers, poets, drummers, dancers, and comics. Joe has a certain acidic wit that holds together through psychedelic hurricanes like a Buddha.

Most people know that at the original festival when they didn't have any performers on site to open the concert due to the traffic, Richie Havens was the only guy in the artist's tent, so he went out on stage and down in history. But also stepping up when no one else was there to do so on the second day was Country Joe. He had never performed solo in his life. Plus, he didn't have a guitar, strap, capo, or pick, but one-by-one they were gathered, and without any preparation Joe began his solo career in front of 300,000 people! When the big rain storm hit on Sunday, it was Country Joe and The Fish who came out and pantomimed their set without electricity, and with sheer enthusiasm and never-say-die gumption, managed to hold the audience together and laughing throughout the three-hour rain-delay. *Twice*, Country Joe McDonald saved the first Woodstock.

And now here he was opening the final day this time. As I slip-slop-sloobied to the rim of the Woodstock Breakfast Bowl, Country Joe was beginning the last verse of his song that stopped the Vietnam War, *Feel Like I'm Fixin' To Die.* There might have been a lot of voices, numbers, votes, and other reasons why that war ended, but I don't know of any other American who got more people to sing the same song, and I'm not talking about singing.

Unfortunately most of this field-camping generation was only beginning to stick its faces out of their morning tent flaps like thousands of white heads suddenly appearing on fat nylon balloons. Pop! Perplexed faces peered out then disappearing inside again. Pop. "What is it?" "I don't know. You look." Pop. Pop.

And up there Joe's doing the song that had the accompanying bouncing ball in the movie, popping along the lyrics on the bottom of the screen. And since most of these kids think the Vietnam War was a TV mini-series, Joe had updated the lyrics to include Saudi and Bosnia and all the other places poor kids are sent to die for rich men's profits. But with only one song for breakfast he wasn't given much of a chance to make his mark.

This being a Sunday, the last day's hour-long

kick-off slot went to the gospel singers were now conducting their Sunday service.

This morning's salvation choir, dubbed the Sisters of Glory, included Thelma Houston, Phoebe Snow, CeCe Peniston, Mavis Staples, and Lois Walden singing the roots of all music. The Spirit. The Sun Rise. The Sisters of Glory.

From their glowing set of traditional gospel music, through WOMAD's World Organization of Music, Art & Dance show, Youssou N'Dour, Zucchero, and The Cranberries, through the history of American music with Bob Dylan and The Band, through Gabriel's hybrid of all forms, we were certainly treated to an educational weekend seminar on the history and future of music.

And while I'm riffing soundbites, to those who complained it was an all-white-Woodstock, do note: the rainbow of Indian tribes who opened Friday, followed by Futu Futu, Cypress Hill, Youssou N'Dour, Salt-N-Pepa, the Gospel Singers, Arrested Development, WOMAD, the Neville Brothers, Santana, Jimmy Cliff and Rita Marley.

Interconnected Woodstock Groups for 100, please: What song did Mavis Staple's wrap in silk in The Band's *The Last Waltz?* Answer located on your home version of the concert.

At many points a cappella, this morning's subtle then bone-chilling cadre of voices woke us from our night and blessed our day. The field of colored tents was gently eased back to life by the lush voices of these morning angels singing *Will The Circle Be Unbroken, Amazing Grace,* and *Got The Whole World In My Hand.* Music unheard by many of your average Green Day fans was shining over us like the morning sun, ringing back to where we came from — before we were about to hear where we were going.

And speaking of going, I must be. It was off to the Media Tent once more, to schmooze with the crews and sniff out the news so I'd know what to choose, like should I store up on booze or go for a cruise to summon the muse to bring the story to you's,

Hoo-hoo, hoo-hoo's.

Suddenly it was time for ...

The Closing Day News-Briefing Blues

Into the Media Tent slides thy,
Determined to uncover the truth vows I,
About roads and rain and buses and you,
About what's been closed and what I can do.

John Scher's swinging like a monkey in glee,
"History's been repeated to a large degree.
The perimeter's abandoned, the rain's slowed us down,
But we've pulled together like any small town."

Promoter Joel Rosenman was just as keen,

Sunday

"These kids are the greatest I've ever seen."
It was nice to hear that whatever the blues,
These guys were still singing some happy news.

Until `Jack Webb' O'Donnell stepped up to the mike,
To deliver the truth like a volleyball spike,
"New roadblocks are in place surrounding the site,
And nobody's getting in till it's over tonight.

"It'll take 24 hours to clear the area,
There's been 14 arrests, and I don't want to scare ya,
But last night a guy got hit by a deer,
I think one of the two was drunk on beer.

"A 20 year-old died from a ruptured spleen,
Only the third death in this riot scene.
We busted one guy for mushrooms at the gate,
He was the only loser to suffer that fate."

A reporter asked why they'd picked on him,
And the officer said, then flashed a grin,
"In Ulster County we won't be tested —
You break a law here, you *will* be arrested."

He went on to talk about the horrible weather,
And how cars were sinking like Gump's floating feather;
The parking lot mud-fields had turned into lakes,
And tents were being swallowed like birthday cakes.

It was getting weirder by the minute,
And all I wanna do is dive back in it.
So I sneaked some juice into my pack,
And hit the road, just like Jack.

* * *

Walking back along the muddy river road in the drizzle, I began mapping out the logistics of the Adventures ahead. "It's beginning to feel more and more like an emergency situation," I smiled, as I noticed no big trucks running me over from either direction. "If food trucks can't get in, and there's a half-million people here already, times three or four meals a day, times crazy moshers," I was calculating . . . "That equals: I could be here with no food for the rest of show. I've been hungry before, but if 300,000 people go scrambling through the same cupboards, the picking could get problematically thin before lunch and I'd have to start eating the acid just to survive."

So I realized — "I better take one last shot at a bike ride for supplies. This light drizzle may be the best weather of the day. And if old Ranger can't make it all the way, she'll just have to get locked up by the roadside."

I skied back to the Coupe along the slopes of Hope Mountain, mounted ol' Saint Ranger, and slid off down the hill. "At least I'll be the only one on the road," I smiled, as my back wheel skidded out behind me. "Deadheads don't fall down, they just keep trippin'," I called out to the omniscient balance referee, and just kept going furthur.

Old Ranger wasn't as pleased with the run as I was. She'd seen younger years, and surfing clay moguls wasn't her idea of a weekend in the country. In fact she was just begging to be put out to pasture. She let me know it every grunting foot of the way, skipping gears and missing years and slapping mud-water up my back like a mill-wheel on a fast river until I finally pulled over and constructed a cardboard beer case mud guard that was so tough it could have withstood bullets and bolted it over Ranger's back with sheer will.

Arrested Development (the working title for this book I'm sure) was playing their Sunday morning worldbeat rap as I navigated the potholes and people behind the stage. They're a great peaceful fun band I've always wanted to see, but this was war.

There were three roads out of the site, and by Sunday I chose The Middle Way: I knew the South Stage route was washed out before the rain yesterday where it ran too close to Beaver Moat Creek — so I crossed that off. The northern exit road had that huge hill that was almost impossible when it was dry, and then it dropped down in that wetlands near the secret cabin that showed sings of regular flooding. It seemed like a dangerous time to test an unknown road, but the only way I'd have any chance at all was straight through the center of the crowd. I had to take it.

It turned out it wasn't water, but the flood of humanity that was gonna swamp my raft! Gushing out of every hole in the fence was a muddy stream of pilgrims joining the ocean already in motion. Some traveled in groups, some walked alone. Some had abandoned everything and were walking naked. Some carried campsites with them, and some were dragging wet sleeping bags behind like a soggy anchor, deliriously unable to let go of their grip. Abandoned and sinking vehicles lined the muddy lane. Food semi trailers were tilting off the shoulders, and you'd need a tug boat not a tow truck to move them.

It was scary not only because of the gloomy, retreating mudpeople, but also because of the canopy of trees creating an eerie umbrella that made you shiver even in August. It was a murky rainforest nightmare of poisonous snakes and deadly mosquitoes with the looming stench of death. No wonder people were leaving. Once you got a whiff of this mortuary air you'd want to break for the highway too.

In fact the dark road out seemed to have become a crackling vein sucking out all the negative-energy people from the field like metal slivers to a magnet, until the whole passageway became filled with voices screaming "ENOUGH!" And if you accidentally got sucked into this parade of the wounded as I did, it was difficult to not start bleeding yourself. It was the only strip in the whole cartoon where the "bad guy" was winning.

When I finally reached the end of the road and

crossed the bridge over the Beaver Moat Creek and broke free from this Swamp Tree Lane of Doom - It had actually stopped raining! Below your feet was still extremely wet, but above your head was completely dry!

I peeled along the highway as fast as old Ranger could peel, but she was fading fast. Her one gear had dropped to about a half-a-gear short of a revolution and the pedal was skipping like a broken record. K'chunk, k'chunk. K'chunk, k'chunk. "There goes that half-witted hippie on his bike again," the scary pitchfork ones were commenting as I hobbled by.

The surrounding highway was nothing like the mayhem of Saturday. I rode past the mural wall where instead of the freshly scrubbed, optimistic faces of yesterday's arriving campers, there was a mob of stumbling raincoats bumping into each other like blind kittens looking for food. The proud parade of Saturday grocery carts of Budweiser had been replaced by armfuls of wet clothes heading in the opposite direction. The crowds of prowling locals who stalked the fence yesterday were simply walking through the open gates today. All security was stopping at this point were cars and trucks, and they weren't even doing that all that well as ol' Johnny was later to prove.

I rode over the Hump to the little retail cluster that owned all three "L's" in location. They all had lines but it wasn't the L.A. riots of Saturday. People were either trapped on-site, or couldn't get closer than 15 miles as of yesterday. Not too many were out buying more supplies for a longer siege. Except, of course, Ranger and me.

The Grand Union Army supply station was surrounded by America's street people making a buck off the cuff by returning hot air balloons full of cans and bottles. I went inside and jammed my Guatemalan daypack to the point of ripping with sandwiches and granola bars and climbed back on my embarrassing bike. It was like pulling out of the parking lot in a back-firing Rambler. But I tried to remind myself that, "Every time that pedal goes round, you're bound to cover just a little more ground."

Half a revolution — skip-CLANK. Half a revolution — skip-CLANK, as I spasmodically lurched in different directions with every heave-hoe, my back-pack-weighted load shifting with every pothole, and the missing gear shaft turning me into a very drunk Mr. Swah Vay I'm sure.

"You know, Ranger, one of us may be on our last legs, and your bell is ringing," I heaved. By the time the two of us made it to the top of the Hump, we decided we both needed a break. This was the high point of the circuit loop and we might as well take in the view. The awful grey sky was beginning to hint at something better.

Before I left the outside world, I decided to check the local papers to see if *any*body got the story right and grabbed a copy of the *Poughkeepsie Journal*. Winners of the Most Enthusiastic Marketeers of the Weekend award, they had actual old-fashioned paperboys out on the Hump every single day hocking copies for 50¢! Every issue had 20 stories, a photo supplement, editorials, and gossip columns. I felt like Madonna reading about myself the next day.

Apparently, I woke up to a muddy paradise, then had fun making breakfast around the campsite. In the afternoon I smoked marijuana, visited the Surreal Field, then went diving in the mosh pit for sunset.

It was a little past High Noon on the High Seas as I Hung Out on Gump's Hump when I finally resolved it was High Time I High Tail it back to the High Ground Homestead to harmonize with the High Notes in the songs of High Hopes.

"Ranger!" I called, as I caught her wandering off down the road after a mountain bike again. "Come here, girl. It's time to go to the show, you gearless wonder. *All I want to do is rock!*" I proclaimed like it meant something and began the coast back down into the madness for the final time.

As I navigated against the tide of exiting refugees who looked like the parade of people in *The Poseidon Adventure* all walking to the wrong end of the ship and there was nothing I could do. I weaved Ranger through the zombies until I got to the end of the Lane where it spilled into the backstage area and the mood was immediately exhilarating again, where a half-million people were having a helluva time.

For the first time all weekend I noticed swarms

of tight-leather biker-babes walking around the stage and I wondered why I hadn't seen them sooner. As I rode past the stage I suddenly heard the tight-leather solos of Dickie Betts and the Allman Brothers playing a bizarrely misplaced noon set.

I powered old Ranger up the final hill to the KarmaCabin and while we were still gliding I threw one leg over her back and coasted to a stop on one pedal. And that was it. Ranger's Last Ride. But it was kind of like dying at Gettysburg: If you have to go down, you may as well go down in history.

I threw the kryptonite lock around her waist, ditched the mud-splattered raincoat, and took off to pick some Allman Brownies. Apparently their handbook specified bustiers and faded bluejeans for the girls, and black leather from hair to boots for the guys. It obviously didn't matter that it was the middle of August. Rules were rules.

Sunshine was actually starting to shimmer in the sky for the first time since the late seventies. In fact, it was turning into a downright nice afternoon if you looked at it right.

With the first hint of the sun, these Allman Optimists were milking the moment, *willing* the light to beat the clouds and win the day. Once again it became Breastfest In America as a sea of women decided less was more, and a lot of their boyfriends decided the women were smarter once again, and followed with their birthday suits.

It was only lunchtime but the mudpeople had

already gone forth and multiplied. The late night and daybreak rains just whetted everyone's appetites and freshened the diving pools. Their Secret Muddian Empire had coalesced through the night and they'd drawn up a Constitution by dawn. They adorned their proud brown uniforms and acted in consort the rest of the concert. They'd become emblazoned, the muddy malcontents, and took to hugging innocents at will. Well, to be fair, some huggees asked for it. That is, they'd ask mud women to hug them, then proudly go around with a mud hug-on all day.

Up on stage the Allmans were wailing away on their fast-paced small-bar tight-jean beer-drinking country-blues rock'n'roll. As I walked in they began their great new hit single right on cue, *Nobody Left To Run With Anymore*, the song an older brother of mine calls my theme song cause I'm the last one he knows still out on the road. Everyone I boarded with or met along the way had long since gotten off the Party Train. After 50 years of faithfully riding the rails, it was gold watch time. In fact it sounded exactly like a song I wrote —

> I'm the last man on the party train,
> Rollin' out of town in the pouring rain,
> Gotta keep movin' or I'll go insane,
> I'm the last man on the party train.

After years of collecting Adventure Cards by hopping boxcars & running from the law, most everyone I knew had gotten off, been busted, or killed. And just to prove I was still here, here I was.

But boy did I feel old. All of a sudden I couldn't see a person who looked over 20. You had to hand it to these old Brothers. These graybeards were whipping off the fastest, most exciting solos of the weekend! They had the entire audience dancing like it was being electrocuted. We weren't at the morning gospel service any more, Toto! And I don't know where all these fellow Kansans came from, but the farm was filled to capacity once again.

And then right when it was totally smoking, they said goodbye and left the stage and you were going, "Holy shit, that was amazing! Where'd they go?" They BOOM, just when you were drifting off into dreamland, suddenly you heard the opening licks of *Whipping Post*!

Like *Freebird*, *Stairway to Heaven* or *Hey Jude*, it's one of those anthems you figure you'll never see performed live by the original artist because it seemed to pre-date music. "Tiiiiiied to the whipping post," sang that gravelly old Gregg Allman as Dickie Betts and Warren Haynes soared like dueling Hendrixs trying to outdo each other while a half-million danced like Janis. No better guitar players shared the North Stage all weekend. Don't lose this Haynes kid's number.

John Scher's comment from a press conference came floating through the 60s-90s dreamscape collage: "This isn't *like* Woodstock. This *is*

Woodstock." And it really was, in every sense of the word. It was a free concert in upstate New York on an impromptu farm during the rains of August, promoted by Michael Lang and featuring Bob Dylan, Santana, the Allman Brothers, Traffic and a horde of hippies playing to a half-million people in the mud. As far as I could tell, the main difference between the two Woodstocks was that I was at this one.

After the Allman Brothers finished helping a lot of people burn off a lot of calories, I stopped in at the Media Tent before Traffic and check the pulse of the pulse-checkers.

The Media Tent was always a noisy nucleus of announcements and salesmanship. There was a constant promise of artists coming down to speak to us — Sheryl Crow, Aerosmith, Joe Cocker, and now The Neville Brothers. Every time you went there somebody was delayed but promised in five minutes. I never waited.

The mile-long rows of tables had gone from unused and pristine to trampled, trashed and toppled. There was one guy from Europe on a small portable typewriter who all the reporters gathered around and watched type, mesmerized like our parents watching us on computers. I couldn't imagine what it was like back in the days when that's all there was and everyone smoked stogies and drank bourbon. Nowadays everyone's on silent laptops with Internet modems and they don't even need no smoking signs because no one does.

I went straight back to the sacred secret corner furthest from the door which had turned into the impromptu Canadian Consulate, in keeping with our self-esteem. "You guys have the whole room. No no, we insist. We'll go way over to the most inconvenient out of the way spot where we won't attract any attention and we'll just watch. You have the stage." There was yours truly covering it for The Gimli Gazette, there was the Global Male, the Toronto Daily Bikini, and the Canadian Press folks.

Julie, the C.P. reporter, and I had become confidants during our several short Canadian Corner Confidentials, always quickly comparing conclusions before we both ran back out to the next event. She'd just been to the Surreal Field, which was a technological futureworld set up like a trade show. It was supposed to be one of the big features of the festival, only it was hidden over a moat, behind a forest, and under a mound of people. I saw the bridge to it once but it was so covered with people you couldn't have even gotten in line without falling in the water.

"Oh it was just jammed," she went on in her sweet Canadian accent. "I waited an hour in line just to get over the bridge, eh? It was awful. And then every exhibit had a half-hour wait." But there she was doing her job. She described The Todd Podd, Todd Rundgren's one-man tent which held about 50 people at a time in an interactive bubble, and he would talk to them during the performance and even allow the audience to play instruments along with him.

This cyber-hippie Epcot Center got us talking about the differences between the first Woodstock and this one.

"ATM Machines," she stated the obvious.

"The backstage pass laminate system," I returned.

"The Surreal Field science show," she said.

"Two stages."

"Cellular phones."

"An Eco Village."

"Disposable cameras."

"Plastic money."

"Pay-per-view," she noted.

"Sound delay towers," I added.

"A CD store," she pointed out.

"Bootleg cash venders," I returned.

"Better prepared audience with better tents," she said.

"Matching umbrellas for the staff," I pointed out.

"Twice as much rain," she said.

"Twice as much mud."

"More port-o-sans."

"More food stands."

"15 weddings and counting," she said.

"15 great receptions," I smiled.

"Metal detectors at the gates."

"Mist machines in the field."

"A fence," she volleyed.

"Giant video screens," I returned.

"Computer graphics," she spiked me.

"Satellite parking lots," I saw her.

"Shuttle buses to get you there," she called.

"Bob Dylan and Sheryl Crow," I laid it on the table.

"Us," she laughed.

Then, just when it was getting good, her C.P. partner came wandering in with his own sleeve-full of aces. He'd been searching for the human angle.

"They found the guy who's wallet was turned in," he smiled.

"What?" Julie and I both said in disbelief. How could you lose a wallet here, have someone find it, have them decide to carry it all the way to the stage, not steal it, but hand it in to some volunteer security guard who doesn't steal it but actually passed it up to the front of the stage where it gets waved around in front of the crowd by this Buck Henry-type announcer flapping it in the wind and asking all day in a really nasally voice, "Did anybody loose a wallet?" So then the exact guy has to be watching at that exact moment or the whole thing doesn't work. Except here it does.

I prodded the young cub for more.

"The wildest thing so far was the mud fight at Green Day. The South Stage is just trashed. Did you see it?" he asked.

"What happened?" we both perked up.

"First Billie Joe started taunting the audience. They responded by throwing mud and hay and anything they could find at the stage. Then Billy Joe started picking the crap up and throwing it back and saying stuff like, `At least I'm not a mud hippie like you,' and insulting them and everything. And then he finally goes, `Okay, everybody say, `Shut the-fuck up,' and we'll stop playing,' and the audience yells it, and they just walk off stage! It was hilarious."

"They walked off?" Julie very reporterly sought to confirm.

"Well, they started to, right? But then all these fans stormed the stage and it turned into a huge free-for-all with the punk-rockers and the mud-covered security guys and the band all going at it on stage," he went on. "What!" we both said in unison as our eyes popped open in disbelief.

"The crowd was getting up on the stage from somewhere right in front, I couldn't see," he said, "And suddenly you'd see some fat linebacker security guard come running across the stage and slam into one of these skinny little Green Day fans and they'd both go skidding all the way across the stage. It almost got out of hand."

Apparently these two Mounties were camping about as close to the South Stage as I was to the North so they became my lifeline to the Confederacy. He'd stuck around for the morning's music while she went off to tackle the giant Surreal Field monster. They were an impressively industrious pair of wire reporters, cutting through the fences and lies of America to see it all, do it all, and to steal the best of it to bring back home and leave the worst in America where it belongs. Damn Canadians, ya gotta watch 'em. They do these selective strikes and nobody even notices. They blend right in, they have fun, then they leave. Meanwhile, they take cars, electricity, movies, and all the cool stuff, and leave us with crack and born-again Republicans.

"Hey! What about WOMAD?" I asked him of Peter Gabriel's world-beat collective that opened the South Stage in the morning.

"Actually it didn't go over that well because I think everyone was there for Green Day," he said. "I don't know if it was my imagination or just that it was slow, but it seemed to go on for hours. It was sort of the Andean Flute Monks following by the Peruvian Tree Brothers followed by the Zimbabwe Tribal Dancers, you know? It was pretty esoteric for the *Dookie* slam-dancers. They sort of put up with it for a while but then it started getting pretty nasty and they finally had to shove Peter Gabriel and Youssou N'Dour out there to sort of calm everyone down," he said. "It was pretty rude," the Canadian reported.

"Country Joe showed up on the North Stage and played the *Fixin' To Die Rag*," I offered as my only North Stage exposé.

"Right, he played on the South Stage too, right after John Sebastian & his jug band and before Gil Scott Heron," he calmly retorted.

"Whaaat!" I said. Beyond all the amazingness I had personally seen, there was even more sound vibration fireworks going off all over the place. No wonder that guy found the wallet. There was more good energy here than a prayer meeting in heaven.

"Gil Scott Heron blew everyone away though," Mr. Goodnews continued. "He closed with something called *Celebrate Your Life*, which sums up the weekend better than anything I've heard so far," he said. "It had this refrain that went on and on of, 'celebrate your life, celebrate your life, call on the spirits,' you know? It was early in the morning and everyone was kind of in a daze and it sort of brought the whole field to life in a way. He begins this 'celebrate' chant and just keeps going until everybody finally gets it and is singing, 'Celebrate, celebrate,' with him. It was *very* cool," he nodded, and we both smiled, the good energy flowing right out of him and covering her and me, the overtones still rippling, and we were all glowing so much we couldn't help but notice it, and broke into laughter.

"Good one," we all nodded without saying anything.

That was all I needed to buzz. It was time to collect more Adventure Cards. Also, I spotted Traffic and Steve Winwood on the pay-per-view monitor!

I worked with Winwood on his *Freedom Overspill* video when he first made his comeback in the mid-eighties. It was shot in Guild Castle on Long Island, one of the crown jewels of the billionaire's club of

America. The entire castle was empty and I snuck all over it including up the scary ladders to the top of the turrets overlooking the ramparts to the endless Atlantic Ocean. Horse stables, secret tunnels, crashing waves, swooping gulls, and silent ocean lapping, until playback would begin and the words "Freedom Overspill" would fill the New York island air.

We all sat around an antique wooden round table one afternoon talking about the state of rock. I remember Winwood rolling his eyes and shaking his head about some different current pop acts. Sometimes he sat silent for long stretches while us non-Cabinet Ministers in the History of Rock n Roll bantered back and forth, and then he'd eventually lean forward, cross his hands, and weigh in with the decisive debate-ending answer.

We all had a lively discussion about Dylan following his Live Aid performance and coming across as somewhat damaged the last several years. Some were slamming him for simple irrelevance, while others thought he'd gone certifiably insane. I was floundering in my argument that there was still good stuff to be gleaned within the erratic madness when Winwood leaned forward. As someone who was in competition with Bob for the Great Artist of the Sixties Award, he simply said, "As far as I'm concerned he can do no wrong," and the thousand words-a-minute the rest of us were spewing seemed silly. After fairly critiquing his other colleagues with well-considered criticisms, only one guy was beyond Steve's repute all afternoon.

I never forgot that. And as I reached the V.I.P. bleachers I realized I was about to hear both of them from the same stage on the same day at Woodstock! "Thank you Great Spirit for bringing this together," I toasted the heavens and soaked up the High Energy of the High-Heeled Boys.

Apparently there had just been a turnover of VIP's after The Amazin' Allmans' set, so I slyly slipped through the legs of the departing adults like a kid at his parents' Christmas party and slid into the third row overlooking an amazing Traffic jam in God's country. Like The Beatles, they were one of those groups that broke up so long ago you never figured you'd ever see them. I know it was just Winwood and Capaldi the drummer, but that's two more than zero.

Except something was wrong.

There was no energy, oh Great Spirit. The whole audience was suddenly standing there like they were in line at the bank.

On stage, instead of Dickie Betts & Warren Haynes sweating out leads so hard it looked like they'd spontaneously combust, we had Winwood looking like a bored L.A. session cat. Perhaps he was already feeling the lack of response and didn't know how to get it back. But here I was all dressed up with a killer seat and no rock to roll. "No wonder I suddenly got such a great seat," I thought. "They're dying."

"What do I do?" I prodding my twirling beanie. ... On the bleachers. Great seat ... bad show

... overlooking this sea of slithering mud ... babes everywhere ... loaded for beer ... with the next band being the Spin Doctors, who were good, but "Do I want to sit in my seat for the next two hours?" I asked rhetorically.

Answer: Colonel Mustard; in the field; with a hit of acid.

"Hi-ho, hi-ho, it's off to work we go," I sang as I marched down the stairs and descended into the street-level ranks of truth or consequences.

The field had thinned out after the Allmans, the seas of mud had parted, and for one brief moment in the middle of the afternoon of the last day of Woodstock you could cross the field. *And I did*, pulling a cross-field exploration examination while the Stevie of Windwoods continued to blow, weaving through the waves like the buoy I am until I came upon the Center of Mud in the middle of the sea. What had once been a river had flooded its banks and become a full-fledged Lake for the Mud People to go about their Muddy Business.

In fact it was clearly recreation week at Camp Express Yourself. By this time it was around 2:30 in the afternoon and everyone already had several hours of rock 'n' roll surging through their veins and the sun was out and nothing was going to stop them now.

In the center of the Mud Lake several hundred mostly naked people were dancing and slithering together, mostly single, but some lucky couples embracing and sliding their shiny flesh against one another, breast to breast, groin to groin in a slippery slidey love fest.   Some were ballroom dancing, embracing each other in their parents' formal mating ritual, in a dance they've probably never done before or since, in something that would be too straight to do any other time, but when you're covered in mud from bean to bone, the far extreme of their rebellion had led them back to simply embracing one another.

Of course this was much to the enjoyment of all the other dancing monkeys who were leaping around the single females in the most primal mating ritual since *Wild Kingdom* went off the air. The unattached members of the species were exploring each other's bodies in a primitive X-rated oozing sex dance that's gotta be illegal in all 50 states.

Surrounding the lake was a circle of paparazzi capturing the best of the nest for future elucidation. Some were official press with seven cameras dangling above the muddy soup like war correspondents leaning into the battle and risking a stumble and instant death to get the shot. Also circling the rim were the amateurs with their disposable Instamatic Whiz cameras clicking at the nipples as they flashed.

If you were around the Lake there was the constant fear that one of the Mudmen was going to spot you standing there and haul you into the soup. You became a Russian roulette contestant on The Price Is High as unsuspecting people circling the Lake would suddenly get grabbed by the mud activists and dragged to a watery grave. And the rest of us would just stand there hoping it wouldn't happen to us but too enthralled by the action to leave.

Or some poor soul would come along and find his buddies had taken the plunge and make the mistake of standing around the edge laughing at them, whereupon their Mudfriends would mobilize, and begin splashing their drier half until it became useless to pretend they were still safe. Or God help them if they made the awful mistake of trying to run, which was exactly what the evil Mudmen were waiting for. Every few minutes a new victim would be chased around the Lake, throwing slippery captors off his shoulders and dodging tackles until he'd become so irrevocably covered he'd have no choice but to turn and charge back at the leader of the posse and the two would embrace like gladiators in the middle of the Lake until one would take the other down in a climactic ker-ploosh and the whole audience would cheer. This initiation engagement went on all day and led to an ever-growing army of Mudmen. And all of it captured on more film than Niagara Falls. It was the bull's-eye center of the field, the nucleus of the atomic Woodstock, the core of the craziness, the freest form of expression and primal exhibitionism since Sodom played Gomorrah in the Cup final.

And all the while Steve Winwood was up there regaining his steam and singing *Dear Mr. Fantasy*, piercing through the video screens, and stinging through the PA system, as the mad muddy choir sang the chorus in harmony, raising their voices like naked wolves to the moon. Ecstasy snapped like a mousetrap in a puddle and what was once a dance became a frenzy, with every one from the Mudpeople to the standing-room-only observation ring singing, no *screaming*, "Make it snappyyyy," and the splashes grew fatter and the waves grew higher and the mud grew deeper and the band rocked harder.

Winwood ended his set with *Gimme Some Lovin'*, the song he originally wrote in 1966 as a member of The Spencer Davis Group. Whether these MTVeenagers knew that this guy was the source of the song, or whether they really gave a flying duck I don't know, but reporting live from center field I can tell you they all broke into a simultaneous bone-bending belly dance like they'd been rehearsing since spring break. Somehow this song has transcended the ages and was still dance-friendly to this latest generation of moshers.

The whole field became one arm-waving gospel choir boogie of testifying believers channeling the chi and dancing for life itself. *"So glad you made it, SO GLAD YOU MADE IT,"* we all sang in celebratory congratulations, and everyone just snapped, spinning out of control, backflipping into photographers and falling on their backs like dancing crabs in the mud.

Mud boys were grabbing Mud girls and singing into imaginary microphones, "Gimme some lovin'," and the two would break into a Mudtango right there in the Ballroom Lake. "Gimme, gimme some lovin," the voices sang, the torsos shook, the tummies shimmered, the arms weaved like snakes through the swampy jungle. Holy most excellent honkness, the Traffic jam finally broke wide open and suddenly everyone was speeding!

And then it was over.

The rock-banging climax suddenly dropped down to a silent field, but all with renewed mud-smiling joy-smacking high-fiving pride. It was the old dream-down slow-down of between set wanderings, past people on broken-down lawn chairs, groups trying to secure camping areas with fences of cans, and fat white whales who'd slopped down in the mud, too drunk or lazy to get up.

And so I wandered, seeking to escape, seeking to find that promised land I knew was here somewhere ... "if I could just find it on my God-dammed map here." I was stumbling blindly poring over coordinates like the Alone Ranger in search of the Fountain of Truth, "which, according to my calculations, should be right around ... *here*," I said, stopping in mid-field and looking around.

It was 3:00. Schedule read: Spin Doctors on the North Stage, followed by Porno For Pyros, followed by *Dylan* at 7:30! "So . . . I really don't have to be back at this stage for four hours," I realized as I flipped to the South Stage line-up: Paul Rodgers, followed by the Neville Brothers and Santana! Not bad. The only hitch was the possible Dylan-Santana timing conflict, but other than that, there was nothing left to do but smile, smile, smile.

Naturally it was time to take the acid.

It was the last day of Woodstock. If this brand didn't kick-in in an hour, I'd still have plenty of daylight to work with before the sun even began to set. "You've got till the end of the Spin Doctors to prove yourself, guys," I said to the little Mr. Naturals as I flipped three of them down the rabbit hole.

And off Adventureman struck into the great unknown final daytime exploration of Camp Woodstock before an onslaught of music would carry us into history once again. But there were still a few more hours to live in real time. I decided to stop at the KarmaCoupe to grab my camera — which ultimately never had film in it, hence the book — and went off to capture the true essence of Woodstock.

I still wanted to see and do everything possible before I was committed to other bands, other stages, other nights, so once again I hiked to the top of Guerrilla Ridge behind the Coupe overlooking the entire site like a scenic vista pullover on Skyline Drive. I found a bunch of fellow spirit searchers lingering in the quiet, overlooking the holy valley below with the reverence of war veterans at battlesites. It was something none of us would ever see again — a full color panorama of light and life dancing all the way to the horizon. Overlooking the site from the same spot on Saturday, everything seemed so new and as though it would go on forever. Now, for the first time, there was a sense it was going to be over soon, and we were catching the last rays of sunlight. It was so beautiful I took some snaps. With a filmless camera.

I walked back down to Main Street until a child of God came rolling along the road to Paradise in his psychedelic wagon being pulled by a large Labrador Retriever in a tie-die T-shirt, accompanied by a long-haired graybeard in rainbow colors, and a pretty hippie woman with the universe painted on her dress. And the acid wasn't even kicking in yet.

Here was a child, his dog, and his parents in perfect harmony simply strolling the backroads of the site and sharing each other. Everywhere around there was music, playgrounds, madness, a crazy claymation of creation, and yet here, far from the man-made fun, was a family choosing to spend their Woodstock together, in peace, on the road and laughing.

People were streaming both ways along the slippery clay road and I could hear the Spin Doctors spinning. Being the last hours of daylight, I wanted to retain height over this situation, so I cut back up the ridge, walking along the fence that divided the regular folks from the High Security Zone (ha-ha).

Part of this dividing wall was a towering 1800s barn with a rough stone foundation and dark brown, thick planked walls. The windows were now dark square holes and just enough boards were missing to make it look dangerous. This was the wise old man who sat looking over us like a grandfather rocking on the porch.

The trees made dancing rays of sunlight that lit different flashes of the forest like laser beams, pow, pow, highlighting shadowy shades of green in a waving, fluid stream. Other naturalists and spiritualists had gathered along the ridge and crouched in silence, mesmerized by the flickering butterfly of sunlight while the biggest sound system ever created thundered beside us.

Just then I noticed beside me was none other than Michael Wadleigh, the guy who directed the documentary of the first Woodstock. With his filmmaker eyes he was framing the very same shot I was. I just watched him watching the world, silently, reverentially, wisely. After a good few minutes of this, and before he vanished, I went over to him, and nodded reverentially, in a way that told him I knew who he was. After a respectful pause befitting Sunday service, I said, "They're here because of you," and I just let that lay for a moment. "Not Jimi or Janis. They're here cuz of that movie you made. That's why they're here." And a slow smile came to his tranquil face. And we both nodded, just enough that we both knew. And after a reflective silence, he just said softly, "Thanks."

And I left him to his moment.

* * *

After a good long spirit soak, I continued walking the path along the ridge stopping at each nice opening to take in the new view, until I'd managed to slip behind the security checkpoint once again and had infiltrated the High Security Zone for about the 17th time. No sooner had I done so, than Michael Lang immediately drove up in his beat-up green Land Rover jeep and flashed me a huge smile and the peace sign just as I was snapping his most excellent picture. Couldn't wait to see how that one turned out!

I continued in my pursuit of the elusive Holy Backstage Grail where all my dreams would be realized or at least maybe I'd meet Sheryl Crow but to tell you the God's honest truth because how can I do otherwise at this point, backstage was nowhere near as fun as the rest of the site. You couldn't really see anything because you were surrounded by huge production trailers and buzzing clipboard people. And you couldn't really hear anything except megaphone traffic directors. So I dodged the stopwatches, cellphones and stressed-out coffee-achievers and took the only road back to Funville.

There was an element of making your own way here, and each day it weeded out more of the weak. There seemed to be people who came expecting not to be inconvenienced and they were loudly voicing their surprise. I always figure you don't step off a diving board unless you're prepared to get wet. The shuttle buses were back up and running by this afternoon and the grumbling were leaving. I'm sure the debate raged for many: Buses leaving — great music happening on two stages. Great show — wet clothes. Happening scene — wet clothes. Until finally the hundredth monkey bus would roll up and your Woodstock story would be over.

I slid into the nearby home base Media Central and the TV monitors were flickering Paul Rodgers' still-chiseled face. The lead singer of Bad Company and Free had put together a special band for the weekend with Slash from Guns & Roses, Jason Bonham from father John's genes, and Neal Schon from Journey. (Editor's parenthetical: Schon played the '69 fest, age 16, as guitarist for Santana.) It was nice to see missing soldier Rodgers back in action. "The career revival of the festival," I wrote in my imaginary *Rolling Stone* column. "'Paul Rodgers comes back after years of seclusion, surprising everyone with a blistering set of textbook rock."

I have no idea. Just being in the Media Tent, you can't help writing ledes.

"Despite the Grateful Dead's absence, several concert-goers appeared to have a good time."

"Mud, mayhem and marijuana dominated as rock fans gathered to rekindle the spirit of more optimistic times. 15-year-old Angela Loonsbury of Hackensack, N.J. said, `This is so cool. We've been totally naked and loaded since we got here. Woodstock rules!' Parents wishing to check on their children should call 1-800-OHH-NOOO!"

Words flew through that tent like notes in

an instrument store. All you had to do was play. I couldn't have been happier if there'd been film in my camera! But the point is, and there's always a point, it's getting late and I needed to report back to the South Stage for the climactic music stretch of Woodstock: the Neville Brothers → Santana or Bob Dylan → Peter Gabriel → the next dimension.

As I headed out of the Media Tent, I could hear wafting from the North Stage, the Spin Doctors singing *Woodstock*, Take II.

"Everywhere was a song and a celebration . . . ."

No kidding! I shook my head in time with the music and amazement at the collective lottery winning. How could you not feel good here? I was stone cold alone, but walking along that road through all those people I've never felt part of so many before.

* * *

The sunset acid was just beginning to shimmer as I strolled onto the South field for the Neville Brothers.

This had been the Peace Field all weekend, and I felt like I was home. Site of the Nevilles, Santana and Jimmy Cliff, the whole field was full of old camping hippies, and families with kids running around their pow-wowing circles. There were fire pits, family encampments and teepees dividing up the land like a settlement post. The first pioneers claimed the front edge of the ridge, while others chose near the concessions, and still others gathered back under the trees. Groups of tents were clustered all the way back to the horizon, with volunteer pioneers working together to make things better in the wide open spaces. Happy faces.

Even the colorful scrims around the stage were more organic and full of Rousseau-like animals than the North Stage. And they could actually lower the curtain wall behind the stage so above the band you could see the trees and moving clouds of a even better backdrop than man could ever design.

The core audience bowl in front of the stage was jammed just like any big rock concert, but the rest of the field was wide open — people camping with lots of room, and tents going back to the moon.

The mud chasm river that ran through the middle of the field yesterday was even wider today. In fact it had become a lake of a watery pudding anywhere from two inches to a foot deep. Some risky Adventurers were out in the uncharted mud had found some tiny patch in the lake where they could spin and swing their arms and the rest of us would watch till they lost their balance.

The Neville Brothers opened with *Hey Pocky Way*, the invocation to make your body rock 'n' roll, the invitation to the dance, the introduction of funk into this festival, the initiation of the spirit into the music. It brought the audience to life like flowers blooming out of their pods in the spring. Slow at first, but by the end of the song they were all blossoming in radiant colors.

If you know what I mean.

The whole vibe of the South Stage was the antithesis of the North, like they were two very different concerts going on simultaneously. The big one you probably know more about than you care to, but hidden over here on the left was the funky adult's folk festival: The Neville Brothers are in their 60s, Santana's 48, and Jimmy Cliff is 47. While on the North Stage, it seemed like some of the acts were just reaching puberty.

But here, here, here my friends, the children played, the long-hairs twirled, and the funk flew. The body of the audience danced as one heartbeat to *Yellow Moon*, the title track of their breakthrough album of a few years ago. Twisted dance, reggae dance, Dead dance, Creole dance, mystic voodoo dance in transcendental time, river valley breezes, blue scrims blowing like flags of a new nation, Nevilles swinging to us all, since the fifties they've made revolutionaries dance, through the segregated south, through bad times and worse, to the high moments, high notes on stages from Jazz Fest to Woodstock. The ultimate party dance band. Wide smiles and dancing so clean it was sexy — reminding me that more demons have been chased away by dancing over the centuries than by all the churches combined.

This wasn't some sports complex rented for the night with meathead security guards and bad sound. This was a blissful wide-open free-for-all park surrounded by a forest with no one but ourselves for as far as you could walk. For in that walk of life what dreams may come true, when we have shuffled off this mortal field, must give us pause.

At the edge of the South Field was a small gorge that dropped down about a hundred feet filled with rich ancient vegetation in the former creek bed stretching maybe a couple hundred feet across. The bank on the far side rose up to the high ground again which eventually led to the North Stage field.

Filling the riverbed gully was a thick maze of bushes about eight feet high. Through the bushes were carved a pell-mell series of paths, non-paths and half-paths like a huge organic house of mirrors. Kids crossed through the gully as a short-cut instead of following the high-ground all the way around. From the ridge overlooking it you could see the players enter the other side and disappear into the acreage of confusion. What was once water was now a lush, swarming river of life, a panhandle full of gold panners sifting for adventure, of lost laughing girls exploring their way until suddenly bumping into a friend and both of them screaming out in surprised laughing amazement. "Whaaaaaaa!" they'd scream and go running in the opposite direction and get lost all over again.

It was like the garden maze at the end of *The Shining*, except this was natural, not sculpted, with nothing but human desire lines and natural forces creating a web of camouflage trails, which for the first time in this Eden's life, was occupied by as many people as plants. I'm sure the flora got the worst of it this weekend — but I'll bet they're still there and we aren't.

A constant flittering ant flow of people weaved through the green bushes until they eventually found their way to the other side — only to discover there was a mud slide cliff that they'd have to negotiate or else hike about a mile down the gully to the next crossing. Ha ha.

Naturally, an impromptu Woodstock Rescue Service formed out of the primordial ooze. As the steady stream of successful explorers found their way out of the maze at the foot of the cliff, the fit teenage boys would see the mountain to climb, get entranced by the challenge, and just naturally scamper up like Navy SEALs, grabbing roots and running up like it was a flight of stairs, while the girls would still be slip sliding away at the bottom, laughing in their mud-splattered blaze. But once the boys got to the top, they'd realize they'd left a cackle of babes below looking up at them, so they'd form an arm-hold chain or actually climb back down and literally carry a girl up. While one guy was helping one back-logged contestant, other guys would find their way out of the maze, and without anyone saying a thing, they'd assume the SEAL role. Then as new girls would find their way to the cliff, the same pattern would repeat over and over with an ever-evolving cast of Fay Wrays and hero Kongs. It was a great unspoken giving that flowed throughout an unconnected maze of people proving once again, when left to our own devices, we're pretty nice to one another.

Meanwhile, in the background it was Sunday Afternoon In The Park with the Neville Brothers and they were weaving their *Voodoo* along some atomic level and affecting everything. Twirling spinning sisters in the field, climbing women over long-haired herculean men, sunny skies warming the soaking earth, and people in every direction flashing the smile of their lives.

Then, through the past oddly, the Nevilles broke out in a *Fever* — the very same song the very Bob Weird played on the same stage at the same time yesterday afternoon (!) — it was one of those Kennedy-Lincoln coincidences. Electric Fever. The tingling chills of fever love, life, fever for the moment, for your eyes, for everything. FEVER indeed through the night!

And a night lay before us like no other. One last night to blow it out on the farm at Woodstock. This will never happen again. Which, come to think of it, was what they thought the first time, but I decided to gobble four more hits of the color-coordinators just to make sure I never forgot this one.

When you find yourself in such a cushy soft playground with a half-million soular cell-mates, a sunny day, an immaculate KarmaCoupe, and some capable minstrels, it's a not a bad idea to step over to the other side while you've got the chance.

Space exploration is never easy or safe. So

you have to pick your flights when meteorological conditions are right. After all the expensive training I've been through, if this Navy Zeal wasn't ready to take the plunge now, he may as well get out of the service. I knew the site. I'd done my research. I'd tested a couple of hits. I had nowhere to drive and nothing to do except see Bob Dylan, Peter Gabriel, and have the best time of my life. It wasn't a Dead show, but I decided to plug in the electric cord anyway and see what lit up. There was only one night left, and having done the whole thing straight as far as I was concerned, it was time to play over there in the other place, where weirder things happen and deeper oceans are lit up like starbursts.

And no sooner had I swallowed the magic potion than the Brothers broke into *Brother John (Is Gone)*, that cajun claves classic to every fallen soldier you care to think of who isn't still with us on the battlefield of human struggle. Pick your own Dear John — Kennedy, Bonham or Belushi, but I heard Lennon at Woodstock again.

And 50,000 people were twirling in a spiritual envelopment, a musical tornado engulfing the moment and spinning us beyond the dancing threshold. Spastic arm-flailing and choo-choo train chugging filled the field like a revival meeting on a full-moon Sunday. Nobody was normal. Nobody was even there anymore. We all lost it, shedding our clothes physically or not, with the pulsing beat of the concert bowl sucking us, sucking us in, closer and closer to the churning engine, the bopping beads of sweat, flashing eyes and the delirious fast-paced tempo of bayou boogie gone bonkers.

Which only fanned us higher into the *Iko Iko* segue, the single funkiest song ever written, or so it seemed at the time. The Mardi Gras bomb exploded annihilating everything but the dancing bears at The Chaos Circus all splashing in the mud — into Jambalaya — *"Gonna Have Some Fun on The Bayou"* — into faces whizzing in circles in crazy exaltation and spinning across the field like balloons losing air.

If such pure joy could be captured on canvas it would be hung in the Metropolitan Museum of Art. But it can't.

And then as if this wasn't enough holy god, mother of pearl, Cyril says, "If positive change is going to come, its got to come from right here in America. So don't cha think its time we put down all our petty differences, and *Come Together.*"

And before I could stop it, I had died and gone to heaven. There was John Lennon on stage playing a white grand piano with the Neville Brothers! We were surrounded by dark green trees, and the stage was like a bright blue sky, and Lennon was wearing that beat-up army jacket, short hair, chewing gum, and somehow he'd gotten the Neville Brothers to be his band, that old jokerman doin' as he please.

It was some fantasy Woodstock starring John Lennon, and it was sunny even though it was wet, and for some reason there was tons of room to dance even though there was a half-million people here, and every one of the strolling young gorgeous bodies was naked, and there was John Lennon banging out the theme on his heavenly white open-hood grand, "One thing I can tell you is you've got to be free."

Check.

And then all of a sudden, as if this wasn't enough, as soon as it's over and Lennon fades to mist, suddenly Cyril Neville was saying, "We believe — matter of fact we know — we're all one family, look around you. I'm looking at one race. *The huuuuman race.* We send this out to every human being walking the planet, or floating around it."

And some sort of transcendental lifting took place again, the kind of thing that can only happen in heaven, where you float, not just you but everyone around you. The Neville Brothers brought out the highest, happiest side of the human spirit all weekend, an unequivocal surrender to the dancing child, the original rhythm inside, and suddenly something more was vibrating through the crowd, more guttural, more instinctual, more inexpressible except by dancing. And thus we did.

Here were The Neville Brothers playing to a tenth the audience of the North Stage, but they were performing some kind of magic right before our eyes. They were eliciting a suppressed joy in everyone that from the looks of things lay dormant for far too long beneath glaciers of repression that was just now blossoming out of the pods in giggling harmony with the other flowers in this fertile garden.

"Let the people go. I'm talking about the black ones, the white ones, the red ones, the proud ones, the yellow ones, the female ones, the little-bitty ones, the old ones. This is America, the home of the brave and the land of the free, But if you ain't got no money life ain't so funny,

And it makes no difference what color you might be if you're broke;

Poverty is slavery;

We got a government of the people,

    By the people,

        For the people,

            You the people,

                Are the people,

                    We the people,

                        Get it together.

Get up, Stand up!   (can you believe this?)

Stand up for your rights.

(I'm dying!)

Since I was already dead I died two or three more times right there cause I always figured Marley was about the most amazing guy who ever lived after Lennon. In fact, WNEW-FM in New York, which didn't play a single song or ad or do the news or anything for at least 12 straight hours after Lennon was shot, the first song they played after it was all over and there was nothing more and we were all just waiting alone without anyone was Marley's *No Woman, No Cry*.

It don't get closer than that. Soulmates in

heaven, and with all of us in that moment in that crowd.

To wrap the rap, Aaron Neville sang an *Amazing Grace* for the encore, but what was *really* amazing was that Bob Dylan was about to step onto the North Stage! At Woodstock.

Sadly and crazily, Santana was due up on the South Stage next. For the first time all weekend there was something of an actual scheduling conflict. For the most part, they never put two bands appealing to the same audience on both stages at the same time. You either had old fogy music for people like me, or head-slamming devil music for the children.

For the first time I was forced to choose between two major acts I came to Woodstock to see. Add to this your six hits of acid where every pro and con takes on such monumental importance that decisions like where to stand can take hours. Or seem to.

I worked a show with Santana in the early eighties and saw him recently on a double-bill with Dylan, ironically, and knew he was a smokin' world-beat rock 'n' roll shaman that few guitarist soulmates could touch. It was working with Santana that I first met Bill Graham, and he and I got to know each other, and I even ended up working with him on the Rolling Stones tour a few months later.

Bill managed Carlos Santana from the beginning until I don't know when, but the way he power-played to get his band on the bill at the first Woodstock is legendary. There's a great photo of him by Henry Diltz from the first Woodstock where Bill's sitting on the stage behind an amplifier while Santana is jamming on stage and Bill's playing air guitar and beaming like a little boy.

It was so amazing that both Santana and Bill's spirit were about to play at Woodstock again, and it brought me flashing back to producing the Woodstock Reunion concerts in River Heights Junior High field in Winnipeg. My whole life in those days was based on Bill's concept of producing an event — creating something out of thin air that would never have existed had you not put it on. This Woodstock would not have happened had the promoters not staged it, nor would the gathering this weekend at Yasgur's farm. Granted one cost $135 a person while the other was free, but the idea of staging an event, no matter how big or small — even asking someone out for a date — is putting people together for a common goal where the chemical reaction outcome is an intangible.

It's one of the things Bill and I talked about when we first met. For some reason he really took to me. Maybe because I wasn't trying to get anything out of him except inspiration. But we stood in this hallway backstage at a Santana show at Nassau Coliseum and talked for an hour, and the whole time out of the corner of my eye I could see this crowd of people huddled around us — people holding tapes to give him, books for him to autograph, just wanting to shake his hand or ask him a question. But the whole time we were engaged in this deep conversation about the ethics and practices of promotion and production. His eyes were locked on me, and that's why no one could get a word or tape in edgewise. He was giving no quarter, no glance, no break of concentration or conversation flow.

He used his hands passionately when he talked, often holding an imaginary globe when he talked of humanity as a whole, which was frequently. And here we jammed, this kid from a town so small, so remote, who could hardly believe a man as great as Bill Graham really existed, a man I'd read every scrap I could about and based my life on what I thought his was, and now here I was talking to the actual person! I don't think most people realize how far removed Winnipeg, Manitoba, is from the rest of the world, but it's further away than, say, Siberia. And colder. Even completing the journey to America seemed impossible, let alone an audience with the King, backstage at a Santana concert!

One of the stories he told me that night was about when he and New York promoter Ron Delsener were both doing shows in Manhattan in the early seventies. Bill used to put barrels of apples in the lobby of the Fillmore so people could have some fresh fruit to eat instead of holding a drink or a cigarette. Delsener asked him if he thought the apples helped sell tickets, and Bill said no. Then Delsener asked him what on earth he'd put them there for. And Bill said to me, "This is the difference between what you and I do and what these other guys do." He had included me in what he did, on the team that he was on. I couldn't believe it. He had taken me in, and we would work together, and I'd never forget him.

Santana, to this day, plays tapes of Bill introducing the band to start their shows. And he was about to do it here at Woodstock.

Meanwhile, behind the curtain of stage number two, we had the Bob of all Bobness, no introduction necessary. On the way to his set I stopped by the Media Tent to see if anyone was testifying at the witness tree but the schmoozaholics were just standing around in full Sunday night card exchanging mode. "Meantime life outside goes on all around you," I'm singing as I leave for the Bobstock.

The North Stage, believe it or not, was actually running ahead of schedule. Porno For Pyros weren't due to be off until 7:00, but by 6:30 it was already quiet. The assembled City of Woodstock was now awaiting the appearance of Pope John Bob II. It was time to cop a spot in the sacred field and hear the pontiff pontificate.

Dylan. Whose mere residency lent the credibility to a town that made it the Jerusalem of a generation. In fact, he was the reason we were all here today if you want to get historical about it. It was Dylan moving to the town of Woodstock that cemented it as a cool musician's enclave (even though Levon & The Hawks, later The Band, parts of Blood, Sweat & Tears, and many others called it home) which prompted Michael & his pal Artie Kornfeld to think up having an annual Newport-like music festival there, and opening a recording studio, and having a concert with Bob and all the local musicians to promote the studio, to which their business partners (John Roberts & Joel Rosenman) thought, "Why don't we skip the studio idea and just do a big concert? We could make a fortune." But it was Dylan in Woodstock that got the whole ball rolling.

And now tonight, the wheel was finally on fire, and I was beamin as I sailed through the Gates of Eden and into the sea of bobbing Bob people.

And a sea it was! I snowshoed across the slippery, sloppy surface in my lead-weighted mud-boots listening to the waves cresting, and surreptitiously evesdropping on the lapping of human minds around you.

"Who was your favorite band so far?" was clocking in as the question of choice with only three acts to go on the weekend.

"Green Day. Definitely."

"*Duuuh.* Trent Reznor and Nine Inch Nails, dude. As-fuckin'-if."

"Sheryl Crow was great on Friday."

"Melissa Etheridge's God. Nobody touches her."

Apparently there were simultaneous epiphanies going down in front of both stages. And I could certainly vouch for mine.

I had to hand it to the promoters. I hadn't heard of half of these bands before I came up, and yet they sold 200,000 tickets at $135 apiece ($27 million gross, largest gate in the history of entertainment), plus as many again came for free. Whoever these acts were, a lot of people wanted to see them. They even had Bob and The Band to keep the old codgers occupied while the kids spent money.

I continued to sail the seas with no direction home, like a complete unknown, vaguely looking to be on my own, but it was 7:00 on the Sunday night of a now-free Woodstock festival, and a few hundred thousand other people also thought this was a good idea. If you wanted to have room to say, breathe, you'd have to find a ridge in the mud several hundred yards from the stage in about row 7,000, *if* there were seats, which there most definitely were not. They all sank along with Atlantis, and this will be like the Valley of Kings in 2,000 years when archaeologists go sniffing through our trash.

> NEW TOKYO (AP) — Thousands of `automobiles' (ancient ground-based location adjustors) were discovered last week, fully intact, as though suddenly covered by lava or a mud slide. A major catastrophe is now thought to have occurred in the region, although the findings appear to slightly pre-date the known implosion of the lost city of New York in the year 2001.

Scientists also uncovered a large collection of green coins imprinted with the word `Heineken'. Debate rages over their origin, some speculating they date back to the Dutch, while others maintain they're less filling. Spokesmen were still drinking it over at press time.

And I don't mind if I do. We'd already been waiting a half-hour for Bob and it was starting to cut into my cocktail hour.

This whole weekend was emerging as one of the great adventures of my life. We all go off in search of the Holy Grail every night of the week, occasionally spotting some glimpse of it here or there, but it's not very often you have three days of peace and music and nothing *but* peace and music. I made it to Sunday night and managed to sleep, shower, live & breathe, and never travel further than a bike ride from the stage. This field had been home since I first crossed its lush grass and hay on Thursday night as ticket-holders were filing in to set up their tents while Dennis Hopper and Peter Fonda were talking at a thousand decibels. And I'd seen it grow from an innocent well-prepared child, to a tough, battle-hardened old man in three days.

Something happened over the weekend that I was just beginning to understand – that all of my life I'd been searching for this in some way. I was so upset about missing the first Woodstock that my whole life

I'd been trying to recreate that moment of history. If only I'd wandered those naked, drug crazed fields of the movie & the pages of *Life Magazine*, if only I'd shared in that apex of the human spirit, I wouldn't have spent the last 15 years smoking and drinking my way to a pale comparison.

But now I was here. I'd made a point of catching most of the large parties America has thrown since 1980 when I immigrated here, from Stanley Cups to World Series, from Inaugurations to Dead tours, but this was in a league by itself. As a professional, I can guarantee you that nothing this free, this open, this wild has happened in America since I got here. This is not a boast — more an act of desperation. What am I doing running around to all these events? What don't I have that I'm dashing back and forth across the country looking for? What have I been striving to achieve by being the wildest guy in any given zip code?

It was this. I know it sounds crazy, but *this* is what I was looking for. There's no question this was Woodstock in a truer sense than I — or anyone — ever thought possible. You can't be the first man to land on the moon, but you can be the second, and it's still the moon. This party, this scene that stretched on for miles in every direction, this surging freedom of choice, this mudfest, this hippie-youth-fest, this do-whatever-you-want-for-three-days-with-nothing-hard-to-bonk-your-head-on-fest, this global symbol of freedom that no other nation on earth could hope to replicate in 200 years, this international incident being beamed from a hundred satellite dishes beside my mobile home cottage to every TV set from Afghanistan to Zaire, this moment, this was the greatest benevolent madness ever created by man, the greatest physical manifestation of the Constitution that we've ever achieved in our 200 year history. Except for another one in '69.

The whole concept of the Constitution was we didn't need kings or armies or churches to keep us in line, but each person could speak their mind, act their conscience, and deep down, if we were given the ultimate freedom of speech and assembly, the best would rise to the surface and we wouldn't hurt each other. Here we were, putting that in practice, policing ourselves by the hundreds of thousands, and it worked. From this moment forward, every one of us would carry this forward like a half-million breaths of fresh air wherever we went for the rest of our lives.

It was almost like a dream — like it didn't happen except in my head — because nobody else I know was here. Was old Johnny on Thursday just part of the dream? Even writing this book could be part of an elaborate fantasy where I imagine I was at Woodstock living in a van beside the stage, blazing on acid in clean dry clothes on Sunday night just before Bob Dylan came on. Yeah right. And what time did the spaceship get there?

I was burying something behind me — a sense of completion of a personal search. I had finally gotten to the place I was searching for. This was not like Woodstock, it was Woodstock. And I was home.

It wasn't just Ranger's Last Ride, it was mine.

I didn't feel anxious anymore. There was a peace, a completion, a resting, a breathing, a joy. Woodstock happened. It was the biggest party ever staged, and it was bringing the curtain down on a long series of them. Retire after the game when you hoist the Stanley Cup. Nothing will ever hold a candle in the mud to this. This was freedom burning on all five senses. All I had to do was stay here for the rest of my life.

Although it was beginning to feel like I'd be waiting for Dylan for the rest of my life! Where was this guy? The mud was getting weary and the master maestro was no where to be seen. I knew I wanted to be in the field for the start, because God knows he's going to come out and say some prophetic thing that will be the single defining moment of the weekend — and if I missed it I'd have to spend another 25 years on the road. Yet I had to retain my perfect moment, and let the magic of the revelations sink in, so I hit the mute during the commercials and got the heck out of there.

"Last Night On The Party Train," I'm thinking as I walked past the crowded refugee bleachers toward the stage-side exit gate. "The climactic night. Make it the perfect divinity, the perfect memory, the perfect moment. Then get to work. This is it."

* * *

I absentmindedly wandered back into the Media Tent like an instinctual magnet just as the final climactic back-slapping press briefing of the festival was getting underway. There was your reporterman on the scene for the final spin indoctrination, doing his level best even under such trying psychedelic conditions to bring you the whole story and nothing but the story so help me God.

The air was crackling with the electric buzz of victory like being in the tent with a post military operation debriefing . . . hosted by the Marx Brothers. All four promoters were assembled in front of their 12 foot "Situation Map" looking like little kids despite being our chaperons for the weekend. They were bouncing off each other like four brothers in a backseat, all bumping and hitting, and hugging and whispering.

Curly-haired Michael Lang was the wise-cracking Groucho, who looked like Dennis the Menace on his way to becoming Keith Richards, who never stood still for an instant. John Scher was Chico with the goofy cap, fast-talking circles around everyone until Groucho would lean in with a punchline. Joel Rosenman was the silent Harpo, flashing his big wide grin, and only occasionally stepping up to honk in a line that would steal the scene. And John Roberts, all straight and tall like Zeppo the straight Marx, nodding like an in-law trying to distance himself.

The main thrust of the briefing was that — by

God — everything was faaaantastic! Everybody made a bundle, we're all going down in history, and they'll have a movie and a record to sell us on our way out the door.

Somebody asked if they handled the rain well, and General Groucho said, "Never laid a glove on us. There were two major fronts, but they both just missed us."

"*Just missed us?*" Chico challenged. "Then what the hail hit us, boss?"

This went on for hours within the next few seconds, until . . .

There were green-eyed monsters and long-neck geese, humpty-back camels and chimpanzees; there were cats and rats and elephants, but sure as you're born, a cop just came out as a unicorn.

Amid flashing bulbs and pushing pencils, the uniformed unicorn read the news today oh boy about some guy from Ontario who was arrested for assaulting a stage worker. What's with these Canadian agitators anyway?

Unfortunately, by this time the fibers in the pages of my notebook had grown into the valleys and forests of an entire continent, and my pen became a giant flowing paintbrush cutting rivers and dividing up meat such that the concept of taking notes from a talking unicorn was inching beyond the possible. Hour by hour through each passing second everything became more liquid until finally I just had to swim out of the reporter's pool and broke for the dryland of daylight.

At some point I passed in front of an extremely full-color face-level flatscreen TV and saw Carlos Santana wailing away on the South Stage. I was suddenly reminded of the grievous scheduling conflict, and panic set in. *My perfect record — Ahhhhh!* For the first time I was missing something I had to see. Ahhhhh! And for the first time I was in no condition to correct it, fry though I may.

I rushed out of the Media Tent but could hear that Bob still wasn't on stage yet so I began defiantly walking away from His Highness's vigil at the North Stage and back towards actual music at Santana. All along the muddy river road, brown cars slowly splashed through the potholes and around potheads dressed in the wildest assortment of get-ups since Halloween in the Village: Torn shower curtains held on by bent hangers; Army fatigues with canteens and camouflage suncaps; Business suits; Bathing suits; Birthday suits. But everyone was smiling, no matter their condition or their fate. Whether they walked alone or in a passel, everyone had some degree of beam on from prankster twinkle to time-of-your-life electricity.

As I kept inching further and further toward the South Field, and Santana came in clearer and clearer into aural focus, it became clearer and clearer that I was missing Bob. *Ahhhhh!* The more Carlos's wailing came into range, the further I slipped from history-in-the-making, from Bob spontaneously spouting our collective edict for the next millennium as soon as he walked on stage like he did at Live Aid. *Ahhhhh!* Right before me Santana was roaring like a rocket with only uncertainty lingering behind. I kept walking. Stepping forward. Determined to dance in Carlos's light, "Definitely going to go to Santana," I convinced myself in the Rain Man's voice. "Definitely going to see Santana. Not going to wait for Dylan anymore. Definitely going to . . ." *Ahhhhhhh!* I turned and ran back towards the North Stage just before my thread tethering to reality snapped.

Splish splash splammy through the heart-racing mud puddles I ran. "Dylan's on, Dylan's on," I'm thinking, "Oh-God, oh-God, I'm missing it, loser, loser, ahhhh-haaa-haaaaa," and I rounded the corner toward the stage about as graceful as a donkey on a skating rink. I'd slipped into high panic gear without noticing it, and was now tearing through the mellow Woodstock walkers like some acid-crazed lunatic, legs wobbling, mind racing.

Needless to say Dylan still hadn't come on yet. But I did hear a tape of Ray Charles singing *God Bless America* which I thought was pretty soulful and thoughtful of the promoters and a kind of funny kick to Ray who it was widely reported wanted 50 grand to play Yasgur's — but it still wasn't enough to lure me back into that muddy mayhem of hormone-throbbing hooligans — egads I shudder just thinking about it.

Instinctively I was heading for the KarmaCoupe where I could freak out in privacy and still hear the stage. The road to paradise was looking pretty frayed at this point in the Sunday night of pre-Bob panic, lemme tell ya. Security guards were still at every checkpoint because the fences were down in so many places that oodles of fans were just roaming around the backstage area, mostly getting deflected from one guard to another in an endless game of pinball until they'd finally bounce past one and win access to nowhere.

"In fact its getting downright spooky," I thought, as strange metallic rings began echoing off the steel stage frames, and music was bouncing off the hillside. Horns and hollering and magnification of technicolor surround-sound spun the world in a wavy circle of maypole dizziness. It became quite clear the world was not flat at this point.

The row of parked white semi-trailers flowed to the horizon like The Great Wall of China. Above the wall ran a giant row of satellite dishes perfectly lined up like plates in a dish-rack and trailing off to infinity like a massive Christo installation.

HOOOONK HOOOONK

Another huge monster roared from behind. It was yet another armored car pushing its way through the people and out of the site with our money, their "take." Well not my money actually, but a whole lot of a lotta people's if they need all these huge steel cash-campers every fifteen minutes. But in my case, not a second too soon, we were back at the KarmaCoupe!

Tea hee for two is all I can say — holy schnooker

dee-dee — I was HOME! It was clearly time to chill the dogs and unchill a Heineken. But as soon as I slid open the door to the van everything looked like an — oh my God — the spin-cycle! All my gear was flowing around in a liquid collage of unfocusable stuff. Every fiber and color of every different fabric was oozing like lava. Anything with texture became an infinite canyon of molecules swirling to the center of the earth where the longer you focused the deeper you could look. The importance or function of an object would flash into focus for a second until suddenly its color would become the most important thing, and it and everything else in view would become pure flowing color. Nothing distinguished by meaning or by distance but only a 2-dimensional wash of pigments until the texture would become the focus and the 2-dimensions would become 3 and you'd see nothing but the molecular structure of how something was made, whether it was cotton or wood and therefore flowed naturally like water, or if metal or plastic in which case there was no organic flow only a repeating geometric pattern and everything would become a flashing collage of molecules swirling in different patterns before you, until your focus would become how far something was to your eyes and the items closest to you would become continents you could hold in your hand and something across the van would be miles out of reach, and all of this takes place in seconds like surfing quickly through channels on a TV and then you can just click on the focus level you want magnified. Only trouble is, normal-vision may be a little difficult to tune in on some sets. Please stand by.

And obviously touching was out of the question! So I had to actually keep looking backwards out the van door while I reached for the cooler, moving my arm like a crane until it clanged on the latch then I threw my whole body forward to open it. Ha! I did something! It was all coming back to me!

But by this time, ground level on the outdoors was becoming a little crowded. A constant stream of people had infiltrated every nook and parking space of my previously private Idaho and it was clearly time to throw The Boys on the tape deck and The Body on the roof.

It only took about an hour to fumble the tape on, but I scampered up the back of the KarmaCoupe like there was a ladder and suddenly found myself out on a beautiful stone patio overlooking the Mediterranean Sea with its crystal blue . . . No wait, suddenly there was the entire field of Woodstock spread before me and I was at this enormous concert! Or sporting event, I'm not even sure. But I ordered a Heineken from the waitress and popped it open with my lighter, sending the cap flipping end-over-end in a slow-motion arc to land in the Heineken-green grass on the far side of the road.

YES!

I toasted, "Thank you oh Lord, oh God, oh Buddha old buddy," raising the dripping green goblet to the spirits, the soldiers and fellow pranksters who made this happen. It was the quintessential co-production: We couldn't have done it without the bands, video screens or masterful revolving stages that kept everything running perfectly all weekend until a guy named Bob came along. Or didn't come along, as the moment's example may be. But it would all have added up to a closed-down drive-in if we all didn't come and out-dance the rain, the mud and the cynics to make it happen.

On the up side of our species, occasionally we work well together. A bunch of homo sapiens gathered here and created a single unified emotion and attitude that can only be made by thousands of people being in the same place, feeling the same way, and bonding through hardship and joy to channel whatever giant force it is that's caught by five hundred thousand antennas all vibrating at once.

Shots of energy were shooting up my spine like electricity. Goosebumps were chilling my arms. And I thought the satellite dishes were impressive! We were beaming signals those things couldn't touch. If you couldn't taste the tangible human energy vibrating across this humming vortex of consciousness you needed to have your acid checked.

From my watchtower, I could see all along the horizon little buzzing helicopter flies constantly circling — probably looking for Bob — while all around me cranked the busiest backstage hive of the weekend. A whole bunch of people who were not supposed to be backstage were starting to move in (if you can imagine such a thing!) A steady stream of humanity was flooding in from somewhere and filing out to the edge of the road along Guerrilla Ridge in front of my home to have their picture taken in front of the endless ocean of humanity. "KarmaCoupe Korners Scenic Overlook, Two-Bits a Shot. Stop in for a beer at the rooftop patio gardens along Guerrilla Ridge at Woodstock."

All around my bird's nest perch an army of news crews were broadcasting their evening reports. Right next door an Argentine TV crew were up on their motorhome roof broadcasting the news. A beautiful dark-skinned woman was delivering her story into a strong wind that blew her yard-long hair in perfect symmetry with the flags of Woodstock behind her.

Suddenly it was mostly photographers in my subdivision for some reason, those fearless goalies of the press, the isolated be-masked soloists who'd face any shot, climb any wall, forge any stream of consciousness to get the picture. I got dizzy watching one guy as he piled one table on top of another *on top of* a semi-trailer and was up there with his body suit of cameras snapping away in the wind like a trapeze artist without a net.

As usual, they proved themselves a breed apart at this Breeders' Cup of Broadcasting. Picture Woodstock and you picture a picture. Brought to you by the Essence-Chasing Photography Corp of the U.S. Army of Reporters. And don't ever let any writer tell you he knows a thing. Photographers are the ground troops in this War of Image and everything you've ever seen a picture of is something they got to first. I toasted my dripping green one to their mud-splattered fatigues.

And then, as quick as I was hallucinating on every fabric of society around me, I became bored of it all. Yes bored I tell you! There I was, bored while sitting backstage at Woodstock just before the performance of Bob Dylan. Then quick as you can say Abraham Lincoln, Mr. Conscienceman showed up again: "So you're bored, eh? (He's Canadian.) There's 7,000 things going on in every direction, you have complete access to the entire molecular universe as well as the free Pepsi tent, what more do you want?"

But before I could get a woird in edgewise, it happened — the white blanket skies suddenly got pulled back and a brilliant orange sunset came bursting out in fiery red streaks arcing across the sky and showering us in crimson glory. Why was this happening now? Because it was sunset? Was this what Dylan was waiting for all along? Or was God waiting for Dylan? Or are they actually one-in-the-same? *Ah-ha!* I suddenly realized I had never seen the two of them in the same room!

But what in the hell was going on here? I mean, was it that the Big Guy was throwing down a gauntlet to the little guy saying, "Yeah I know you're good, tiny poetman. But can you . . . paint the entire sky orange! And then perhaps . . . turn it PURPLE! Ha-ha-ha-ha." He was obviously up there having the time of His life just like We were! Then He broke out His new box of 64 Crayolas and decided to show off. "How about, oh, a little dandelion right here, with perhaps a shadow of burnt sienna around it. And then oouu how about some vivid tangerine over here. Ha-ha-ha-ha . . ." He laughed, sounding a little too much like Cesar Romero's Joker to me. And I thought the computerized video screens were good! Holy rainbows all over my dreams, Batman, the sky's the limit!

Empires of smoke were exploding all over the place as the sun caught each cottonball and filled it full of fire. Talk about bombs bursting in air, this became the peace revolution's Fort McHenry, and the flapping blue stage scrims our Star Spangled Flag. Francis "Beam Me Up Scotty" Key may have made the 1814 show, and Jimi "I Can Bend It Furthur" Hendrix may have completely revolutionized the concept of sound at the '69 show, but tonight we had the best damn sky-washer in the business painting with all eight arms before some guy name Bob was supposed to play.

Then guess what? MORE natural explosions of color went off. Then more and more and it made Aerosmith's fireworks seem puny, my dear Watson. Absolutely crazy sky flames in every direction. Golden eruptions of light would go off in the darkest quadrants of your eyes, the places where nothing existed before would suddenly explode across the the heavens with a paint-bomb balloon of some color you couldn't even name. And eventually each cloud-puff would dissolve like cotton candy into shivering angels, sprinkling their tiny slivers all across the universe in a soft wash of gold.

Good God! Veeery good God. Thank you for this, Big Fella, or can I just call you Big?

And can I just say right here that there was this pulsating energy center all around me! And that it was just beginning to dawn on me — What a long time I've been sitting on this roof!

Dylan was due on stage about three weeks ago, and here I was still nursing a beer in the airport lounge waiting for the Air Bob departure. Motto: "The Flight Times They Are A-Changin'." Ergo — when the mood strikes. Air go — not very often. Fly Air Bob. Guaranteed nuts!

How many roads must a man walk down, before he gets to the show?

And how many beers must I drink here, before he lets us know?

Yes and how many suns will come and go, before he starts to blow?

The answer, my friend, is Bobbin' in the wind,

The answer is . . . Has this guy flipped or what?

Porno For Pyros went off stage at 6:15 and it was now about 8 million o'clock. The stage has been empty since yesterday, back when things were actually running *ahead* of schedule. But that was B.B.

(Before Bob.)

Who else in American culture could have held up a huge show like this?

Up top, the pastel light show was dripping like ice cream over the mountaintops. Inside, my motor was purring with sunset centeredness. "Bombs bursting in air," I thought as the sky continued to explode with sunlight.

Wait. One country had the Revolution, Walt Whitman, Jerry Garcia, *and* Woodstock? Not fair. Plus New York, Abe Lincoln, Bob Dylan, and the Grand Canyon? *No way.* I want one.

I'll take Cool Countries for 100, please.

Invented jazz, rock 'n' roll, and the convertible. What is —

"We've waited 25 years to hear this. . .

. . .Ladies and gentlemen, Mr. BOB DYLAN!"

Holy shit! Bolt upright!

"Bob's on!"

And I had an audience with the jokerman by the second verse.

"So swiftly the sun sets in the sky ...." he's singing as I walked into the field. Well sure, *now* it does, Bob. We've been watching that drip drop for hours, if you catch my poetic license.

What a joker he is!

Bob, in his never-ending attempt to suck-up

to an audience, proceeded to dismiss all the women present with *Just Like A Woman* — his pigeon-holing of a whole gender in a single song. Dylan-heads will tell you after several (thousand) listens and beer sandwiches it's *not really* sexist, it's sensitive, and I'm Chopin. Fortunately, tonight's assembled masses were pretty much ignoring the obvious. There wasn't a person near me who wasn't talking or just gazing around at the naked people.

"Oh-oh," I'm thinking in my newly reactivated rock 'n' roll brain, "If Bob just does one of his typical Dylan tour shows and gets strange and mumbly, we're in trouble."

But y'know, he came out of the gate playing pretty intense versions of the first few songs. It just seemed no one was listening. I mean, almost literally completely no one around me.

What a unicornball the guy is — skinny as he was at 20, tight black pants, cowboy boots that he twists around in on his toes, with this puff of hair that catches the light just like the clouds did, creating this fuzzy halo around his head. Touched or what? And tonight it seems the joker's twisting out every word and, savoring every phase like a master chef cooking a monster feast.

And P.S. who in the heck was this band? Some wild Rastafarian on drums [Winston Watson], and two desperados in fedoras and suits [Tony Garnier & John Jackson]. Where did he *find* these guys? It was like a dread-lock Jamaican Keith Moon thunder machine meets the Tennessee Mountain Hoods, with Maestro Halohead conducting. Then over in the corner there was this one utility player [Bucky Baxter] on peddle steel, lap steel, and mandolin. In the words of Jim Carey – "SMOKIN'!!"

And then, to add to the circus, walking through the crowd were all these TV reporters looking like clowns in pancake make-up and flat ironed David Byrne suits shushing around the mud people trying to "get the story." Dylan was the first news out of this place since the news of Dylan not being here, and now all the reporters were finally stepping out of their protected trailers and walking for the first time all day. In a field where people have been living and eating mud for days, suddenly these gooby make-up phonies said, "Excuse me," as they pushed on through looking straighter than your parents walking into the middle of a Saturday night free-for-all at high midnight. Many of the frail girlie-men looked terrified and were dashing back as best they could over the mud to their air conditioned cubicles and pancake girls. And I'll bet more than one of the Mr. Joneses got taken out on the way by the old rolling slide-dive.

Then suddenly his Bobness launches into *All Along The Watchtower*, which will be in the movie so you'll see it there, but it's the whole new arrangement where he rushes all the words into the first half of each line!? I turned open-mouthed to the people around me to share a, "Whoooa — what the heck is <u>this</u>?" look, but nobody even noticed. This certainly wasn't a Dylan concert like I've ever been to before. Usually I'm surrounded by fanatics who are hanging on every nuance and I'm the clueless one in the clique. Here, no one was even registering this completely new rendition of a classic song, a song, come to think of it, that Jimi Hendrix made famous, the guy you never stopped hearing about all weekend. He-llo?

But something caught them. Maybe it was the wicked, searing, string-stretching version they played that seemed to solidify the band, and in turn, us. Half-way through one song he'd taken an inattentive crowd and yanked them into his world, as if saying, "Yeah maybe some other cat covered this, but lemme show you where it came from."

Suddenly this guy who I was almost feeling sorry for because nobody was paying attention was single-handedly playing a half-million people like marionettes. He didn't smile, he didn't talk, he just slayed the field like a warrior, and took back the night with a single song.

The video screen mixers had certainly mastered their craft by now and were freely splashing electric colors over his electric music, adding a highly fluorescent accent to an already brilliant display. Wave after wave of color washed over the screen with each new phrase of a solo, occasionally revealing Dylan's face as he sternly led his band trance-like through something that began to give the night, the show, the weekend, a sense of greatness. Everything before this had been wonderful and exciting, but finally the

Grand Master was honkin'. By the end of *Watchtower*, those blank faces around me were screaming in wide-eyed rock 'n' roll ecstasy.

Meanwhile, the skies were still blazing like a western campfire. It was the first time since about June that it was nice out, and there was J.C. Bob wearing the halo and singing *It Takes a Lot to Laugh, It Takes a Train to Cry* while pink, orange, red and purple streaks danced across the ceiling like an Alvin Ailey ballet. The flashing fingers of light above mirrored the fluttering, colorful happiness below.

The Main Field was less than completely full for the first time. People must have been drifting out before Bob, because this was definitely no Saturday night. The thicket in front of the stage was still packed, but everywhere else was pretty free-flowing, so I took the opportunity to move through the crowd, digging deeper and deeper into the core of the Dylan night, negotiating the crowd streams that had sprung up all over the property, until I found myself next to the soundbooth tower in the center of the field with a perfect view of both the stage and the blow-up video enhancers.

Dead center, Dylan acoustic, *Don't Think Twice, It's Alright*. Oh it was more than alright, thanks! Once again my feet had gotten me to a very good spot and my ears were pleased they did. There were flashes of Bob doing *Chimes of Freedom* from the steps of the Lincoln Memorial during the Clinton Inauguration, another very good event to attend on acid if you ever get the chance. Just like that, here was Bob singing with just his acoustic guitar, with video screens so people in Toledo could see, history in the making, and everybody in a really good mood. And no screaming idiots. When was the last time you were in a crowd of a half-million people and there were no screaming idiots?

There had been some turnover at the Cafe Mudpie. Most of the Saturday beer nuts had been eaten by the Sunday dinner crowd. There was more standing room, but you still had to wait for a table.

It was funny to watch the difference between the all-weekenders and the Sunday drivers. Certain clusters began mysteriously appearing throughout the field with lawn chairs and donuts and clean clothes. The only thing they left at home was the TV, so they watched the video screens. They did bring a cupboard-full of crackers, Aunt Josie's pound cake, and more condiments for eating than I even own. Pass the mayo, Gordo.

And then you'd switch the focus channel and there'd be this dark pond full of leaping human gorillas splashing the water and grunting in a primordial sacrifice ritual involving fat white people with clothes on.

Backpackers were wandering through the maze in search of, well I don't really know, but there was a flurry of activity in general, this being the final hour of daylight. Everyone was jockeying for position for the darkness, and searching for something indeterminate, just like me.

In other major news: Dylan launched into *Masters of War*, which is about as direct as he gets about the Industrial Military Complex. But unfortunately the acoustic music lost the audience. Just when the kids got on their rock 'n' roll shoes of course Bob puts down his electric and picks up the acoustic just so no one settles too comfortably into a blissful rock 'n' roll show or anything.

The quick-cut video kids immediately lost interest and broke back into their discussion groups. Looking around, I could no longer spot a single person actually listening even though I was standing at the heart of Woodstock, New York.

What an idiosyncratic idol this guy is. Who the hell can be this anti-social / anti-showbiz and still be so popular? Black suit via Johnny Cash, never smiles, never speaks, shows up two hours late, often sings in a way to obliterate his poetry, has no sex appeal, a nasal voice, and isn't a virtuoso on any instrument! Yet he's influenced the music of this century more than any other living American songwriter, can twist a half-million disinteresteds around a single song; and is bigger than Jesus in a back-to-back height test.

In the last half hour he'd seared our ears, and now was giving the audience — whether they wanted it or not — a bluegrass display direct from the mountains of Tennessee. With mandolin, upright bass and acoustic guitars — the only time those instruments were unpacked at Woodstock all weekend

— he played the lineage that got us here. He took a chance by leading this exuberant troop of shirtless Gen Xers into the woods, but here's Bob at 53 still making people listen to instruments and music they would otherwise wouldn't. "Songmaster, songmaster, sing me a song; twist me a twist, spin me along."

The mandolin player switched to steel guitar and he finished the acoustic set with *It's All Over Now, Baby Blue* and I realized once again that what was happening here wasn't normal.

I know it's tempting to look for meaning in everything after a couple of hits, but right after I realized this weekend was the culmination of a particular search, a time to get off the road, settle down and have a couple of books, here was the Messiah on the Main Stage singing, "It's all over now, baby blue."

Then right after he sang about coincidence . . . and then a poor painter . . . out of the crowd in front of me suddenly appeared a paint-splattered artist! And he was actually carrying a palette of wet paint and brushes! I'm getting chills just remembering it.

Why do these things happen? I'll tell you why — it's The Spirit. The Channeling. The Chi. The renting of vans. The not lying, cheating, or stealing. Not being mean or bitter or greedy. At least it's a start. The Collective Unconscious: Synchronicity, "Meaningful coincidence" as Jung called it back when.

It's all over now Baby B.

And what a Last Night it was about to be!

God Knows.

My mind was racing. This all took place between about two notes, but I was carving the conclusions in the stone cliffs of my brain, staring unblinkingly at Dylan defining my life.

I'd never listened to the song before even though I'd heard it a million times. "Why now, why now? What's going on?" I'm thinking. It's as if he's reading my trepidations, doubts, fears and aspirations. This powerful laser beam was shooting out from center stage and nailing me in both eyes. You don't get this cumulative sign sealed and delivered very often. Too many bread crumbs led to this place. When he ended the song with "*Go start anew*," I realized tonight wasn't the end of something, but the beginning.

It's not very often a song changes your life, but I was getting the feeling this one had.

I don't know why he chose to play it on this night, or why I heard it for real for the first time, or why that damn painter walked right in front of me with his fresh palette, but just like the signs on the way to the lighthouse, you can deny the first couple, but if your eyes are open, you can't miss them all.

Who puts them there? And how come sometimes there's none, and other times there's too many? Is it a human who's tacking these signs along our paths, or is it, as others speculate, a large white rabbit in a waistcoat?

God Knows. Which, when I zapped back in from the stellar inner voyage, was the song Dylan was singing.

"Where the hell was I?" I wondered as I danced, realizing I hadn't seen anyone here for a long, long time. I'd been so focused on Bob and me that I thought it was just us! Suddenly I saw the mud and remembered there were others here. But I kind of liked it better when it was just the two of us.

By Sunday, some of the field encampments had become extremely well supplied because the gates were down. Some rebel troops had moved in heavy provisions to reinforce their line with beer, pretzels, sodas, wheel barrows. Many camps had erected 20 foot steel flagpoles flying the multicolored troop insignias.

Flags would rise and fall just as flags would disappear over the field of battle as a platoon fell or surrendered. The constant ebb and flow of the field of battle could be seen by watching flags changing position and moving across the field, like the time the one Canadian flag and its troops started out on the far side and for about an hour slowly fought their way across the battlefield inch by inch until finally the regiment was front & center.

But the crowd had completely come back to life and was in full mosh heaven for *God Knows*. Up on stage, the regal Bob was holding court, the reverential poet serving up the delicacies of the language, while right in front of him workboot-wearing tattooed teenagers were dropping themselves on their heads for fun.

This was clearly Dylan's early moshing period.

Watching from the little rise I'd found near the sound towers, this other-worldly sea of mud seemed so impossibly far from home, from New York, or anywhere else. Nothing in the real world could prepare you for this other mudworld with music and psychedelic movie screens and topless girls kissing mud-covered boys and everyone living in tents not knowing what's going to happen next while entertainment is ongoing on two different stages while simultaneously ambulances and helicopters and school buses are circling you like a cloud of gnats for 2 or 3 days or weeks I'm not sure but it was all going to end in two more acts.

Then he breaks into *I Shall Be Released*, which, I don't want to put too fine a point on it, but ! ! ☺ The sacred hymn written a mile from here at Big Pink started rolling over the rock 'n' mosh fans which gradually slowed everything down into one giant sway. Even the mud people began waltzing.

Here he is, at Woodstock, giving the most articulate and focused performance I've ever seen him give, and every song seems to be about seeing one's light come shining. It certainly has this weekend in so many ways. What kind of a succession of blessings this has been, of dreams exceeded, of perfect-bliss-moments ten-to-a-day. Of Bob hitting it out of the park after a two hour build-up. And now here I am, still in perfect shape, with a full tank of gas for the climax. Perfect execution. The only mistake was missing Santana, which we won't tell anyone about.

Bob breaks into *Highway 61*, the thrashing, knock-out rocker to climax his set, which always reminds me of Bill Graham putting bleachers out in the sun, and everything being so easily done certainly seemed to be summing up my Woodstockian magic.

You know . . . that's what makes taking acid fun: Things that don't usually happen, happen quite naturally. And when they do, you can cut away the surface and see the core like you're wearing a backstage pass to essence. Just like the valleys between the fibers of paper, there's depths to our experiences we don't always perceive. Physicists and spiritualists will tell you that all the levels are always there, but personally, I need three or four hits.

The band left the stage, and came back out for the encore about 15 seconds later! As if they were gonna make us wait around again! And as you may have heard by now, he played *Rainy Day Women*, the song everybody thinks is called, "Everybody Must Get Stoned." I was wrong. *This* will be in the movie. Forget *Watchtower*, check <u>this</u> out!

Suddenly Bob was leading a half-a-million mudpeople in a massive swaying sing-along of delirium. I don't know what the kids were thinking during this, whether they'd even heard it before, or heard it but didn't know it was Dylan, but the whole place went bananas in a very loud way.

Suddenly, here was some guy they'd heard their parents talk about, singing about getting stoned! You might say it went over well. Not that anybody was stoned or anything. Not that anyone ever gets stoned or anything. But there was a whole lot of Flintstones fans who were very excited their theme song came on. Almost too excited you might say. In fact, everyone was screaming out the line every time Bob even started a verse! And that was fine. At least they were showing some interest in something.

Here we were with classic Bob — throwing out his meaty bone for the monster moshers to mash — and devour it these hungry dogs did. Everything in the garden started popping off like popcorn all around me, POW! POW! POW! — even the normal-looking people suddenly started exploding. And here was Bob, clearly not playing to his own audience — even though this was Woodstock — yet still sending chills through every body in the house.

This wasn't the rock 'n' roll fever of *Watchtower* — it was something a step above that, when every single person, no matter their stripe, condition or age, was channeling the energy and their body was vibrating the way it knows best and everyone from the dad with the papoose to the naked loogan was in their fullest bop mode while Bob put everything into it and the video screens were swirling like psychedelic washing machines and everyone lit a joint so the air was so thick with herb that by the time Bob brought it back around to to the chorus again, another round of dynamite went off firing up the troops past what they could handle and spontaneous combustions started happening everywhere — KA' POWIE! KA' POWIE! KA' BOOM! KA'BOOM!

It really was over-the-top on the old scale of over-the-top musical moments.

Then Dylan made his now-famous, off-hand remark:

"I'd just like to say that I hope that some of the money that's raised, maybe one or two million maybe, be used to free some of the pot farmers in this country."

This of course was the catalyst for a series of benefits to pay Willie Nelson's legal bills.

He followed the electric mayhem rock 'n' roll with the fluttering acoustic angels of paradise to close the show, changing his instrumentation once again to the upright bass, lap steel, acoustic guitar band.

All he did was play *It Ain't Me Babe*, a song I had no particular interest in before, nor most of my fellow campers I assume, yet every one of us stood in rapture as Dylan soothed the audience of bouncing moshers with wooden music that had everyone transfixed, heads cocked in a freakish collective moment of contemplation. The wild rumble was suddenly hushed for the first time since the Indians blessed the field on Friday morning.

There was no reason this should work. When he'd taken the crowd up to the electric rock 'n' roll heights earlier in the show, the audience tuned him out during the acoustic follow-up. But this time every spinning top was frozen even after the frantic dancing "stoned" — they were now glued to his every word, every wooden riff, every escalating run.

Just when it seemed like the final note had been struck and the night was over, Dylan unexpectedly stepped forward and started up one more refrain that took off into the longest, most enchanting instrumental I've ever heard Dylan play in over a decade of cat.

On this run he took the audience away on a harmonic, hypnotic journey that rekindled every challenging musical exploration I ever heard a player work through. He was alternatingly soft and gentle, then furious and troubled, like Cecil Taylor. He was actually taking the lead on the acoustic guitar, but he ended up leading the band and all the rest of us by the hand through the night into the light and then out of sight!

With just an acoustic guitar & harmonica he silenced a half-a-million people — the only time I saw that happen all weekend.

And it was more than that. He played his roots, and made them compelling. He believed in where he came from, no matter how odd and unsuited it seemed, and he stayed at that world until he got it right. Like the lead he was working through in front of us right now, struggling, fumbling, but still playing, staying, working, and finally carrying all of us with him over the precipice and into a heaven of harmony and connectedness that's still in me today.

And his parting sentiment of "It ain't me"

wasn't lost on this sailor either. "The fault, dear Brutus, is not in our stars, but in ourselves," I smiled. Bob may have taken me to about 15 places I didn't think I'd ever see, but it was I who got on board and held the railing through the storm, not him. And when I got back to dry land, it was I who was going to have to act on what was seen, cuz Captain Bob's going back to sea. It was me who was going to have to stay off the Party Train and build the house, sharpen the skates, and write the book, knowing that dreams come true cuz if Woodstock could actually happen again in the middle of a mosh pit in the middle of a rainstorm, anything was possible.

When it was over and people from far away to right beside me were screaming "Bob! Bob! Bob!" I knew I had to get out of there before they turned into pumpkin punk rockers.

What could possibly follow Bob? Well, apparently somebody figured the Red Hot Chili Peppers were a good idea. But that's not my movie. I was in heaven, and intended to stay there. It was time once again to join the Perfect Moment Protection Program.

All weekend I'd been Mr. Cartographer surveying the scene, learning the facts and drawing the maps. Now it was time to operate within those maps.

Coming out through the backstage gate onto Main Street was like stepping into the Mississippi bayou. Dripping thick trees were casting giant moving shadows over the mysterious underworld. For the first time all weekend there was no second stage to go to. There was no alternative to the alternative music. The South Stage was over for the weekend and there was nothing to do until Peter Gabriel. In fact Woodstock was virtually over.

I so badly wanted to scooch along the backstage road to the south stage and see Neil Young. Or Aretha Franklin. Or maybe even Alice Cooper. I mean, I'd only seen the Gospel Singers, the Allman Brothers, Traffic, the Neville Brothers, and Bob Dylan all in one day — and I'm upset there's not more? There is something wrong with me, I know that. It's fatal, it's futile, it's a fungus. But it's a fun fungus.

As long as I'm nowhere near the Very Loud Chili Poppers I'll be fine. "Silence and solitude" became my mantra as I worked my way through the wasted weekend warriors wearily wandering the roadway. I tried to avoid any break in my bliss-thoughts by holding old Halo-head's image in my mind and replaying his words and chords like a hologram memory chip.

Trucks, cars, people, flashing lights, go here, can't go there, clip boards, walkie talkies, long blond babes walking with cell-talking suits, faces hidden in darkness until jeeps' bounced headlights lit their faces like the paparazzi.

It was the same kind of insane surrealism as when I first pulled in. Nothing made sense. Never did. Now worse than ever. If anybody ever tells you any of this made any sense, they're makin' it up.

The Main Street road was very alive with hyperactivity as everyone was trying to cram as much fun in the dwindling hours as they could. It was closing night at The Shining Hotel and Jack was grinnin' crazy.

As I reached the back of the stage, a rather exciting catastrophe was in full bloom. There was only one road running through this town of Woodstock, which except for some mud slides the staff had miraculously kept flowing all weekend. Until now.

And who might be at the center of this catastrophe? That's right, you guessed it. Bob. The omnificent, omniscient, ubiquitous Bob. And what was he doing — you won't even believe it. Instead of turning his bus around in the football stadium-sized parking lot they built behind the stage to do just that, he was trying to back his space shuttle bus-train out and around and up the wazoo. He had not one, but two giant oversized Supercharger buses, each with a dinky dinghy trailer attached like he's hauling his beach toys around or something. Plus there's one car in front like a police escort and an army of support vehicles in back. And so this whole entire entourage monster decided it had to pull out immediately and the freaking Secret Service was brought in to do it, and suddenly there were walkie talkies in the middle of the road, and yellow jackets and blue jackets, and Hell's Angels in full colors, and for the first time all weekend the main road was completely shut down.

First the security guys had to stop all the traffic on the only road out of the sight. Then they had to put this mile-long snake of cars into reverse cuz they didn't stop the cars soon enough. Just when there was enough room for Bob's Jumbo Jet to taxi out, an impatient throng of people had formed in both directions on Main Street, all trying to get past during their climactic Sunday night fun, then as soon as the bus would be all ready to back up one more inch, some twit would walk right in front and stop the whole process.

And every second there's this growing line down the entire single lane road winding through the site, probably leading all the way to Manhattan by now. For miles back, bus loads of wet and tired people were asking, "What's the problem?" And here, all the way at the front, one calamity after another is happening as the bus backs into a ditch, then gets stuck, then tries to pull forward but has no room and they have to clear everything for it to back up one more time, then there's that twit again, and nothing, no matter how hard they squeeze this bus will it fit out the exit. They're trapped, we're trapped, the road backs up, and Grrrrrrr. And meanwhile Bob's inside going, "Are we there yet?"

So this goes on for hours, I could tell you a lot more, but it was only a comic aside to the very serious mission I was on which was searching for inner-peace and tranquility. I was searching for a mountaintop. I was searching to protect my perfect moment. I was searching for, oh heck, a cold beer and a chair at this point would work.

Usually after monumental experiences I wander alone in Central Park absorbing the silence in solitude. Tonight I had to settle for the dripping, eerie, back streets of Woodstock, where shadows moved like movies and ghosts skirted the periphery. Clouds were blowing past a brilliant crescent moon just enough to set the werewolves to howling and prowling through the woods in the darkness.

God Knows.

I stuck to the streets, which were like an old west town, where roads were paved with mud, people lived by the Code of the West, and nobody had to play sheriff. The trailblazing cowboys rode through town, and wild west girls would flash them some skin. It was the freedom just before civilization moved in.

Like a homing magnet, the touchstone buzz center of the Media Tent was pulling me in again. It was the Grand Central Station of information and people and energy and things. If the van was my bedroom, this was my office. It was the chance to pass Go and pick up your next Mystery Adventure Card. I never did find the $200.

As I slid down the sloppy runway into it I saw the video monitor and omnificent "Holy cats! Jimmy Cliff's on! *What?!* There's still more music!? Those crazy Rastas are still playing?!" I blurted, as I rushed out of the tent and along the backstage road to Cliff's pulsating tribal drums, weaving through Dylan's traffic jam of ragged clowns and roving gamblers to catch My God! the final act on the South Stage! The two-stage Woodstock fantasy was still alive — once again ringing the bell of the Dream Come True meter!

It was around 10:00 when I rushed into the field and the entire rhythm of my body and the earth slowed right down to the funky groove of reggae-time, mun.

All dressed in black exactly like Dylan, Cliff was bouncing all over the stage as he sang. This guy is all Spirit. After the intellectual whiteboy music, here was a soulman chanting and flipping his body like a possessed medicine man.

Samba Reggae is a hybrid of Brazilian and Jamaican rhythms, and there isn't better dance music. I couldn't believe I was seeing this in the dark mud spirits of the night. I always knew the guy was touched, and thought it was so cool that it wasn't gonna just be him, but — it was Jimmy Cliff's All Star Review! featuring Rita Marley, Toots, Eek-A-Mouse, and lotsa friends. And here he was in front of us proving why they were all in his band and not the other way around. He had the whole field in a frenzy. And there was Sunday night dancing room! And people were using it! From in front of the stage all the way up the hill and outta sight roving spotlights illuminated the smiling faces of a swirling, dancing, energy flow.

"Don't watch the clock; We're rockin at Woodstock," Jimmy joked to the organic audience of people who didn't want to catch Dylan or anyone else. Here, hidden away in the South Stage pocket late on Sunday night, were spiritual travelers lost in the same trance that was started by the Neville Brothers this afternoon, maintained by Santana, and now conducted by Maestro Cliff leading the faithful over the top. These were the soulful, the radiant, the divine. The ones who came to Touch The Earth, to feel her pulse, to dance for joy. All you had to do was step onto the field to be under the spell of these collective witch doctors.

"You know, I'm getting to like this guy," I'm thinking, as he broke into *Wonderful World, Beautiful People*. It was all too much, but I was still holding out hope for *The Harder They Come*, although I knew he'd been playing for an hour so it was probably behind us. But simply seeing Jimmy Cliff was always a dream of mine. And right after seeing Dylan at Woodstock! Back-to-back Dreams-Come-True. *Double points.* And on a Sunday. On acid. *Bonus!*

Dilemma: Going from the best steak dinner of your life with Dylan, then somebody puts a plate of the best looking sushi you've ever seen right in front of you. You're stuffed, but what do you do? You're screwed! You either ruin your steak by eating, or you pass up the second best meal of your life. Guess what I did?

Ha-ha. I over-ate. Stuff me! I'll sort it out tomorrow. 'Scuse me while I kiss the sky. Losing it to a reggae beat. Marley — no, wait, Cliff — was dancing like a lava lamp on high, floating across the stage on waves of rhythm from his amazing 7,000 piece band. Naturally being what Jagger aspires to, this guy moves like he *is* music, every fiber swinging with Charlie Parker cool. He's the rainbow organic Dylan of reggae music, dancing his heart out to us, singing his heart out, praying, making us *move*. He's been making people dance for about as long as Dylan has, and he's still doing it tonight, skinny as a honky joint, singing and shining brilliance. Who'd-a-thunk this at the first "hope-I-die-before-I-get-old" festival?

And then with no one at all giving the slightest warning, he broke into *The Harder They Come!* "YES!" I screamed, leaping fist-first in the air like a teenager, followed by several minutes of bongo bonkers crazy dancing. There in the climactic mud of Woodstock, Jimmy Cliff began singing about the sun shining and everybody sharing.

It was the whole essence and key to Cliff, the movie, his life, the greatest reggae song that Bob Marley didn't write, his *Like A Rolling Stone*, the magic culmination, the final music card in the reggae deck to complete the set. Being free, I'd rather be.

Uncontrollable hyper-active reggae frenzy dancing, spinning in circles, bouncing spell back and forth between all the surrounding reggae spirits. The mud, the people, all slip away, and a unified chanting rhythm blissfully assumed control. "The harder they come . . ." we all sang without trying. Hyperspeed head-shaking lost-motion space-like elastics snapping back – one and all.

Good God of all spiritual beings, I feel you! Sacred center, pull of the earth, the music, every heartbeat, every spinning twist, every surging vein of truth serum cleansing the soul and turning the wheel of tranquility. Dizzy spinning triple axles, uncontrollable beat-keeping frenzy of Mother Nature's energy, good God, yes, God ... YES!

Two over-the-tops were more than I could handle. Didn't need to see more. Couldn't. Had to get out of there and preserve what just happened. Still working on *It Ain't Me Babe* — now *this!* Too unexpected. Jimmy Cliff! The greatest living reggae song. God help me. Can't go on much longer. I stumbled for the exit. Find trees, find a field, find peace. The dancing swarms, the crazy cross-pollinated reggae dancers tantalizing every foot of the field, more energy to channel in every direction, but I had to take what I had gathered from coincidence and hold onto it. A divine moment of energy infusion, of something tranquil hitting the soul, and I didn't know what it was. I had to get out and let it settle.

I made my way out of the muddy river field in search of the hidden valleys in the fiber of Woodstock nation. The mud, the walk, the tranquil focus in a slippery world again. The peace of moving among friends. Survivors of the rock 'n' roll wars. No matter my condition of peaking frenzied acid insanity, I didn't look any weirder than anyone else. For once.

Every person was beyond the edge in one way or another, and we all respected and accepted each other for that.

The human river road of hope was flowing through Woodstock, every tiny drop on its way to destiny, whether to more oceans of Adventure or home to the city. Everyone being themselves, mud equalling all. No polo shirts, no-out-of-place anyone. No class, no power, no stature. Everyone on equally slippery footing in an irrational mudworld. You could imagine all the people living life in peace. For one moment the door opened and a few thousand more walked through it. There is a chance. Lines of communication were getting clearer. There were more of us. More minds to drop into. More reasons to celebrate. I know it was only one weekend, but there were more obstacles on this survival course than on most of the 18 holes I've played. Getting to Sunday was like crossing that marathon finish line — where you shiver a tingle with everyone who made it.

Then out of the haze, while drifting along the road in paradise, I heard, "Cold beers. Two bucks. I'm serious."

Holy shit. No way!

"Beer's on."

I looked over. A dusty red car was half off the road. No hubcaps — oh my God — it looks like it's — check the plates — Friendly Manitoba! It is! Johnny Dodger's wide eyes and open arms were rushing across the mud towards me!

"Hassett!"

"Johnny!"

I was suddenly embraced in a massive spinning bear-hug, and Woodstock was twirling in a drink-splashing swirl. Winnipeg. Johnny. Johnny Dodger! River Heights! At last! He's alive and well. And selling beer! Not only did he get his car in, he's opened a business!

"It's you! I can't believe it! You're here! Where you been? How long you been here?"

"All weekend. I've been here the whole time. Here and everywhere else. Except Friday I went to Bethel."

"You went to Bethel?!?!"

"You want a beer?"

"How was it?"

"Oh it was great, buddy. Neil Young was going to play today, or Saturday, I'm not sure," as Johnny went on with his daily affirmation that Neil Young was going to show up somewhere near him. He'd been doing it for years even before it actually happened, and the two of them ended up smoking a joint sitting on this very car back in the Peg, but ever since then, like Elvis, Johnny sees him everywhere. "And Bono, and Pearl Jam . . ." Johnny was still going on about all these people he wanted to believe were going to be there at Yasgur's.

"Why did you come back?"

"It was shitty. Plus I had this," he said proudly holding out his Press laminate. I'd worked all my life to get mine, or at least a made a few phone calls, and now Johnny had one too?!

"How did you get that?" I asked, surprised though I shouldn't have been.

"It was a long night involving a lot of rum and some really cute girls," he laughed, handing me a Molson Export with one hand while he sold a Miller with the other. There was a constant stream of people buying beer at his ridiculously low price of $2. I'd already seen him rake in a mint since I'd been standing there, but I also saw the last beers of my generation distributed by madness and dwindle down to about 12, so I immediately shut down his operation in the interest of future liquidity.

On acid you can operate on a razor's edge of timing perfection with everything falling neatly into place without a thought about it. If I'd stayed for one more song at Cliff, Johnny would have been sold out of beer and wandered away. Acid makes the mind and body work at a different speed than usual. It can slow things down so you can catch falling objects like they're standing still. Or you can slip through doors that only open for an instant.

It connects people who need to be or want to be brought together, whenever they want to be. I hadn't seen Johnny since we got separated Thursday night, then I take acid and Boom, there he is! The molecular pull, the instinctual homing to the person or place that's the same as you. It proves it can be done. Telepathy becomes a fact of life and just another way to communicate. Energy becomes tangible and visible. And if it's tangible and visible, you know it's still there when the acid wears off. You've seen what's possible, and then you can make the choice to go play the rest of your life in the energy gardens you discovered on your trip.

"I'll have two, please."

I copped a squat on "the Neil Young seat" on the hood of his car and somebody in the circle of people that always surrounds Johnny twisted a fern and started telling his story. Johnny and I smiled at each other. We've heard more weird tales in more weird places with more weird people than with anybody else I know.

"So you're not gonna believe what happened, right?" this guy begins. "I was selling grass, quarters for fifty, eighths for twenty-five, and I'm doing great. People are buying. Made, like, $700. Then I'm over in the Eco-Village right? near the mud slide down to the riverbed, and all of a sudden I feel this little tug around my waist and this guy undoes my fanny-pack with all my cash and takes off up the hill! And it's like, 'No way,' right?"

"So I take off after him, but it's like way-muddy, and I'm slipping all over the place and yelling, and then all of sudden I'm going too fast and it's super muddy and there's this whole, like, *family* sitting there all on the ground and there was no way I could stop and I just ran into the first guy and just went flying! It was really fucked up, man. There I was laying in the lap of this like . . . *mother*, and some guy's taking off with my wallet. And these people are screaming at me, and the guy I hit is all bent over holding his back yelling, 'Get his name, get his address, you're not gonna get away with this!' And she starts feeling me up for my wallet, but I'm like, 'Lady, somebody just *stole* my wallet.' And they're like, 'Yeah right,' and they're not even gonna let me go and meanwhile this cat with my wallet and all my money and everything is in like fuckin' Kansas!

"So anyway, my life's like totally over right? Everything's gone. It's hours later, I've been living off these stupid plastic coins they have here," he says holding out a handful of the Woodstock scrip. "Which I don't even know what's the deal with *these*. Here, you want some?" he says, handing me a palmful of real fake money. "And all of sudden this dude tells me they found a wallet right? 'Like, maybe it's yours.' And I'm like, 'No way.'"

And *I'm* like, "No way." Don't tell me this is Mr. Lost Wallet they were talking about from the stage all day!

"So, finally I go over to the security office, right?" he goes on. "And they've, like, *got* my wallet! And the whole $700 is still in it. Every cent! Can you believe it?" he says, flipping open the wallet and showing all the money and family photos and old withered stuff he'd obviously carried with him for years. "This is my whole life, man," he said. "The guy must of dropped it while he was running or something, and somebody turned it in. Is that the coolest thing or what?" he asked, his red, frenzied, passionate eyes looking up into mine, bleeding with sincerity and tearing at the edges like someone who's been through too much.

I looked over at Johnny. He was smiling and shaking his head.

But it was Johnny's head, Johnny's face, that wide beaming smile that had laughed through every memory I ever had it seemed; the twinkling, sparkling eyes that danced through my every teenage milestone; that I had produced Woodstock reunion concerts with. This dream of my life was talking to me.

"Hey come on, let's go for a stroll," he said, and we loaded up a half-dozen freezing Molsons and left his car with a cackle of people still sitting on it.

"This is amazing!" I said, bopping up and down in the mud. "How long have you been here? How did you ever get *your car in here?*"

"Hi John," some young cutie says as she passes.

"Oh you're not going to believe it," he begins, nodding his head to the strange girl and starting his next story without missing a beat. He told me how he scammed the pass by staying up drinking all night with the girls in charge, how he snuck his car in by pretending he was with a film crew, and sneaking back out to get more film, then looking for beer to sell backstage. He had every detail down, and could remember every girl's name he'd met for three days.

"So finally after driving about 20 miles I find

one guy selling cases of Millers for 30 bucks. 24 for 30, you know? So I bought four of those."

"So you laid out $120 for beer right there?!"

"Yeah, yeah, just knowing that I could resell it, of course," he said, as some curly-haired high school student walked by.

"Hey Johnny," she smiled. I just looked at him in disbelief.

We were approaching the busy hive behind the North Stage. Survivors were buzzing all over the roads in various directions. "Should we drop in on the Chili Peppers for half a song?" I bounced, figuring he'd probably know everyone there.

"We should, but we shouldn't, you know?" he said in a famous Johnnyism. He had a perfect, simple wisdom for everything. He based every action on instinct and what feels right. He has a simple honesty of action with a sure compass, and a firm but loose grip on the rudder, you know? The Peppers were history going down before us, a hand we could always play in future Adventure Card poker games, but Johnny held the one-on-one moment in the same esteem I did.

"Hey, lemme show you where live," I said, as we happened to be facing down Main Street toward it.

"Great!" For the very first time I was actually going to be sharing my Thoreauian cabin with a fellow wandering woodsman of this sacred Walden Pond of Woodstockian Mud. And it wasn't just any wanderer — but the principle roving, raving Woodstock Ambassador from my homeland! The guy I used to stage Woodstock reunion concerts with every teenage summer was walking beside me at a real Woodstock, in New York state, where Bob Dylan just played, and we were backstage together with a satchel full of ice cold beer waiting for some really good band to come on. Or was I dreaming? I looked over at my apparition.

"So then I had to *beg* this guy I bought the Millers from for ice," he was still talking as I zoomed back in. Nope. This is real. I couldn't even be *dreaming* this. "But the guy wouldn't give me any. And I was just, 'Ah shit, you've got ice, sell us some,' but he wouldn't. So I drove down the road and there's no ice *any*where. Everything's sold out for miles. I've got 96 Millers for $120, which was the last money I had, and they're warm as piss.

"So I get back to the entrance, the guy recognizes me, and I'm in! So I drive up to where you saw me by the South Stage, and all of a sudden I see some staff guy pulling this wagon of ice! He was walking by the South Stage tents and canteens, eh? So I run after him, and I go, 'Look can you sell me some ice?' And he sold me some!" Johnny said, clapping his hands together and smiling. "Quite cheap. A dollar a bag! I bought four and just piled them in the cooler."

"A dollar a bag?! He could have sold them for twenty!"

"I know, I know, it was great," he smiled. "So I sold half the beers really fast — made $100 American and went over and caught Dylan."

"Fantastic!" I toasted, and we both tipped up

our cold ones in unison like kicking Rockettes.

Then suddenly we were right in front of my van. "Check out the view," I said, sweeping my hand across the misty nighttime audience. Spotlights filled the field with eerie light, highlighting the smoky wisps that were blowing across like gunsmoke after the bombs bursting in air.

The lights from the stage were turning all the faces from red to green to blue to yellow as we watched in silence from quiet Main Street as swells of cheering rose from one section and rolled across the endless audience like an ocean wave. And I just soaked in Johnny soaking in the spectacle for a Woodstock Minute.

Then we turned around and I introduced him to the KarmaCoupe.

It was like showing your old teacher your graduate science project. "See, here's what I made after I left," holding out your hands in pride. Here was my friend Johnny, sharing in my home and making it real for the first time because someone else saw it. He immediately fit right in, stepping up on the door frame balcony to survey the field with the roof as a table and a beer in his hand. Just like me. Or was I just like him?

I'd been so blissfully alone all weekend, and now I had my oldest friend in the world here to sing out the climax. I'd preserved my peace of mind, focused my search, maintained my home, and now here was a friend to give it life and context in the final act.

After a long beautiful silence, I finally suggested, "We should probably go do one last site tour before Gabriel. We'll be able to hear the Chili Peppers from anywhere," I smiled.

"Sure," he said, interrupting only briefly another story about some other cute girl he'd met. "Oh she was just perfect," he was saying. "But she was kind of way too young. Or she wouldn't have been way too young if her mom wasn't there!" and he was off. "She was 17, gorgeous, and just mmmmm," he said, shivering at the memory, as I led him up the hill towards the backstage showers.

The hillside had been beaten in. The repeated successions of rain and people had gorged the land to gooey, sticky clay suction cups, but we kept plodding through it, Johnny slip-sliding away but never breaking his narrative. "And her *mom* was at the original Woodstock, and she's *in the photograph*! One of the photographs — the guy had it on display – and *there she is*!"

We got up to the highest road on site and looked back at the muddy masterpiece — like the set for *Apocalypse Now* with a *Star Wars* spaceship of a stage under a mountain of low hanging clouds.

We walked along the high road sharing Adventure Cards in rapid succession, me pointing out the secret showers, he pointing out it wasn't raining, me pointing out the security guards to the performer's area up ahead, he pointing out we should turn our passes around so the backs show and we smoothly walk through with the cluster of other luminaries ahead. It was nice to be with a fellow pranking pro again. Johnny just laughed. "Kay, just act normal, ha-ha-ha."

"Absolutely fucking normal," I thought, as we plodded down the hill toward the dressing room trailers, the spotlights illuminating this high security zone making it look more like a penitentiary. There were guards in every direction and we were walking straight through in our fake uniforms like Billy at the end of *Midnight Express* where any moment someone might notice and yell, "Hey you! Stop those men," and there was nowhere left to run to anymore.

"Hey!" Johnny suddenly blurted. "I was in here before!" he exclaimed, all happy as a child. "It was this *guy* . . . he was half-Japanese, half-English, he looked sort of like John Lennon."

"*John Lennon!*" I thought. "You met a guy who looked like *John Lennon?*" I asked.

"*Yeeeeees,*" he stressed. "He was this total character, knew everyone. We met at the bleachers, and . . ." Johnny was off on another story, but I was thinking, "John Lennon? What's he *doing* here all weekend?!" And I looked up in that big sky above me and remembered the snow falling over his memorial service at the bandshell in Central Park.

We came upon a party outside Michael Lang & Company's trailers, so naturally Johnny and I were on it like flies at a picnic. Surveying the cluster of closing-night late-night hard-core crazies milling about with their cocktails and cameras, Johnny immediately zeroed in on the prettiest girl who wasn't taller than him and started talking to her, "This is great, eh?"

"It SUCKS," she said.

"Alright. Good start, Johnny," I stage whispered right behind him.

"I'm totally pissed. I want to be seeing the Red Hot Chili Peppers but MY STUPID DAD just keeps talking to people and now I'm going to MISS THE WHOLE THING," the little girl said really loud in the direction of a circle of bald spots.

"Oh come on," Johnny said laughing. "You must have seen something you liked earlier. Catch Dylan?"

She turned really slowly with that rising anger of some Linda Blair devil-child and screamed, "I HATE BOB DYLAN! HE'S OLD AND *STUPID*."

"Oh," Johnny said, sounding dejected, but still laughing. "Kay. See ya ha-ha-ha." And we both snuck away like we just broke something.

"Who do you want to talk to now, Mr. Cool?" I asked. But I didn't have to. He'd already spotted a cute Long Island brunette and was moving in like a cat on a bird.

"Do you know where the Gabriel trailer is?" he asked her.

"Why? Who are you?" she asked. We both suddenly noticed she had a few extra laminates dangling under her jean jacket as though she might actually do something.

"I'm John," he says, sticking out his hand. "We just came down from Canada. Well I did, he lives in New York," he whispered for emphasis. "What's your name?" And she's looking back and forth between me and Johnny and I'll bet part of what she was thinking involved, Who are these clowns?

"I'm, ah ... What are you doing here?" She was fairly to the point, and we like that. Sometimes.

"We're with a Canadian film crew, eh?" he said. "We've just had a great time. Everyone here's been so nice. What do you do?"

"I'm a director of security," she said, shooting him between the legs.

"No waaay," Johnny laughed. "You look so small to be a security person. Well, you know, you'd expect the security guy to be ... well, a guy for starters," he laughed again. "We're just waiting for one of our reporters to come back. We're heading back to Yasgur's. There's a half-million people there too."

"What?" the increasingly sexy federale said. "I thought it was dead."

"We were there. We saw it," he went on out of nowhere. "Neil Young played this afternoon, and Eddie Vedder's playing tonight."

"You're kidding," she said, looking back and forth between us like we're suddenly her two best friends.

"Yeeeeah," Johnny insisted. "There's more

people there than here. That's why we're going back. But you have to leave during Gabriel or you'll never get out," he said, as though he was passing on the tip of the weekend.

"I'm working," she said. "Neil Young played today?"

"Yeah, that's what three different people who were there told me, *including* the guy at the hotel where he stayed," Johnny went on. "You think the roads are bad around here! Cars are driving all over the fields over there, and the state troopers are trying to get it under control, but its a total mess, so just be careful if you go," he said.

"Thanks," she said, lost in thought. "Okay, you guys take care now, and good luck getting over there," she said, walking off as though trying to figure something out.

Johnny was making funny faces at me and laughing without making any sound. I shook my head at the ease with which he improvised, and wondered why he did it. He intentionally puts himself in strange situations, then makes them stranger just for the fun of it, then extracts himself Houdini-like whenever he wants. It's a fairly peculiar particular skill, but he has it.

"Lets get out of here and have some fun. These people are too straight," he said, waving his hand around this CentCom. "Let's go find more fun people."

So we wandered over to the Center For Non-

Working People — the V.I.P. Tent — which was still half full of straight-streets at 11:30 on Sunday night. Johnny insisted we sit down at one of the empty tables and collect the Adventure Card for the tent by smoking a bomber, drinking a beer, and watching the Chili Peppers on the crispy monitors.

It was like being at the end of a big wedding when some people are passed out on chairs, and the rest are passed out under tables. Even Johnny, the human conversation machine, was silenced. "You know what this is?" he leaned forward. "Bored kids waiting for their rich parents to drive them home."

I looked over his shoulder at the awake ones sitting in chairs watching TV, and wondered what kind of a life would lead you to be sitting in a tent while sex, drugs, rock 'n' roll, and majic were going on all around you but you'd rather watch it on TV.

"We better keep moving," I suggested. "We gotta keep one step ahead of whatever this is. It looks degenerative."

"And I prefer progenerative any day," Johnny declared, standing up for himself and leading us out of Sick Bay.

We sashayed back into the silliness of the night. The Häagen-Dazs tent seemed to have a smidgen more life to it, and just as we were about step inside, some dude in a giant cone costume appeared out of nowhere and says, "I'm sorry you can't come in here."

"Oh really?" Johnny said.

"You need an invitation."

"What do you have to do to get an invitation?" he asked.

"Well, basically sell Häagen-Dazs ice cream," the cone buzzkill said.

Oh. As we turned around to leave, I began hollering, "HÄAGEN-DAZS FOR SALE! COME GET YOUR COLD HÄAGEN-DAZS ICE CREAM HERE. HÄAGEN-DAZS!" And Johnny and I took off before the cone could grab us.

When we got back behind the stage again, everyone from security guards to party buffalos had had very little sleep since about Tuesday and a lot of the scene was functioning on hand signals at this point. The drivers knew the roads and the pedestrians knew the ropes and everything flowed with a little less friction. Even the ever-popular battle between "The Big Drunk Guys Trying To Crash Backstage vs. The Big Drunk Security Guys Who Say No" had devolved into a soft, puffy touching of the tummies, like two doughboys bumping into one another and bouncing off in slow motion then drifting through outer space.

While I was watching the floating spacemen, I realized I was using Johnny as my lifeline to Earth. He was allowing me to be more free because there was at least one pair of non-acid-spinning eyes. I took the opportunity to let him direct my traffic while I sat in the backseat and hallucinated like crazy.

"So that was Friday night, and I ended up sleeping in the coat check room at the Tuck, until the owner came in in the morning, and ..." Johnny was still rolling on while the lights of the stage were fire breathing dragons blowing rainbow colored flames into the clouds of smoke that were ominously drifting everywhere like some movie bad-guy was about to appear.

There was this gigantic futuristic spacestage like some 2001 space station — two times the size of a rocket ship, steaming smoke everywhere, with all these shiny metallic poles and painted scrims and lightning rods shooting up to the sky, and here I was, one tiny human next to this pulsating Enterprise. It was about to indoctrinate us by sucking us into its gaping maw and we'd never be the same again, ha-ha-ha. And it was following me!

I turned away real quick cuz if you don't look at bad things they go away. Or at least they do on acid. If only life could be more like acid. Note to self.

It was a spooky dark wet night under dark wet trees. It didn't seem possible to be slopping through mud in the crudest backwoods hog-pen farm while next to this technologically futuristic billion-dollar Disneyland erected in the middle of it. I turned back once more cuz who can resist one last peek and saw the lights and heard the roar and it seemed like the spaceship was about to lift off right then. It just didn't seem possible the two worlds could be existing in the same place. Performers had the most high-tech sound system and computerized video screens ever invented while the audience lived in the mud with less shelter than farm animals.

"And *then*, I met up with this guy who did the insurance for this whole thing," Johnny was saying as I noticed we seemed to be back at the KarmaCoupe.

The final cocktail. The final moments. The final band to close Woodstock. And here's my oldest friend in the world, I suddenly remembered. Talking. "But he was a *hoooowl*, eh? He was just an old drunk, and he'd stay up till six in the morning trying to hustle up the women in the lobby, and he was just this *character* to hang out with till about six," Johnny told me. "Beyond six he was a nightmare."

I pulled out two ice cold ones from the cooler and raised one to him. "Good Adventuring," we tinged.

The Chili Peppers were over and we could hear the echoes of distant stage announcements. "*Ahhhhhhh*," Johnny screamed, laughing. "This is great!" as he scrunched down for emphasis. "So what was your favorite performance of the weekend?"

I thought for a second about Sheryl Crow and Aerosmith and the seven John Lennon sightings, but it was still no contest. "Mother Nature's rainstorm on Saturday, and that encore sunset tonight."

I slid the van door open the rest of the way in her honor, and Johnny stepped up and stood on the runner. We both looked over at the smoke blowing across the dark field. We were surrounded by million dollar production vehicles stretching for miles, and the biggest stage ever constructed by man. And millions of people. And yet it was eerily quiet — like an encampment of soldiers awaiting battle. The assembled, the millions, the minions, the troops; the field full of tents and troopers, survivors, and warriors by the thousand — but it was hauntingly quiet. How could so many people make so little noise? Spooky. But we had a great box seat and could stick our heads inside the van when we got scared.

After some silent soaking reverence, Johnny leaned his bottle over and tapped mine. "This takes initiative, Hassett," he said. "To be here now," as we both reflected on all the hoops we had to jump through to share this moment.

We stood in silence on that van runner as strange barks of people interrupted the night like howls anywhere in America. Inaudible stage announcements rumbled in the distance like a New York subway. But mostly it was silence. Silence and bliss . . . in the really late Woodstockian night.

"Crick, cric-crick. Crick, cric-crick."

"You hear that?" I turned to Johnny. Yes! Crickets.

The farm was starting to take itself back already. We invaders weren't even done with our fun, but the slightest weakening in our forces and nature was right back in here again. "Driven little critters," I thought.

"Crick, cric-crick. Crick, cric-crick."

We both stood in the cricking silence looking

over the field, and listening as more and more of them rose their legs to the rhythm and a stronger and stronger groove grew until we were both bopping our heads to their beat. Once again my favorite performer was making us rock.

These were the last moments I would spend with Johnny, who I staged these things with in a schoolyard in my youth, and here we were, together around my van with the final band yet to come, the last moments to savor before the final unknown would be known.

You can't buy that.

Then Earth-link Johnny at Mission Control, monitoring the airwaves and his cosmic AWACS, picked up that the Angel Gabriel was approaching. I could feel the tug of his lifeline pulling me back to Spaceship Earth. I had to trust him — perhaps there *was* something more interesting on earth than the Buddy Holly crickets and sacred leaves of grass surrounding the sacred van that got me to this sacred place. The next thing I know we're slip-sliding along the muddy trail of Main Street, hand-in-metaphoric-hand to the last waltz.

It was midnight on the final night, and sure enough, in the distance, the spaceship had landed, baring the Angel Gabriel, noises whirring, lights spinning, and we were all about to be taken to a place far more beautiful than we'd been all weekend.

Then wouldn't-you-know-it but Mother Nature came through again with *The Crickets' Last*

Reprise (for Buddy Holly) — this time they're actually, yes, working *with* the spaceship . . . in this kind of — *rhythm.* I don't know who was working with who (or "whom" as the owls hoot) but the whole cricket tribe of the farm had risen up and were joining in with their human invaders in a massive backing choir to Gabriel's *Come Talk To Me* drum beat overture, grounding us to the earthen mud while a technicolor child was swirling and birthing to life before us, as the rainforest canopy hanging over Main Street amplified their delicate song better than any million dollar sound system could, as we walked through the Gates of Gabriel into the oozing mass stretching out to the horizon.

Everything became approximate. In fact I doubt I'll be able to hold the signal much longer. "She's breakin' up, Captain." Lord Sydney was taking over and making the ground shake just for the fun of it. And just for fun, I followed Johnny . . . right along the front of the stage into a brand new world of tall mud-graffiti-covered walls in front of the stage as tall as the Empire State it seemed completely covered in writing: Sparkey's Acid Shop, Fortunes $1, Backrubs for Beer, Hugs are still Free!

An entire strip mall had sprung up in the heart of the city. And it had seen some serious decay already! Deep holes were pounded into the earth. Casualties covered the ground. The wall was Berlin, with layer upon layer of graffiti obliterating successive generations. A walkway ran along the edge so you could visit each of the stores and admire at the artwork of mud on the wall.

Of course from here you couldn't actually *see* Gabriel unless he came out and leaned over the front of the stage, and after Adventure Captain Johnnyman tried negotiating a passage for about 15 seconds, we both decided instead of this cramped approach we'd opt for dancing and seeing.

As we shadow danced back out from the inside, you could see all the faces lit up from the stage lights, and peer secretly right into their thoughts — their fears at not having it together, their joy that their hero was on stage before them, their wishing their boyfriend would hurry up and *what's he doing?* — all skipping past like telepathic channel-surfing.

Following like a water-skier in the wake of Johnny's boat, I shushed along until we found the perfect island in the middle of the wavy ocean, the sacred spot, barely a hundred feet in front of the stage, the closest I'd been for a major act in hours, and we immediately set up the equilateral triangular sightlines with the perfect split-view of the stage and the animation screens.

And boy was Gabriel huge! The back-of-the-field routine was so yesterday baby — tonight everything was wide open. Except for the hardcore pit right in front of the stage, everyone had dancing room all the way to the horizon. Perfect view. Perfect space. Johnny's face.

"How about this stage?" I asked him, this being

the first act we'd seen together and likely the last, what with the scheduling and all.

He rolled his eyes to heaven. "Best thing I've ever seen, no doubt about it."

"Best thing I've ever *even seen a picture of*," I countered.

"Yep, you're right," he said, the two of us nodding like professionals in the field.

"Or ever even *heard* of," I said.

"No, you're right," he nodded again, concluding the issue.

After a few more tumblers fell into place I said, "So that makes this, what we're looking at, the most beautiful stage ever built." I couldn't let it go.

He paused to consider it a thoughtful moment, and then finally turned and uttered these words I live by: "I think you're right."

If only more people could live by that simple ethic, we'd all be so much better off. Or at least I would.

Then Gabriel broke into *Steam* from his new album and showed why he had the Jimi Hendrix slot. The coveted closing spot had fallen to a man few of us would have picked in advance, but who could write, play, sing, arrange, inspire, and cut across the decades like an ageless sage.

Where The Band excelled at the honest lumberjack jamming roots of rock 'n' roll, Gabriel was a computerized conductor of orchestrated perfection. And obviously he's been hanging around the world beat in 80 ways, cuz Englishmen just don't come this funky.

In 750,000 watts of clear digital sound, he sang about dreamers dreaming in a repetitive chant and I just kept thinking how this whole spectacle was *my* dreamer's dream: Even to this moment in the late Sunday madness, everyone was smiling to one another, young to old, women to men, person to person. All across the universe of the battlefield a oneness was blowing though everyone's hair, a hard rain kissing our faces and connecting us all with God's green spaces, our ancestral traces, linking the races, making us holy, and making us high. MUSIC!

High tension, high wire, high hopes of holding it together when Peter keeps turning up the *Steam* — real as any thing you see — I dare say, as the Cat in the Hat suddenly bounded by with a white rabbit in tow.

Out of the front of the stage industrial bolts of steam were shooting out like James Bond's evil villain's secret fortress, filling the landscape with billowing clouds and obliterating half of everything you saw.

The audience had rallied behind the extravaganza and it was the most unified response of the weekend. There was no one else we were waiting for, so you were into it or you were gone. We all knew this was it, and Gabriel was up there painting an electric, eclectic cross-generational masterpiece. Ageless, he shone through the years like the flame of hope, with no barrier, no exclusions, only this cumulative celebration of rock 'n' roll to charge your batteries for the next 25 years. Everyone who was left was singing the words, punching the air, and screaming out their joy like laughter personified.

"This is more than I can take," he seems to be singing in that funkiest of all bridges, my whole body twitching like a Marcel Marceau strobe dance without the lights in some sort of spastic release of limbs expressing themselves and following the muse of the music wherever it took them. And the ground began to disappear as the thumping bass kept my heartbeat and the melody drove my mind which was operating on no function whatsoever except actually *becoming*, no longer alive, no longer a man, an energy field of color, light, infinite space, blue, white, energy, MUSIC!

And before you knew it he's playing *Digging In The Dirt*, which had two or three different meanings you could think of right off the bat *besides* the Woodstockian mud — the places we don't want to look at, the scary bits when we know we're wrong and we've got to change our lives, opening up the wounds, no locked rooms, the self — sticking your whole face in the gaping maw of your own truth, as he keeps singing and I keep digging and Johnny keeps dancing and Peter keeps demanding we look.

Then to make the point, he puts on a helmet with a built-in camera sticking off the front of it like the light on a miner's hardhat, but it was on a flexible pole and he would bend around so the fisheye lens was pointed right at his face, broadcasting absurd close-ups on the giant video screens as he was singing about looking inside ourselves.

At some point in this dreamscape soul-escape Youssou N'Dour appeared — a rich layered honey voice harmonizing in the fluid energy, liquefying molecules and adding another flow.

Johnny and I were both giddy and had lost each other, at least conversationally. We danced, nearly crying for joy, caught in the headlights of oncoming magic and overtaken by a blockbuster neither one of us anticipated.

"Mind-boggling," Johnny leaned over, crazed and sweating, barely able to extract the word, lost on the other side. We were both nothing but blooming energy now — colored leaves soaking in the Gabriel light and guzzling the liquid sound.

"I'm glad we're in the audience and not the bleachers. It's better here," I managed to get out to Johnny, pointing at the ground and trying to interact to prove I still could. But it was useless. We were both goners. I wanted to share some thoughts, but the archangel Gabriel had lifted us both to heaven and it didn't seem English was spoken in that purely molecular universe.

"I'm just tripping right now. Seriously," Johnny finally said, even though he hadn't taken acid in years.

"Early signs of an epiphany," I figured.

Realizing he was next up for an audience with

God, and being a deeply religious man myself, as well as actually blazing, I happily took the opportunity to re-enter the solo dancehall — which is pretty much where I stayed the rest of the night, weekend, and my life, come to think of it.

But back at Woodstock, Gabriel was *talking.* Yes! He was telling some story like a giant-sized Hans Christian Anderson (meets Max Headroom) about "an Apache brave who was running away from a trumped-up murder charge, sort of like Leonard Peltier," and he told a whole story about medicine men and having visions on mountaintops, and at the end, the last thing I heard Johnny say was, "Alright. Here we go." And the universe of man began to blissfully slip away.

No more were we honking in the same flock. I had been set free by the angelic haze of incommunicable bliss between us — the chance to soar away solo and explore the possibilities Peter was pronouncing. YES! Squeaking myself free from any kind of restraint, the restless prankster within kept rising up, and I found myself inching toward the door like a teenager with keys to the car.

"Johnny," I tapped his dancing arm. "I'm going exploring," I hollered through the heaven. "Meet at your car after Gabriel," I said, and he nodded, completely unconcerned I was leaving. We were brothers without the blood, and had shared the trenches before. Whole lives of personal journeys lay ahead for both of us and we didn't have to stay in the same seats, not when there was all of Woodstock to explore.

Johnny was mesmerized like he was watching a magician mid-trick, and I knew we'd both be fine finding our own gods and gold in the glistening miracle of the night, and all was good in the universe. So I faded away, into the unknown audience, the screaming heads, the dancing girls, and the infinite landscape of the final act.

It's entirely possible that he played *Red Rain* in here somewhere, but frankly my dear I was too zippered to record the record. Somewhere in here God almighty opened up. Somewhere in here the heavens parted and the future gleamed like the sun around an eclipse.

Suddenly Gabriel's significance in so many pivotal moments of my life came rushing back in a flood. My best friend's suicide attempt. Playing *Don't Give Up* for her — and it working and she's still alive! So many times playing it when I'd lost hope myself. So many times when "*So*" flew through my Walkman and saved me, yet I'd never sought out its author. Till now, till here, scrawling his signature at the bottom of my Declaration of Independence was the voice of the last decade, stepping forth and redefining himself as someone so key to a healthy soul.

He was bringing back *Big Time*, about coming from a small town to the big city. About Johnny, New York, immigrants like myself, striving, struggling, starving, but being part of America.

Somewhere in the spaces of memory and

emotion one writer had filled the void more than I ever realized or admitted. And now that very archival archangel was singing to us all.

I left Johnny and was blissfully floating solo again, listening to the healer who healed me, as I wandered among the swaying and testifying parishioners in this church, where all the pews seemed to have been overturned, and perhaps there'd even been a flood.

Then softly, the first wisps of *Solsbury Hill* began to waft over the horizon — the chilling, haunting, hopeful hymn of independence. As he sang about the blowing wind of change I stopped in the mud and soaked in the connection between one man and a hundred thousand. With the inflection in his voice, he could raise us off the ground until we were hovering mid-air like hummingbirds, or blow us back like a hurricane. No other artist all weekend had that range of subtleties or the power to inflict them on his audience at will.

The difference may have been the absence of moshers or drunks or crazies, I don't know. Maybe they all had their peak during the Chili Peppers and left. But this audience was at peace, and one with the singer, who was one with the song. He was certainly taking us home, and set the hummingbirds a'fluttering again, our light spirits — Light Spirits — whisked away with the singer even if our bodies remained ostensibly the same.

Earlier in the night, Oxfam (the international

disaster-relief agency) had passed out thousands of candles to light as a symbol of hope to the survivors of the mass murders in Rwanda. All through Gabriel's set the field was twinkling with the sparkler dims of candlelights flickering like stars across the sky.

It probably confused the birds all to hell. They'd go swooping up to the stars — but fly right into the ground! Although at this hour they turned out to be swooping bats! The barn bats of Saugerties were on their nightly screech, and fluttering black wings would swoop past your head in the already surreal belfry of the weekend.

I continued wandering though the passionate parishioners of the candlelit church, wanting to experience as much as I could while it was still alive. There were lots of warm bodies, worn bodies, persevering spirits, willful warriors, women and men alike, hair mud-encrusted, chests tattooed with hand prints, the earned medals of this playful skirmish, the badges of courage from a weekend war — the more mud, the more distinguished. They were all brave soldiers who'd fought for their mud and wore it proud. I was but a flag-waving civilian in their war on convention. Many of their generals went back to New York City in full uniform and hit the streets of Times Square for a little R&R. It was the only place they could think of to not be noticed.

And then Gabriel used his *Sledgehammer* to crack open our heads and our hearts, and wouldn't every artist love to have one of these in their repertoire?! A very horny number, and I don't just mean the brass section if you catch my Georgia O'Keeffe. How could they ban *Louie Louie* but let *"Sledgehammer"* become Number 1? It is a wacky world after all!

Every MTV viewer has seen this video a thousand times, so it was pretty recognizable even without the melting graphics. Although I was still certainly enjoying them. ;-)

The computerized banks of lights were constantly mutating the stage into different flowing shapes and colors. The gradual transitions from van Gogh yellow to Renoir blue to Monet green made you tip forward as one color would pour into the next.

And speaking of getting dizzy, there were more naked bodies exposing themselves than there were people, or so it seemed. I could go on about it for pages, but it was all a surreal dream . . .

You're at Woodstock. You're walking through an enormous crowd of people. You stop, and look at the stage. Peter Gabriel is performing. You feel good. Everything is wonderful. You start walking again but you notice every person in the crowd around you is completely naked.

God — It was such a weird dream!

As the singer's singing about shedding his skin . . . as massive change was in the air . . . as every poet kept reminding us all weekend. This wasn't all fun and games. There was life in transition.

"This next song is for the spirit of Jimi Hendrix. It's called *Secret World*," I heard Gabriel say, evoking the second-most referenced guiding Woodstock light after John Lennon this weekend. But he would have been more on-target citing John. I'm sure the following may be sacrilege in some denominations, but all night Gabriel was sounding like The Beatles would if they'd kept going. I suppose that's the highest praise you can give a rock 'n' roll band, but tell me *Secret World* isn't *Tomorrow Never Knows* at a nineties pace, with its hypnotic cycling rhythm, Lennon's haunting optimism and McCartney's popping bass.

And all the while the band's running around in throbbing strobe lights which you could watch for about five seconds on acid before the whole world began pulsating in flashing lights and jerking time with everything staggered and *nothing is real.* Peter, Paula Cole and the whole band were doing a Rockettes meets the Juluka South African Dance Celebration while the strobes turned everything into a silent movie with only a partial view of the dancers every other second which was magnified into hours while the on-stage lightning storm kept cracking with snippets of the scientists at work.

I had to start moving again! Mud I could handle. It was mostly one color and it stayed somewhat still.

People were dancing in bliss, in a transcendental shape-shift soul drift. It felt as though Gabriel's set may have ended around here somewhere because I remember wandering for what seemed like miles as the crowd kept cheering without music, exploring my way through the vines of peace hanging thick in the air like moss in the bayou, weaving invisible through clapping arms and whistling fingers until at last I came out on the banks of the deep muddy river that ran through the site, sparkling alive with the starry night candles. This quiet, gentle Mississippi of ours unassumingly began in the dark hills beyond and was quietly rolling past people having the noisiest night of their life.

In the center of this delta of dreams was some sort of altar on an island in the water, some sort of fire rising from the earth, and circled around it was a peaceful cluster of muddy monks standing shoulder-to-shoulder in silence while up to their shins in water.

And as I wove into their mix, this sacred circle was surrounding a giant peace sign made of hundreds of the Oxfam candles. And each of these solemn saints was engaged in the unspoken task of lighting all 500 candles at once so the entire peace sign would burn united — but as one would gently bow to spark a light, his body-breeze might extinguish a lifetime of birthdays. Or a soft whisper of Mother Nature would quietly hush through their legs and nearly snuff out their dream completely. But no. These pious mutes were not deterred, united in hope, united they stood, searching and striking, bending and lighting, bonding and enlightening each other in a steady procession of action, solidifying themselves against the storm, once more, bend, once more, bend, once more, bend, until . . . THEY'VE DONE IT!

Making peace! 500 candles burning at once in harmony in a circle in the mud. And surrounding the flames flickered the beaming faces who made it happen, cheering together their united flame in a sea of mud.

Beyond this circle we'd been burning together all weekend — now we were pulling it off in the mud again — thousands of lifelong friends who finally met, all playing the same game without frontiers or rules being stated or winners declared.

And as we were cheering this Great Flame of Peace, off in the distance Saint Peter came back for an encore. Somewhere far away a drum beat began, a slowly rising heart beat playing a tribal rhythm, a patterned intro of — YES! — *In Your Eyes*! And in our ears came Youssou N'Dour's angelic voice, pouring into the song like cream into coffee as the audience began to catch on and rise with him in a chorus of flame-flickering joy, of river-bodies dancing naked whether clothed or not, of our collective subconscious exploding in the twilight's last gleaming of Sunday's night.

As all the reaching out from the inside that this song has ever evoked suddenly came rising through my throat, through my eyes, right in front of me, I was unavoidably facing the unfaceable, every moment of not speaking, every battle not waged, every voice not raised, every step not taken, rising, through my eyes, rising, from the inside, rising, every strength of conviction convincing me now — not again — every moment of truth doubted — never again! — "I reach out from the inside" — and come alive! — reborn from the center, from the truth, from the heart, from now on.

Whether this song, this weekend, or something more, somehow everyone became whatever they wanted — at least for a night or a weekend ... with the possibility of life — free of all that ever confined — whatever dream was yearning to reach out from the inside — there was spark enough here for life-long ignition.

Somehow through the magic swirling ship of *In Your Eyes*, I found myself standing on the very top row of the V.I.P. bleachers again overlooking the cheering field for the final song of the final set of the final night. I was perched on solid ground for the first time in days, and my heart was racing to the beat of Gabriel's quest.

There was no turning back.

Somewhere out of the jungle darkness a new rhythm arose, a haunting rhythmic native drum, a distant tribe, a beating trance, a call to all to dance tonight. And echoing through the shimmering canyons came a voice:

"25 years ago,
People believed,

You could change the world,
If you fought for justice,
If you fought for what you believe in,
If you fought for your dreams.

This is your Woodstock.
These are your dreams."

And the spirit of *Biko* rose from the earth,
summoning us from the bell towers of revolution and
revelation, ringing through the night, chiming in the
freedom spirit and calling us to the village green.
The soul of independence flew in circles
above our rabble-rousing candle-bearing
uprising, our pitched voices, our tuned forks, our
half-million-voiced choir gathered before an altar
of music, holding flames on high to all those before
us, who wrote, sang, and played before us, who died
for the freedom of flight before us — our chanting
singing spirits soared.
"If you fought for what you believe in" kept
echoing echoing echoing now, no body no more —
releasing the Spirit Balloon and drifting from the
earth, from the body, by a drum, a voice, a haunting
tribal jungle beat in a chanting mystic nightfall heat,
drifting high through the mist like a dream, a drum,
a drum, Macbeth doth come, double, double, toil and
trouble, fire burn, and cauldron bubble, floating,
floating, free as spirit, fire burn, here and near
it, above this earth, above Woodstock — through

kaleidoscopic prisms scattering moonlight into rain, splintering sunshine out of pain, shattering dreams into streams of ringlet reams twirling over the flower glades of all yesterdays making new todays.

Wild scenes flew open like shutters in a storm — flashing mud-clay sculptures baking by candlelight — tribesmen dancing entranced in circles — flame-flickering faces smiling in bronze — weaving and swaying, believing and staying, enhanced by moondance and trialed by fire. A mighty midnight breezing blast billowed our sails and hoisted our hearts — not extinguishing flames but blowing our dreams like saxophone solos through the skies of our songs, scattering our spirits like stardust in the wind, floating as one to the horizon beyond, and joining the stars, the pearls of the heavens, the stardust we are, the golden we glisten.

Saint Peter was singing like a fluttering angel in the clear sky night as our Spirit Balloon floated back to where people were swaying gently in a lullaby cradle at the rocking hand of God. Colored spirits spiraled up with the smoke, embers flickered in the starry night and blazed in the hearth-fire heart-center of our soul. Thunderous bone-shaking drums held a million as one, sending us off in boats on a river with tangerine trees and marmalade skies, where sugarplum fairies make dreams come true and visions dance on watershine.

As Gabriel sang in the winds of change blowing through the trees, through our souls, through our

cells, through ourselves, through the world, behind
our sails, behind you now, behind tomorrow when
you rise, behind your comeback when you fall, behind
your dreams, unseen by all.

"This is your Woodstock.
These are your dreams,"

he said of the ones that come true on top of
the mountain, within your heart until they spark in a
neck-tingling leg-dancing shiver-me-timbers that
spikes your soul, strikes your life and makes it whole,
beaming the goal of your character's role. No one
else sees it, but you, you've got it, you see it, nobody
else, but you, you know it, nobody else, you see it,
nobody else, inside you ... now, flickering flickering
flickering now —

"And what happens now,
is up to you,"

as the mystic minstrel waved goodbye. "And
what happens now, is up to you," a drum beats in
the distance, and what happens now, a drum beats,
a drum beats inside, "And what happens now, is
up to you," a drum beat begins to fade to cheering
as candles flicker, and out of the candle's flicker,
glowing and growing from the field of life, the field
at night, a glowing ring of fire begins to take over,
a flaming ring of flickering peace, a raging circle

of dancing men, a rising voice of singing women, a
thousand voices merging together — human voices
rise, rise, rising above the field, human voices rise,
crying out, out on a limb of pious pagans dancing
in tongues around a circle of light, a sign of peace, a
resounding choir, rising, from the field, rising, from
the field, pulling us, pulling us, pulling us God help
us in — to the chanting circle, to singing unbounded,
to free me, free me, free me for real, free me for
once, and all we are saying, all we are praying, all
the spirits are swaying, the field all as one, all we
are saying, John is here smiling, all we are saying,
all we are swaying, locking arms, spinning faster,
locking arms, spinning faster, with the spirit still
faster, arm-in-arm with God in the mud, with God
in the light, spinning faster, and all we are saying,
all we are swaying, all we are praying, it's all in our
hands, and all we are holding, one and sister brother
lover all, one in a million — to a million are one, in
a mud-splashing arm-locking swirling dance twirl,
and all we are saying is let's stay together, and all we
are saying is joined at the heart, and all we are saying
is kindness to all, and all we are saying is spinning
together, and all we are saying is burning inside,
and all we are saying is no turning back, and all we
are saying is raging inside, and all we are saying
is keep it alive, and all we are saying is stoke the
improbable, light the impossible, fan the invisible, be
the invincible spirit you are.

When I was writing this book, my girlfriend bought me this peace sign candle, because everything at that time was about peace & love.

It sat within eyesight as I wrote the book you just read. Then as I was approaching the climax — writing the last few pages you just read, I finally lit that sumbitch — didn't want to jinx it beforehand — didn't want to have it burned out before the book was done. And those last few pages went pretty fast — I was in The Zone.

She was in the other room reading pages written earlier in the day, and when I got to the end, I walked in with I dunno *what* kinda look on my face. "It's done," I said, and we hugged, and cried, and shook. And then I blew out the candle so it would always be frozen in time at the moment this book was finished.

All Band's
Times on Stages
and
Path of the Narrator

Friday

North Stage only   (Friday was a late add, so there was not anything scheduled on the South Stage)

Acts caught in **bold** (approx set lengths in minutes)	location of narrator
10 AM **Opening Ceremony** (60)	in front of stage
12:30 Roguish Armament (20)	at press briefing
1:15 Futu Futu (30)	behind the stage
2:00 Lunchmeat (20)	in KarmaCoupe
2:30 Paul Luke (20)	on bike ride
3:00 Peacebomb (20)	in secret abandoned cabin
3:30 The Goats (20)	back on bike ride
4:00 Orleans (30)	at Cheri's fixing flat
4:45 Blues Traveler (40)	in motorhome with models
5:30 Jackyl (40)	on bike ride
6:15 Del Amitri (40)	on road into site
7:00 Live (40)	KarmaCoupe ReCampment
8:00 James (40)	penetrating backstage
9:00 King's X (40)	in V.I.P. Tent
10:00 **Sheryl Crow** (40)	in field and ecstasy
11:00 Collective Soul (40)	watching monitors in Media tent
12:00 Candlebox (40)	sleeping
1 AM Violent Femmes (40)	dreaming of Las Vegas

Saturday

North Stage

12:00	**Joe Cocker** (75)	in V.I.P. bleachers
1:30	**Blind Melon** (60)	wandering the field
2:45	Cypress Hill (45)	driven from field
3:45	Rollins Band (75)	at South Stage seeing The Band
5:15	Melissa Etheridge (60)	at South Stage seeing The Band
6:30	**Crosby, Stills & Nash** (90)	in field
8:30	Nine Inch Nails (90)	in Media Tent; then napping
11:30	Metallica (90)	dreaming of Gimli
1:30 AM	**Aerosmith** (90)	in field and bleachers
4 AM	**(fireworks)** (30)	melting in bleachers

Saturday

South Stage

12:00	The Cranberries (45)	at North Stage seeing Cocker
1:30	Zucchero (45)	at North Stage seeing Blind Melon
2:45	**Youssou N'Dour** (60)	in the field
4:30	**The Band** (150)	dancing on the edge
7:30	Primus (60)	at North Stage seeing CSN
9:00	Salt-N-Pepa (60)	absorbing Adventure Cards

Sunday

North Stage

9:30	Country Joe McDonald (5)	heard from van
9:35	**Sisters of Glory** (60)	saw from front of stage
10:45	Arrested Development (45)	at press briefing, and on bike ride
12:00	**Allman Brothers Band** (90)	saw from field
1:45	**Traffic** (75)	saw from bleachers and field
3:15	Spin Doctors (75)	exploring backstage
5:00	Porno For Pyros (90)	at South Stage seeing Nevilles
8:00	**Bob Dylan** (75)	saw from field
10:00	Red Hot Chili Peppers (90)	site exploration with Johnny
12:00	**Peter Gabriel** (90)	saw from field and heaven

Sunday

South Stage

10:00	John Sebastian (5)	at North Stage seeing Sisters of Glory
10:15	Country Joe McDonald (5)	at North Stage seeing Sisters of Glory
10:30	Gil Scott Heron (15)	heading to Media Tent
11:15	WOMAD (150)	at morning press briefing
2:00	Green Day (45)	at North Stage seeing Allmans
3:30	Paul Rodgers (75)	saw on monitors in Media Tent
5:30	**The Neville Brothers** (60)	saw from field
7:00	Santana (120)	waiting for Dylan
9:15	**Jimmy Cliff** (90)	saw from field

Some of the original cassettes recorded in the field that have survived.

And the floppy disks where the original book files were discovered and recovered.

Acknowledgments

Mainly I have to thank my old girlfriend at the time this all went down. She kept a massive binder scrapbook while I was away at the festival with all the multiple New York newspapers' clippings, and was supportive by the day, reading the pages as they came out of the typewriter (printer), and I could hear her laughing in the background as I kept writing.

Also to —

My NYU professor-become-best-friend Walter Raubicheck who read this and everything else I've ever written, and we spent thousands of hours dissecting it and honing my craft;

My writer / roof-climber friend Mitch Potter for the same kind of hours of detailed explorations of every part of every paragraph through eternity;

And of that similar vintage my old collaborative partner still Will Bill Hodgson who gave this book encouragement and suggestions back in the day, as well as in the present tense as we've rekindled our jamming;

Jose Kilometers for being part of our first Woodstock Reunions in River Heights field and down at "the river" . . . and then being the only person I knew to actually make it to Saugerties!

And the great Winnipeg spirit John Kendle for assigning me to cover it!

My current sweetie Sky for keeping the Woodstock spirit alive in my life and encouraging us to keep living it at home and On The Road;

My brother Gubba out in B.C. who I constantly felt in the room with me reading this book over my shoulder and chortling and cheering the whole way through.

And to —

Michael Lang for creating the first Woodstock — and this one!

and John Lennon for writing songs played by a half-a-dozen bands over the weekend.

And of course my partner in books, the mighty Michelangelean David Wills, who I've now co-created four books with in the last five years.

Index

Index

Index

Who's On First, 141–42
WOMAD, 82, 193, 210, 329
Woodstock '69, 190, 207, 223, 242, 254
Woodstock Lessons, 37, 62, 80, 131. 136, 141
Wray, Faye, 228

Yasgur, Max, 40
Yasgur's farm, 7, 8, 9, 15, 39, 51, 52, 53, 65, 235, 247, 281, 292
Young, Neil, 5, 15, 94, 122, 272, 281, 283, 292, 293

Zucchero, 193, 327

Also by Brian Hassett —

The Hitchhiker's Guide to Jack Kerouac

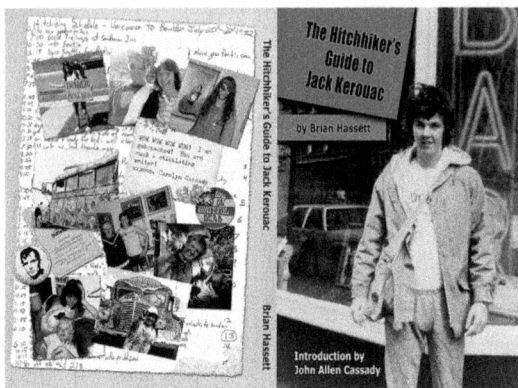

"You did a fine job of bringing this back, far finer than my own memory, and I thought I had a decent one."

Dennis McNally
Kerouac & Grateful Dead scholar & author

"This book is a youthful memoir with all the never-to-be-recaptured frantic zest of a young man. Everything is wonderful in the Hassett world, even bad luck. Every cloud he sees has a silver lining. This attitude takes him far. It's the sheer unbridled enthusiasm that pours from Hassett that is so engaging."

Kevin Ring
Beat Scene magazine

"Both Kerouac and Hassett worked incredibly hard to seek out truth and beauty in this world. And then sit down to tell us what they found. Read the *Hitchhiker's Guide* for the history. But don't miss the larger lessons within."

Kurt Landefeld
author of *Jack's Memoirs: Off The Road*

See also front of book for more quotes.

How The Beats Begat the Pranksters
& Other Adventure Tales

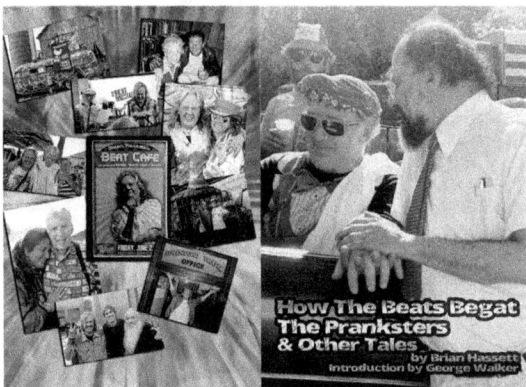

"Brian Hassett has made it his life's work to present to all of us the insights of the Beats and the Pranksters, and all the history, all the important things that came out of that, which have been perpetuated by the incredible vision, the incredible energy, of this man who is now one of our prime spokesmen, and we are so fortunate for that."

George Walker
original Merry Prankster and practicing Neal Cassady

"This is an excellent new addition to the collective cultural canon from the people's Prankster Brian Hassett, Beat evangelist and voice of the living Dead. Our rocking roisterer and bebop brother has done it again!"

Simon Warner
author of *Text Drugs & Rock & Roll* and *Kerouac On Record*

""Brian Hassett doesn't just write ABOUT the Pranksters! He IS one! This book is great insider stuff about Ken Kesey and the Pranksters, about Jack Kerouac and the Beats, and especially about the late, great Neal Cassady, who did more than "bridge the gap" between those two points in the Bohemian universe — he closed it!"

Lee Quarnstrom
author, journalist & original Merry Prankster

On the Road with Cassadys
& Furthur Visions

"Brian Hassett tells stories like no other, and this book of adventures with my family does not disappoint. I recommend all of Brian's books for fun, energetic jaunts that will keep you entertained and uplifted. Brian does us Proud!"

>   Cathy Cassady, daughter of Neal & Carolyn Cassady

"This book is a masterpiece! It's brilliant. I want everyone I know to read it. It's a modern classic."

>   John Allen Cassady, only son of Neal & Carolyn Cassady

"This is the third book in the highly acclaimed and entertaining Beat Trilogy. Everyone should check out all three of these. There are very few people in the world who know as much about the Beats and the Pranksters as Brian."

>   Jerry Cimino, founder & director of The Beat Museum

"Hassett has perfected the art of getting backstage and into the world of the musicians, writers, actors & directors. He's always in the middle of the action, and his sense of camaraderie, spirit of fun, and knowledge has him embraced by all. This makes for unusual insider stories that are all a testament to the author's perseverance and fascination with all things Beat. And it is all so much fun to read."

>   Kevin Ring, Editor, *Beat Scene* magazine

BLISSFULLY RAVAGED IN DEMOCRACY
ADVENTURES IN POLITICS
1980 - 2020

"I loved this Hip Herodotus History of Happenings! You really nailed the whole era, in addition to a crash course in Pranksterland and your account of the afternoon tribute to Abbie. You show a new generation your take on the relationship of the THEN and the NOW, and that's the whole idea!"

David Amram
jazz bandleader, classical composer & Kerouac collaborator

"This book brings an insider perspective to what politics looks like on the ground, the human interaction. What is the reality of people involved in politics and how has it changed over the years? That's one of the interesting things that you get down in this book. It's continuing the theme of what you do. You're the Gonzo journalist type who's attracted to very interesting, colorful personalities, and you join them on their travels, and are able to communicate it so the reader feels like they're with you on these Adventures. It's a really fantastic thing that you're doing with your literary voice."

Mike Flynn
WUML DJ, musicologist, Beat scholar & festival coordinator

www.ingramcontent.com/pod-product-compliance
Lightning Source LLC
Chambersburg PA
CBHW060241100426
42742CB00011B/1604